The
Myth
of the
Britannica

The Myth of the Britannica

Harvey Einbinder

Grove Press, Inc.　　New York

To my wife with love

"When all treasores been tryed treuth is the beste."

Piers Plowman

Contents

Introduction

A Personal Note

I AM a consulting physicist. I provide technical assistance to defense contractors engaged in missile and space projects. Several years ago as a release from the pressures of consulting work, I undertook some spare time activities. One of these was an attempt to launch a series of educational television programs that would explain the achievements of modern science to the general public. In gathering material for this series, I occasionally consulted the *Encyclopaedia Britannica*, which I had not used in the past. Like most people, I assumed that any information in the set would be reasonably accurate and up to date.

In the article on Galileo, I read that he disproved the theory of ancient philosophers by dropping weights from the Leaning Tower of Pisa. Later I came across a book by Lane Cooper of Cornell which showed this account to be fictitious. Galileo never mentioned the experiment in any of his writings, and it was not recorded by any of his contemporaries. The story was first presented sixty years after the experiment was supposed to have occurred. Professor Cooper noted that this legend is offered as a true story in the *Britannica*. I was surprised to find that although Professor Cooper's book was published in 1935, the *Encyclopaedia* continued to reprint the Galileo legend for more than twenty years.

This disturbing experience led me to examine the 1958 edition, where I discovered obvious flaws in the entries on Heat, Vaporization and the Compton Effect. If there were errors in an exact science such as physics, what was likely to be the case in other fields where truth and fiction, opinion and evidence, could not be so readily separated? To answer this question, I inspected a large number of articles in different fields.

So many defects came to light during this preliminary survey that I decided to write a book that would systematically discuss the *Encyclopaedia*'s limitations. This study was not supported by any foundation, grant or fellowship, but was the result of my own initiative and concern. In examining the set, I compared articles with entries in earlier editions. This permitted individual articles to be dated, and clarified the changing character of the work during the last three generations.

Checking the accuracy of the set was a time-consuming task which required an extensive search through many books. This would not have been possible without the resources of Columbia University and the New York Public Library, which served as a giant encyclopedia in verifying the *Britannica*'s information.

When I began, the 1958 *Encyclopaedia* was the latest edition available, so it served as the basis for my critical study. It was fitting that this edition was chosen because it coincided with an outburst of publicity and promotion for the "Great EB." Despite annual revision, a great deal of the criticism of the 1958 edition applies with equal force to later printings. However, the aim of this book is not to supply an exhaustive catalogue or inventory of errors. Rather it seeks to examine the quality of the *Britannica*'s scholarship and its editorial standards. Examples have been chosen because they illuminate fundamental issues, or deal with subjects possessing a wide interest and importance. They represent only a sample of a much larger number of entries that could be discussed. But they provide a framework for evaluating the goals of *an* encyclopedia. The 1958 *Britannica* is the basis for the present study, and references to articles are to that edition, unless specified to the contrary. However, *any* recent edition would yield similar conclusions, even though the particular cases might be different. This is demonstrated in chapters 18 and 19 which consider the 1963 edition.

Heaping up errors and omissions is not enough in analyzing an encyclopedia. Its size makes it necessary to deal with broad characteristics, as well as individual entries. Different areas must be treated systematically, and articles selected to illustrate basic problems. Since an encyclopedia is a mirror of contemporary learning, it offers a valuable opportunity to examine prevailing attitudes and beliefs in a variety of fields. Consequently a thorough study of a major reference work inevitably becomes an exploration of modern knowledge and the means of presenting this knowledge so it can be understood by educated laymen.

An effective critique must consider the functions of an encyclopedia and the audience for which it is intended. It must deal with such varied topics as the shifting tide of critical opinion, the nature of historical evidence, and the role of science as a humanistic discipline. In addition, the *Britannica*'s position as a reference authority and educational institution must be discussed in the light of contemporary values in American society. As a result of such diverse material, this book is more than a study of a particular reference work. It is a broad survey of the current intellectual scene that may be of interest to those who value the life of the mind.

[1]

The Myth

During the last generation, there has been an explosive growth in almost every branch of science and scholarship. Research is now an organized activity involving an army of trained investigators, whose progress is recorded in a flood of books, monographs and technical papers. Knowledge is expanding so rapidly that it is impossible for an individual to keep up with the results of this incessant activity. Therefore practical methods are needed to enable us to assimilate the discoveries of contemporary science and scholarship.

Encyclopedias are useful for this purpose because they provide a distillation of modern learning in a form that can be absorbed by educated readers. Jacques Barzun has observed that the problem of constructing a new world encyclopedia "appears as the embodiment of the greatest intellectual problem of the age: to keep the bulk of human knowledge common property by keeping it communicable." This is a challenging assignment because editors and authors must forge a common language with their readers at the same time they are instructing them.

Since encyclopedias survey the entire domain of learning, they are useful instruments of education. They supply an introduction to unfamiliar subjects, enable teachers to supplement classroom material, and offer information on inaccessible topics. They are particularly valuable in backward countries with meager libraries and limited educational facilities, because they distill contemporary knowledge in a form that can be readily transported. This was recognized a few years ago when the Rockefeller Foundation and the U. S. Government made funds available to place the *Britannica* in overseas libraries so that students in foreign countries would be exposed to the "best" in American scholarship.

The *Encyclopaedia*'s large, heavy volumes are a familiar sight on the library shelf. Encased in their rich maroon bindings, they are identified as an accurate, up-to-date source of information on a wide variety of topics. They are employed by the public as a comprehensive summary of learning whose authority is accepted without question.

The *Britannica* is more than a reference work. Over the years, it has become an institution in American life that is constantly consulted in settling factual questions. Many Americans regard it as the last word in contemporary scholarship, and its publishers state that for nearly two centuries it has been recognized as "the reference standard of the world." Although it is written primarily by scholars, the work is intended for laymen. It is conceived by its editors as a continuing link between the academic and the lay worlds, designed as a source of reference and a major instrument of popular education.

Advertisements describe the *Britannica* as "the greatest treasure of knowledge ever published," and claim it "will provide instant and authentic information on every conceivable subject of thought." Each year the Company announces that a "new edition" is available, thus catering to the desire for accurate, up-to-date information. However, few consumers realize that a great deal of material is several generations old—an aspect of the work that is not widely publicized.

Many articles in the 1958 edition—and the 1963 edition as well—have been taken from the famous eleventh edition of 1910–11. They include the entries on Jonson, Smollett, Fielding and Pope; Schiller, Lessing, Pushkin and Lope de Vega; Mozart, Liszt, Rossini and Schumann. Old essays appear on such varied subjects as Genealogy, Heroic Romances, Lyrical Poetry and Serpent Cults; Legal Maxims, Possession in Law, Syriac Literature, and Fathers of the Church. So many of these articles are prosaic accounts that it is difficult to believe they have been retained because of their literary brilliance or scholarly excellence.

Even more surprising are reprints from the ninth edition of 1875–89. Such material, whose average age is seventy-five years, includes the entries on Shelley, Macaulay and Scott; Hesiod, Pindar, Rhetoric and the Sophists; as well as Machiavelli, Mazarin, Mirabeau, Medici and Mary (Queen of Scots).

Obsolete essays can sometimes be recognized by an old bibliography or outmoded footnotes. Another reliable sign is the absence of initials identifying the author of an article. When these initials are missing at the end of a long entry, this almost always indicates material from the ninth, tenth or eleventh edition, since their omission conceals the age of an article by eliminating the names of deceased contributors. Examples include the biographies of Hadrian, Tiberius, Turgot, Renan and William Morris.

In the 1958 edition, the initials of well-known authors have been dropped, as well as those of obscure figures. The biography of Sainte-Beuve is an abridged version of an essay prepared by Matthew Arnold, but he is not identified as a contributor. The articles on Montaigne, Racine, Voltaire and La Fontaine were written by the Victorian critic George Saintsbury for the ninth edition, but his initials were eliminated from these entries. Yet paradoxically, they were retained in the essay on Balzac which is openly identified as a reprint from the eleventh edition.

A different approach is followed in the case of Swinburne. His article on Congreve is identified as a reprint from the ninth edition, and his essay on Beaumont and Fletcher carries a long footnote explaining why it was retained:

> Recent research has resulted in some variation as to the precise authorship of some of the plays commonly attributed to them; but this article, contributed to an earlier edition of the *Encyclopaedia Britannica,* remains the classical modern criticism of Beaumont and Fletcher, and its value is substantially unaffected.

This note was added to Swinburne's essay in 1910. It states that the "results of later research are epitomized in the Bibliographical Appendix"; but this appendix is fifty years old—and the essay itself is more than eighty years old.

Sometimes fanciful tales are presented as if they were true stories. The celebrated poaching incident is described in the article on Shakespeare in the following fashion:

> . . . There is a tradition which comes from a double source and which there is no reason to reject in substance, to the effect that Shakespeare got into trouble through poaching on the estates of a considerable Warwickshire magnate, Sir Thomas Lucy, and found it necessary to escape the results of his misdemeanour.

The first source of this legend was the Reverend Richard Davies who reported about 1700 that Shakespeare got into trouble stealing deer and rabbits. This story was subsequently elaborated by Nicholas Rowe in a biography of the dramatist written almost a century after his death. Rowe vividly described how Shakespeare was apprehended while poaching deer on the estate of Sir Thomas Lucy. Unfortunately for this story, it has been established that Sir Thomas had no deer on his estate. The poaching legend was indignantly rejected 120 years ago in the seventh edition by Thomas DeQuincey who declared, "The tale is fabulous and rotten to the core"; and today serious scholars reject this colorful portrait of Shakespeare as a youthful delinquent.

Old articles in the *Britannica* make it difficult to identify the set with modern scholarship. This is particularly true in the field of history where a great deal of material has been taken from the ninth and eleventh editions. In the 1958 edition, and the 1963 edition as well, this includes the essays on Feudalism, Guilds, Villeinage, and Village Communities; Goths, Huns, Vandals, and Teutonic Peoples; and Media, Scythia, Phoenica, and Seleucid Dynasty. In addition, biographies of many important historical figures have been reprinted for decades. Among the entries that may be cited are those on Frederick the Great, Moltke and Metternich; Savonarola, Garibaldi and Mazzini; as well as Robespierre, Richelieu, Talleyrand and Louis XIV– XVIII. These examples are only a small sample of the *Encyclopaedia*'s antiquated contents.*

Many of these articles contain information discredited by later historians. The essay on the Waterloo Campaign repeats the story that after the flight of Napoleon from Waterloo, the Duke of Wellington and Field Marshal Blücher met on the battlefield at "La Belle Alliance." This story, however, is contradicted by Wellington who states categorically in his *Supplementary Dispatches* that they met in the village of Genappe, five miles away. The Duke adds: "Anyone who attempts to describe the operation of the different armies will see *that it could not be otherwise.*" The entry on Wellington carries a footnote listing two possible dates and places for his birth. This footnote was originally attached to the article when it appeared in the ninth edition seventy years ago. It has been retained for three generations—even though it has long been established by the evidence of contemporary Irish newspapers and the sworn testimony of Wellington's parents that he was born in Dublin on May 1, 1769.

The *Encyclopaedia* frequently fails to keep up with current events—and sometimes is painfully behind the times. The article on Nürnberg in the 1958 edition is accompanied by a plate of photographs illustrating some of the leading sites of the city. One photograph shows the old fortress castle with a Nazi banner

* A list of 666 old articles is given in the appendix, pages 363-373.

waving over its ramparts. The same edition gives the population of Tarnopol in Poland as 35,831, half of whom are Jews— figures gathered in 1931. Below this entry is a note on Tarnów in Poland whose population (based on 1935 data) is listed as 42,235, of whom 40 percent are Jews. Such antiquated figures can even be found in the treatment of major cities. The article on Warsaw states that nearly 70 percent of its population is Polish, and nearly all the rest are Jews. Obsolete statistics! What morbid thoughts they rouse. . . .

Although there are notices on many leading corporations, a busy executive may not find them very useful. Data for the three Chicago railroads are given for 1950, but the freight and passenger revenues of the Atchison, Topeka and Santa Fe are 1939 figures. For others, such as the Erie, no statistics are included—and strangely enough, the nation's two largest carriers, the New York Central and the Pennsylvania, do not receive separate entries. Finally, the assets of Armour & Co. are presented for 1934, although the company is one of the largest enterprises in the city of Chicago, where the *EB* has been published for the past thirty years.

The *Encyclopaedia* often neglects the efforts of scholars to unravel the uncertainties of the past. An instructive case is the attempt to determine when Abraham, the first Hebrew in the Bible, lived—something that can only be established by inference, and not by direct proof. According to the article on Abraham, he lived about 1550–1450 B.C. in the dark age that followed the fall of the Hyksos kingdom. These dates are based on archeological findings published in 1924. However, subsequent excavations in Transjordan by Albright and Glueck beginning in 1929 have uncovered an important line of cities destroyed by foreign invaders about 2000 B.C., and which lay in ruins for more than a century thereafter. Archeologists connect the destruction of these cities with the invasion by the Eastern kings that resulted in the looting of Sodom and Gomorrah, as described in the fourteenth chapter of Genesis. Since this event occurred during Abraham's lifetime, many scholars believe he lived about 2000 B.C., or five hundred years earlier than the dates given in the article on Abraham. Furthermore, they tend to associate the dark age after the Hyksos dynasty with the exodus of the Israelites from Egypt, rather than with the time of Abraham.

A reader who consults the *Britannica*'s index can discover additional material on Abraham in two other entries. The essay on Judaism follows the discoveries of Albright and Glueck by recording that he lived about 2000 B.C., but the longest discussion of the question is given in a section on Old Testament Chronology which carefully examines the evidence for both 1500 and 2000 B.C.—and concludes that both dates seem equally probable. Consequently the information presented on Abraham is, to say the least, confusing and contradictory.

There is no information on the Lascaux cave paintings—the remarkable treasury of paleolithic art found in southern France in 1940—and other lapses occur in archeology. In 1894 Arthur Evans began to uncover the once legendary palace of King Minos in Crete. During his excavations he discovered hundreds of clay tablets covered with a strange script. For more than two generations the contents of these tablets remained a vexing riddle. Then in 1952 the puzzle was solved when a brilliant thirty-year-old architect, working in his spare time, succeeded in deciphering the form of Minoan known as the Linear B script. Michael Ventris deciphered this script in a remarkable feat of pure linguistics without the aid of a bilingual text. He identified it as a form of archaic Greek and confirmed this interpretation by means of recently discovered tablets containing words and pictures. This major step in recovering the language of ancient Crete has aptly been called "the Everest of Greek Archeology." It was announced in a prominent three-column headline on the front page of the *New York Times:*

TABLETS ANTEDATING HOMER DECIPHERED

This feat is not reported in the 1958 edition; instead the article on Aegean Civilization offers an outdated prophecy:

> History of an inferential and summary sort only can be derived in the absence of written records. The latter do, indeed, exist in the case of Cretan civilization and in great

numbers; but they are undeciphered and likely to remain
so, except in the improbable event of the discovery of a long
bilingual text, partly couched in some familiar script and
language.

The importance of the Minoan script is noted in the article
on Greece which asks, "Were the creators of the Minoan and
Mycenaean civilization Greeks or were they not?" It then
replies:

> The excavations at Cnossus have yielded thousands of
> tablets written in the linear script. There is also evidence that
> a script, although a different script, was in use among the
> Mycenaeans as well. If Greek was the language spoken at
> Cnossus and Mycenae, how is it that all attempts to decipher
> the scripts have hitherto failed?

Since this section is fifty years old, it concludes that until the
scripts are deciphered or new evidence is forthcoming, no final
judgments can be reached about the origins of Minoan and
Mycenaean culture.

Information on that other momentous recent discovery—the
Dead Sea Scrolls—is limited to two brief paragraphs noting the
discovery of an Isaiah scroll and a Commentary on Habukkuk.
One paragraph appears in the article on Palestine and the other
on Asia, but there is no inkling of their importance. When William Albright, the Biblical archeologist, first saw a portion of
the Isaiah scroll which had been found in a cave at Qumram
in 1947 he wrote: "My heartiest congratulations on the greatest
manuscript discovery of modern times. What an absolutely remarkable find!" Here at last was a Hebrew manuscript of the
Bible written twenty centuries ago—one that antedated the earliest previous Hebrew manuscript by a thousand years.

The Dead Sea Scrolls have inaugurated a new era in Pales-
tinian archeology by providing for the first time written documents that are two thousand years old. They have shed new light
on the Biblical text, but their existence is ignored in the section
on the Manuscripts of the Bible, which was not touched for a
generation. Finally, the essay on the English Bible fails to discuss

any twentieth-century translations, but merely concludes with a pious defense of the Revised Version prepared during the reign of Queen Victoria.

Sometimes one hears an echo from a bygone era that evokes a quizzical smile. The private life of Charlemagne is described in the following terms: "Though a devoted husband to three of his four wives, he had illegitimate offspring by five mistresses."

The essay on Calligraphy offers sound advice:

> The pressure of life to-day tells heavily against decent hand-writing. Writing too much and therefore too quickly we corrupt the shape and become accustomed to low standards. We may find a way out by practicing two hands, a rough scribble and a ceremonial script. . . . To inculcate a good modern current hand, Mr. Hewitt's *Oxford Copy Books* are to be recommended.

Finally the article on the Classics declares:

> Although the classics no longer enjoy their old monopoly in education, the study of the Greek and Latin writers seems to flourish as vigorously as it has done at any time, and at the present moment, so far as the evidence goes, the prospects of classical scholarship as an indispensable force in education appear to be singularly bright.

Perhaps this explains why the entry on Cicero contains eight lines of Latin and the article on Sophocles four lines of Greek without translation, while the biography of the Roman poet Horace presents fifty lines of his verse in Latin.

Because of the *Britannica*'s reputation, many writers assume it is an accurate source of information on inaccessible topics. Sometimes, however, their faith is rudely upset. Alec Waugh, the popular British novelist, relates an unfortunate experience in his book *Love in the Caribbean*:

> If one cannot trust the *Encyclopaedia Britannica*, where can faith begin? Because of a reference to it in that august authority, I had long been anxious to visit the Dutch West Indian island, Saba. The reference is brief; but how it whets the imagination! Saba, I was informed, produced the finest

boatmakers in the Caribbean, but since it has no beach, the boats had to be lowered over the side of the cliff. I was most curious to observe this industry.

Saba was, however, hard of access. . . . I had often seen Saba, shadowy on the horizon, a single cone-shaped mountain like Vesuvius, but I had failed to fit a visit there into my schedule. So when I wrote a comprehensive book about the West Indies, and came to Saba, I had to content myself with copying from the *Encyclopaedia.*

To my surprise, I received a letter from a correspondent assuring me that there was no truth whatsoever in that paragraph and calling my attention to an article contributed by Charles W. Herbert to *The National Geographic* magazine in November 1940. "Saba," Mr. Herbert wrote, "has no natural timber and if the material was imported, it is hard to believe that men would struggle to carry the massive timber fifteen hundred feet up to the top and be faced with the colossal task of getting the completed schooner down to the salt water." It was very clear that whatever else I might miss on my next trip to the West Indies, I must not skip Saba.

Now, having kept that promise to myself, I am convinced that Mr. Herbert was right and that the *Encyclopaedia* was wrong. . . . Having been all over the island and examined its remarkable conformation, I doubt whether boats have ever been built on Saba.

Alec Waugh derived some benefit from his encounter with the *Britannica,* since it led him to explore an unfamiliar island in the West Indies and write a stimulating essay on his findings. Other writers, however, have not been so lucky. A historical novelist attempted to refute a reviewer who had questioned the accuracy of her book dealing with the Maori Wars. She protested against his criticism in an indignant letter to the editor of the *New York Times Book Review* (November 15, 1959), saying: "I cannot allow him to shake my publishers' belief in my reliability. I regret he has particularised on only one point, the Maori Land League, but for proof of his error in that, I refer you to the *Encyclopaedia Britannica.* . . . I should dearly like to know the names of any historians who have at any time suggested that anything so undeniably factual as the land league could ever have been regarded as a 'myth.' " The reviewer replied that recent research had demolished the story of the Maori Land League. The *Britannica* asserts:

> The native tribes, brave, intelligent and fairly well armed, tried, by means of a league against land-selling and the election of a king, to retain their hold over at least the central North Island. But their kings were incompetent, their chiefs jealous and their tribes divided.

Although the article on New Zealand contains data as recent as 1955, this passage—as well as the entire section on the early history of New Zealand—has been reprinted from the 1911 edition. Yet the historian Keith Sinclair demonstrated in 1950 by examining nineteenth-century newspapers that the traditional account of the Land League was a myth invented by government officials who wished to justify British colonial policy by blaming any trouble with the natives on seditious Maori resistance.

In consulting the *Britannica,* one never knows when it may supply misleading information. The brief entry on Tobago reports, "Daniel Defoe used Tobago as a setting for Robinson Crusoe." Other encyclopedias identify Crusoe's island with Juan Fernández in the Pacific. Both claims overlook the origin of *Robinson Crusoe* as a fictional narrative composed from a variety of sources. In the first edition in 1719, Defoe's name did not appear on the title page because the book was offered to the public as a true story written by Robinson Crusoe himself. The editor announced in the preface that he "believed the thing to be a just history of fact" and this assertion aided the popularity of the work. But Defoe, in creating his account, drew upon the adventures of Alexander Selkirk who had stayed on one of the Juan Fernández islands, four hundred miles west of Valparaiso, Chile. In his book, however, Defoe stated that Crusoe was shipwrecked on an island in the Caribbean, but he endowed it with such imaginary characteristics as penguins and mountains covered with snow.

Despite such fictional elements, Tobago has maintained that it is the site of Crusoe's island, and authorities have designated a cavern on the island as Crusoe's Grotto, after a well-known incident in the book. But Defoe never visited the Caribbean, and he recorded that Crusoe landed on an uninhabited island in 1659, at a time when Tobago had already been settled by Dutch colonists. These discrepancies, however, have not disturbed a profitable fiction that has led tourists to visit the island. Oddly enough, the author of the entry on Tobago is the same expert who reported that boats are built on Saba.

Encyclopedias may be led to emphasize salesmanship rather than scholarship because their contents are rarely subjected to critical scrutiny. Each week, magazines and newspapers devote many pages to the latest novel, biography or bit of political journalism embalmed in hard covers, but very little is published about the reference works that are a major investment of the book-buying public. The merchandising of these works is a silent business beyond the reach of criticism, and their success often depends on the skill and ingenuity of salesmen rather than the quality of their contents.

It may be understandable that textbooks are seldom reviewed because they are evaluated by school administrators, teachers and professors whose professional training presumably enables them to discriminate between competing texts. But more than 90 percent of the encyclopedias sold in the United States are acquired by laymen who are not in a position to judge whether they are getting fair value for their money. One reason why reference works are rarely evaluated is that critics are intimidated by their sheer bulk, and usually avoid the arduous task of examining their text to determine their usefulness and accuracy. Consequently most reviews are merely a form of free advertising. They record obvious features, but generally omit any comparison with competing works that would aid consumers.

This was illustrated in 1960 when the *Britannica* offered the complete twenty-four-volume set to newspapers reviewing the work. Almost without exception, they simply repeated the publicity material distributed with the set. On March 20, 1960, the

New Haven Register carried a long feature article which noted the contributions of Yale faculty members and reproduced a section from the third edition of 1788 describing the state of Connecticut. Liberal extracts were quoted, including the following elevated passage:

> A thirst for learning prevails among all ranks of people in the state. More of the young men in Connecticut, in proportion to their numbers, receive a public education, than in any of the states. Dr. Franklin and other literary characters have honoured this state by saying, that it is the Athens of America.

The review concluded by observing that Connecticut receives very ample attention in the 1960 edition, although not in the same glowing terms as the 1788 essay. Unfortunately, however, the *Register* did not refer to the entry on New Haven. Had it done so, it would have discovered that the *Britannica* reports the city is served by coastal steamers and inter-urban trolleys—a bit of obsolete travel information which has been reprinted for thirty years.

The examples presented in this chapter may suggest that the *Britannica*'s popular reputation is open to question. Of course, an encyclopedia cannot be expected to be perfect, since even with scrupulous care, some errors and omissions are bound to occur in a work containing millions of words. However, once its level of accuracy and modernity falls below a certain point, its value is seriously impaired because readers can no longer rely on its information. When this is true, it merely becomes an imperfect guide, rather than an authoritative source that can be consulted with confidence.

The *Britannica*'s contents have been influenced by its past history and ownership. In addition, its organization and outlook have been conditioned by the development of the encyclopedia as a library tool and synthesis of knowledge. Therefore it is fruitful to trace in a chronological fashion the evolution of the encyclopedia and the growth of the *EB* before analyzing the modern set.

[2]

Encyclopedias—
Old and New

IDEALLY an encyclopedia distills the information contained in a giant reference library. Each successive edition represents a landmark in the history of culture by mirroring the interests and opinions of its time. The idea of collecting the wisdom of the ages in a set of books has fascinated many people. Thirty years ago, H. G. Wells began to agitate for a World Encyclopedia which would bring learning into closer contact with existing social and political realities. He felt "it would not be a miscellany, but a concentration, a clarification, a synthesis." Such a work, he believed, could be "a general summary of thought and knowledge which will serve as a basis for common understandings between specialists . . . and so become a guiding center for the intellectual activities of mankind." Unfortunately, Wells' ambitious vision was never realized because he was unable to secure the funds required for such a project.

Encyclopedias have been honored in many countries as

vehicles of national culture and learning. The various Conversations-Lexikons in Germany and the Larousse in France have long been recognized as national reference works. The utility of such works as organs of propaganda was recognized when the *Enciclopedia italiana* was completed in the 1930's. It carried an article on Fascism with a section by Benito Mussolini that disparaged individual freedom and democratic ideals. When the second edition of the *Great Soviet Encyclopedia* was launched in 1949, its editors were instructed by the Council of Ministers "to show with exhaustive completeness the superiority of socialist culture over the culture of the capitalist world. Based on Marxist-Leninist theory, the *Encyclopedia* should give the party's criticism of reactionary bourgeois tendencies in various fields of science and technique." The editors faithfully followed this directive by attacking American foreign policy and presenting a warped view of life in the United States.

The modern encyclopedia is such a convenient tool we may take its existence for granted, yet it is the result of a long process of evolution. Although "encyclopedia" is a Greek word meaning "learning in a whole circle," or a complete system of education in the arts and sciences, the modern idea of an encyclopedia was unknown to the Greeks. The word was first used in the title of a book by Johann Alsted in 1620, and when Sir Thomas Elyot introduced the word into the English language, he defined it in 1538 as "that lernynge whiche comprehendeth all lyberall science and studies." Today it merely signifies a work that treats various branches of knowledge by means of articles arranged in alphabetical order.

Perhaps the first and greatest encyclopedist was Aristotle, the Greek philosopher who expanded the intellectual horizons of the ancient world by examining and codifying the knowledge of his time. Virtually every field pursued by the Greeks received the vital imprint of his analytical mind. Whenever he touched a subject, he transformed it from a collection of miscellaneous facts into a unified body of learning. His investigations, which ranged from abstract questions in logic and metaphysics to a detailed study of the life history of animals, dominated European thought until the Renaissance, so that Dante could justly describe him as "the master of those who know."

The oldest extant encyclopedia is the *Natural History* compiled by the Roman, Pliny the Elder, in the first century A.D. It consisted of thirty-seven books containing over a million words. Its preface stated that more than 20,000 facts were gathered from the writings of hundreds of authors, and one of its outstanding features was a detailed treatment of animal life. It discussed the diseases that can be cured by medicinal herbs and described many lost masterpieces of Greek painting and sculpture. In addition, it preserved many colorful tales of antiquity by recording the adventures of Appelles and his pictures, Cincinnatus and his plough, and Cleopatra with her pearls and poisons.

A major drawback of the *Natural History* is the absence of any systematic organization that would unify its diverse mass of material into a coherent body of knowledge. Lacking Aristotle's genius for penetrating beneath the surface of a subject, Pliny was content to heap up information from ancient authorities. As a result, his treatise resembled an enormous collection of stones that have been quarried from the ground and stacked into separate piles according to their size and shape, rather than a coherent architectural structure.

Pliny's major asset was his exuberant energy as a collector of fact and legend. Whenever Pliny traveled, he was accompanied by a retinue of slaves who would read aloud from the latest books acquired for his library. The compulsive drive of his scholarly activity is suggested by his belief that physical exercise was a foolish waste of time that could be more fruitfully devoted to study. His naïve faith in the infinite power of nature led him to affirm the existence of miraculous and extraordinary creatures. Thus his catalogue of the animal kingdom included the unicorn, the phoenix and the griffin, as well as mermaids and tritons—who were sketched with the same care and respect accorded to the lion, the crocodile and the elephant. This preoccupation with prodigies of nature reached its zenith in the geographical sections of his work which listed the inhabitants of distant lands. It recorded the existence of mouthless men subsisting on the fragrance of fruits and flowers, and centaurs with the torsos of men and the limbs of horses. It stated that there are men in India who cover their nakedness with their giant ears, as well as hybrid creatures with human bodies and the heads of dogs.

These figments of ancient imagination lent an air of romance to the *Natural History,* and it enjoyed an enormous vogue in the Middle Ages. Monks laboriously copied it by hand to satisfy the requests of wealthy readers, so that more than two hundred medieval manuscript copies have survived as testimony to its popularity. The first printed copy was issued in 1463, and soon editions were published all over Europe to satisfy the insistent demand. During the sixteenth century, almost a hundred different editions were issued in a variety of languages, and during the Renaissance, Pliny's compilation was recognized as a leading authority. Indeed, its influence persisted until the end of the eighteenth century—truly a remarkable record of longevity for a reference work compiled during the reign of the Roman emperor Vespasian.

During the Middle Ages a number of encyclopedias were completed, of which the most famous were the *Etymologies* of Isidore of Seville and the *Speculum Majus* of Vincent of Beauvais. These works illustrate two different principles that have contributed to the development of the modern encyclopedia. One mode is the anthology in which extensive passages are taken from earlier writers; the other is an extension of the dictionary in which information is presented by examining the meaning and significance of key words, rather than special subjects. Isidore followed the latter method in compiling his *Etymologies* about 600 A.D. His treatise was highly favored by medieval grammarians because it discussed thousands of Latin words and helped codify the language that was to serve as a primary vehicle of written communication in the Middle Ages.

Many of Isidore's etymologies were quite farfetched. He reported that fish receive their names for sexual reasons—thus *musculus* (mussel) is the masculine of whale because this monster is said to conceive by union with the mussel.

> The Salamander is so called because it is strong against fire, and amid all poisons its power is greatest. It fights against fires, and among all living things, extinguishes them. For it lives in the midst of flames without pain and without being consumed, and not only is not burned, but it puts the fire out.

Despite such definitions, Isidore's treatise was an indispensable part of every respectable library, and the twenty books of his *Etymologies* represented the sum of human knowledge for many centuries.

The *Speculum Majus,* or *Giant Mirror,* of Vincent of Beauvais sought to reflect the entire spectrum of medieval learning within the confines of three huge folios. It employed long extracts from more than five hundred authors in what was essentially a glorified anthology drawn from Greek, Latin, Arabic and Hebrew sources.

The transformation of the encyclopedia into a giant anthology reached its logical conclusion in China where it was converted into a vast storehouse of ancient learning, classical literature and traditional scholarship. This process was a natural outgrowth of the high value placed by Chinese ruling classes on the intensive study of a small number of literary and philosophical classics. Their attitude encouraged the common practice of collecting all the sayings and writing of revered sages and teachers within the confines of a single work. The resulting exaltation of study and traditional wisdom was foreshadowed by Confucius, whose *Analects* began with a prophetic aphorism:

> The Master said, "To learn, and at due times to repeat what one has learnt, is that not after all a pleasure?"

The followers of Confucius raised scholarship and learning to a way of life that dominated the subsequent intellectual history of their country by making a thorough mastery of a selected body of Confucian classics the road to imperial preferment.

Throughout Chinese history there was a close association between literary learning and individual advancement. This was largely due to the intellectual refinement of China's emperors, whose scholarly and cultural interests led to a number of outstanding encyclopedias. Created under imperial auspices, they served to perpetuate the name and glory of the emperor in much the same way that the pyramids immortalized the Pharaohs of Egypt. These anthologies, known as *lei-shu,* were designed primarily as repositories of existing literary and philosophical texts—and, unlike Western encyclopedias, made no effort to provide new material. The tradition of collecting classical texts was already well established by the tenth century A.D. when the *T'ai Ping Yü Lan* was completed. It consisted of one thousand sections distributed among fifty-five separate topic headings; and the entire work is said to have been produced under the personal supervision of the emperor who devoted a year to critical examination of its text.

The founding of the Manchu dynasty illustrates the reverence for learning that elevated the encyclopedia to an important place in Chinese literary history. The Manchus were a nomadic, warlike people who invaded China from its northeastern frontier provinces. After successfully driving out the last of the Ming emperors, they assumed control over all China. In their desire to be accepted by their more civilized subjects, the Manchus eagerly adopted Chinese manners and customs, and, to refute the charge that they were barbarians, they encouraged an intensive revival of classical scholarship. Their first emperor, K'ang-hi, commissioned a new encyclopedia to portray the glory and splendor of Chinese civilization that was being revived by enlightened Manchu rule. This encyclopedia was printed from movable type in 1726 A.D. during the reign of the emperor's successor, Chien Lung. It is divided into 5,020 books—and a copy possessed by the British Museum requires more than seven hundred volumes to house its contents. This giant anthology is still widely used by contemporary sinologists. Each subject is presented by means of lengthy excerpts from recognized authorities arranged in chronological order. These passages are followed by elegant extracts in prose and verse where the subject may be merely mentioned or treated parenthetically, and the articles conclude with anecdotes and incidents drawn from the rich lore of Chinese history and mythology. Consequently they supply a panoramic view of changing literary preoccupations and philosophical conceptions as seen through a perspective of twenty centuries of accumulated wisdom and tradition.

By far the largest and most comprehensive reference work ever compiled in China was the *Yung Lo Ta Tien,* created by the decree of the Ming emperor, Yung Lo, who reigned from 1403 to 1425 A.D. This ambitious ruler decided to collect in a single work everything of significance that had ever been written on four major subjects: the Confucian Canon, History, Philosophy and General Literature. He appointed a group of officials who directed the labor of more than two thousand scholars who were employed for more than five years on this monumental project. After its completion, it was known as the *Great Standard of Yung Lo* in honor of the emperor who commissioned the work. It contained more than 20,000 separate sections occupying more than 900,000 pages, and its 367 million characters corresponded to some 500 million words—so this product of Chinese scholarship was more than fifteen times larger than the modern *Encyclopaedia Britannica.*

Perhaps the most famous of all encyclopedias was the great French *Encyclopédie* which sought to infuse a fresh spirit of reason and enlightenment into the intellectual life of a nation hobbled by the absolutism of church and state. This project was launched by Diderot and D'Alembert who wrote many of its principal articles and secured as contributors some of the keenest minds in France, including Voltaire, Rousseau, Montesquieu and Turgot—men whose ideas were to exert a profound influence on the subsequent direction of European thought. D'Alembert in his "Preliminary Discourse" to the *Encyclopédie* eloquently expressed the value of such a work:

> What an advantage it would have been to our forefathers and to us had [the knowledge of] the Egyptians, the Chaldeans, Greeks, Romans etc. been transmitted down in an encyclo-

pedia; and had they delivered at the time of fame the real principles of their respective languages. Let us do for succeeding ages what we regret was not done for us. If the ancients, who accomplished many great things, had elaborated such an encyclopedia and if this manuscript alone had escaped from the fire that destroyed the Library of Alexandria, this would have been sufficient to console us for the rest.

The *Encyclopédie* swiftly became a spokesman for the new spirit of the Enlightenment that was disturbing the philosophical foundations of French society. This spirit was reflected by Diderot's declaration in his article on Political Authority: "No man has received from nature the right of commanding others. Liberty is a present from Heaven, and every individual . . . has the right to enjoy it as soon as he enjoys reason."

A prospectus of the *Encyclopédie* was issued in 1750 and the first volume appeared the following year. Diderot and D'Alembert were convinced it would profoundly influence the intellectual conceptions of their countrymen, and this hope was vividly conveyed by Diderot in his article on the word "encyclopédie":

> . . . the purpose of an encyclopedia is to assemble the knowledge scattered over the surface of the earth; to explain its general system to the men with whom we live, and to transmit it to the men who will come after us; in order that the labors of centuries past may not be useless for the centuries to come . . . and that we may not die without having deserved well of the human race.

The elevated aim of the *Encyclopédie* was not merely to codify existing knowledge, or to supply information on a wide variety of topics—rather it sought to lead men away from the superstition of the past toward the enlightenment of the future. By advocating religious tolerance and the right of men to think according to their conscience, it incurred the hatred of those who defended clerical dogma and the entrenched interests of society. No other encyclopedia has exerted such a deep political influence on the history of its country, or occupied such a conspicuous place in the literary and intellectual life of its century.

Its reputation and notoriety steadily increased as successive volumes were issued. It was examined as a source of information and as a disguised commentary on contemporary French life. Its friends saw it as a light dispelling the darkness of popular ignorance and superstition; or if they were more daring, they regarded it as a battering ram against the privileges and institutions of the aristocracy. Its enemies viewed the work as a source of dangerous political and religious ideas, and their fears mounted when the *Encyclopédie* hinted that religious dogmas should be subjected to critical analysis. A crisis was reached when the seventh volume was issued in 1759. It contained an article on Geneva by D'Alembert, praising the Protestant reformers led by Calvin who had made Geneva a center of religious activity. This was a dangerous heresy in Catholic France, and Louis XV reacted swiftly in response to Jesuit pressure by suppressing the work.

Although volumes could no longer be issued publicly, the encyclopedists were able to continue their endeavor secretly because they had powerful friends at the Court who supported their venture. As a result, the encyclopedists were allowed to proceed in obscurity and solitude, hidden from the inquisitive eye of the public. At best, they were silently tolerated; at worst, their work was threatened with seizure and destruction. They suffered a major setback when D'Alembert decided to withdraw as a co-editor—weary of the sermons, the satires and foolish censors who had hampered his efforts at every turn. Diderot was left as the sole editor—and he labored for seven years, until by his industry and perseverance he successfully completed this enormous undertaking. The seventeen volumes of the text were finished in 1765, and the eleven volumes of illustrated plates were secretly delivered to subscribers in 1772.

Diderot had toiled for more than twenty years on this project, so it represented nearly a lifetime of intellectual activity. During the final decade, he shouldered the heavy load of editorial labor virtually without assistance. As the set was nearing completion, he had occasion to consult the article on the Saracens, which he had written some time previously. When he examined the printed text, he found to his astonishment that his article had been gravely mutilated by a series of deletions and alterations. Hurriedly Diderot examined other entries he had prepared and discovered they too were emasculated. Angrily he demanded an explanation from the bookseller printing the work, only to learn that he had been tricked by a wily publisher. Fearful of royal displeasure, the printer had devised a scheme that would deceive Diderot and satisfy the royal censor. He took the original articles and set them up in type. After Diderot returned the proof sheets, he secretly cut out or altered all those passages that might cause offense. To make doubly sure that this editing would be effective, the printer destroyed the original manuscript as well as the proofs of Diderot's articles. Thus while Diderot might storm and rail against the perfidy of the publisher, there was nothing he could do about the mutilation of his work. To the end of his days, Diderot could never forgive this cowardly defacement of the edifice to which he had devoted so much of his life.

Diderot predicted the *Encyclopédie* would be a great success because it furnished information that could not be found elsewhere. He defended the practice of including certain historical expositions on cooking, fashions and clothing by saying with a touch of irony, "the most succinct articles of this sort will perhaps save our descendants years of research and volumes of dissertations . . . an essay on our modes which is today thought frivolous will be regarded two thousand years from now as a learned and profound work on French costume, a work very instructive for men of letters, painters and sculptors."

Today the *Encyclopédie* is remembered primarily because of its brilliant contributors who advanced ideas that were to furnish the intellectual capital for the French Revolution. D'Alembert said it would be remembered because of its philosophical spirit, and Diderot predicted, "The thing will surely produce a great revolution in the human mind."

The *Encyclopédie* marked a major advance in the evolution of the encyclopedia as an instrument of scholarship by providing an exhaustive treatment of science and technology on an unprecedented scale. This was due to the vision and philosophy of the encyclopedists who exalted scientific knowledge and peaceful industry. D'Alembert explained in his "Preliminary Discourse" that the aim of the editors was to execute Bacon's plan for a Universal Dictionary of the Arts and Sciences. Their ambition was to elevate the artisan, the craftsman and the engineer, and to draw them closer together by explaining their contributions to society. The editors realized they would be unable to achieve this lofty goal if they relied only on information printed in books and periodicals. They left the cloistered solitude of the library and went into the world to obtain what they required by interviewing men energetically pursuing their vocations.

Diderot played a major part in this activity. During the day, he would visit leading workshops and factories in Paris to learn about the latest mechanical inventions and technical processes; then at night, he would write up the material he had collected and commission artists to prepare careful drawings of the most interesting machines he had seen. His fruitful labor is reflected in the pictorial volumes of the set which contain more than three thousand splendid illustrations covering all phases of industrial and mercantile activity. Prepared by skilled artists on copper plates, they offer a valuable record of eighteenth-century science and technology, and provide a visual museum of a bygone era.

Of course, the *Encyclopédie* was far from perfect. Its entries were of varying merit because it was often difficult to secure writers who possessed an adequate knowledge of their subject. The editors asked the composer Rameau to prepare the articles on Music, and when he refused, they assigned this task to Jean-Jacques Rousseau. After his early articles appeared, they were bitterly attacked by Rameau for their "errors." Such deficiencies were frankly acknowledged by Diderot when he declared:

> Some parts of the *Encyclopédie* are inflated and exorbitantly diffuse; others meager, flat, dry and jejune. . . . A good-natured man purchases our work, and being troubled with the cramp, turns immediately to the article "Cramp"; he finds the word, but is referred to "Convulsion"; he looks for this, and is directed to "Spasm," where after all he learns

nothing about the cramp. This is, I confess, a most ridiculous neglect, and I have little doubt that we are guilty of twenty similar ones.

After its completion, the *Encyclopédie* was widely acknowledged as a monument of French culture. Its influence extended beyond its narrow circle of subscribers because thousands of copies were sold abroad in unauthorized editions. This led individuals in other countries to undertake similar projects.

In 1768 the *Encyclopaedia Britannica* was quietly launched in Edinburgh by two enterprising Scotsmen, Andrew Bell and Colin Macfarquhar. One was an engraver, the other a printer; and they decided to embark on this venture because of the extraordinary success and notoriety of the French work. Since they were unable to secure anyone with a European reputation to serve as editor, they chose William Smellie, a local intellectual who was noted as "a veteran in wit, genius and bawdry." This colorful, whiskey-loving editor was responsible for most of the articles in the first edition, and he often boasted that he had made a Dictionary of the Arts and Sciences with the aid of a pastepot and scissors by snipping out material from books in his library.

The *Britannica* was not the first alphabetical encyclopedia in the English language. This honor belongs to the *Lexicon technicum* published in 1704 by John Harris, the first secretary of the Royal Society. It was followed by a much larger and more famous work: Ephraim Chambers' *Cyclopaedia*, which appeared in 1728. Although Chambers excluded history, biography and geography, he attempted to treat subjects as "so many wholes and so many parts of some greater whole." He sought to draw upon the whole commonwealth of learning in compiling his two massive folios. He noted that one man's wit could only go a small distance in such an undertaking—and he confessed, "Nobody that fell in my way was spared, antient or modern, foreign nor domestic, Christian or Jew or heathen."

Chambers' *Cyclopaedia* was extremely popular, and it went through a number of editions. It was a direct predecessor of the French *Encyclopédie,* and was undoubtedly used by Smellie in assembling the first edition of the *Britannica*. This edition, completed in 1771, consisted of three volumes containing 2,659 pages and 160 engravings. The title page announced that it was compiled by a "Society of Gentlemen in Scotland"—a pleasant fiction invented by the publishers to add distinction to their work. From this modest beginning, the *Britannica* rapidly grew in size and scope. When the second edition was completed in 1784, the three volumes of the first edition had increased to ten volumes containing 8,595 pages. A decade later the third edition was issued in eighteen volumes, and when the fourth edition was finished in 1810, the set had grown to twenty volumes and 16,033 pages. This rapid expansion made it possible to cover the entire circle of learning in an increasingly comprehensive manner. The owners were encouraged by the response of the public, and during the nineteenth century they sought to keep the set up to date by issuing a new edition about once every twenty years. Some of these editions merely consisted of a number of supplementary volumes added to an existing edition, while others represented a complete revision of the work.

Although other encyclopedias were launched during the eighteenth and nineteenth centuries, the *Britannica*'s unbroken continuity, its famous contributors and commercial success established it as the leading general reference work in the English language.

[3]

The Growth of
a Tradition

THE first edition of the *Britannica* was published in installments in Edinburgh in December, 1768. They appeared as slim pamphlets costing sixpence each. During the next three years, as successive numbers were issued, little attention was paid to the work by the leading wits of the town. Thus Boswell, who was well informed of the latest intellectual events in Edinburgh, never mentioned it in any of his writings. This neglect was probably due to the emphasis on practical topics, which was succinctly expressed in its preface:

> Utility ought to be the principal intention of every publication. Wherever this intention does not plainly appear, neither the books nor their authors have the smallest claim to the approbation of mankind.

In line with this practical outlook, there was a thirty-nine-page essay on Farriery, the art of curing diseases in horses. The editor explained that the subject was covered so fully because most individuals treating horses were illiterate and "the practice of this useful art has hitherto almost entirely been confined to a set of men who are totally ignorant of anatomy." This utilitarian emphasis created certain difficulties. When a detailed account appeared on Midwifery, many subscribers were offended by the accompanying plates which graphically illustrated the normal and abnormal delivery of babies. Some readers felt these pictures were "obscene," and indignantly removed them from their copies.

The editor hoped his work would benefit a large number of people rather than a limited group of readers, for he said: "We will, however, venture to affirm, that any man of ordinary parts, may, if he chuses, learn the principles of Agriculture, or Astronomy, of Botany, of Chemistry, etc. etc. from the *ENCYCLO-PAEDIA BRITANNICA*." Despite these large claims, however, the first edition was a modest achievement. The letters A and B were covered in the first volume of 697 pages, but the rest of the alphabet occupied two volumes containing less than two thousand pages. Long treatises dealt with particular subjects, but most of the entries consisted of brief definitions since the work was essentially a Dictionary of the Arts and Sciences. Thus Japan was described in a single sentence:

> JAPAN, or *Islands of Japan,* are situated between 130° and 144° E. long. and between 30° and 40° N. lat.

Although the *Britannica* subsequently became famous for its comprehensive coverage of literary and historical subjects, there were no biographies or historical articles in the first edition. Poetry was discussed in a mere five hundred words and drama in seven lines, yet more than fifty pages were devoted to a treatise on Book-keeping that included a set of sample ledgers. Today some of the brief entries in the first edition make quaint reading. Thus we learn:

> HEIRESS, a female heir to one who has an estate in lands &c. Stealing an heiress, and marrying her against her will, was declared a felony by 3 Hen. VII.

OMELET, or Amlet, a kind of pancake or fricasse of eggs, with other ingredients, very usual in Spain and France.

Sometimes articles were a model of conciseness. The entry on Woman required only seven words, to wit: "WOMAN, the female of man. See HOMO."

The publishers of the *Britannica* were inspired by commercial motives. They had no wish to emulate Diderot and D'Alembert by disturbing the established order of society, and the conservative tenor of their work was accentuated by the violent excess of the French Revolution, which seemed to confirm the danger of bold philosophical speculation. Consequently when a two-volume supplement to the third edition was issued in 1801, it was dedicated to George III and stated:

> The French *Encyclopédie* has been accused, and justly accused, of having disseminated, far and wide, the seeds of Anarchy and Atheism. If the *ENCYCLOPAEDIA BRITANNICA* shall, in any degree, counteract the tendency of that pestiferous Work, even these two Volumes will not be wholly unworthy of Your Majesty's Patronage. . . .

Diderot did not receive a biographical entry in the third edition, but the supplement contained a long article that bitterly attacked his principles and those of his associates:

> It has been completely proved, that one great object for which the philosophers, as they called themselves, undertook the compilation of the *Encyclopédie* was to sap the foundation of all religion. This was to be attempted not directly and avowedly; for bare-faced atheism would not then be suffered in France. A cloak, therefore, was to be worn, and the poisoned dagger to be concealed under it.

And the article concluded that "to draw a formal character of this wretch is surely superfluous."

During the early part of the nineteenth century, English encyclopedias featured comprehensive essays on scientific subjects recording the results of original research. Many scientists employed this medium of communication because the number of technical journals was quite limited at this time. Booksellers were unwilling to issue treatises on mathematics and physics because there was no market for such works. Therefore long dissertations on scientific topics were a common feature in early reference works. Matters were somewhat different in the humanities where it was often difficult to secure authors of established eminence to write on popular subjects such as literature, history and biography which already claimed a wide circle of readers.

The early role of the encyclopedia as a vehicle of scientific communication is illustrated by Thomas Young's remarkable contributions to the *Britannica*. Young, like Helmholtz in Germany, conducted research in many different fields. He made important observations in human anatomy and physiology, engineering, physics and linguistics. In 1805 he wrote an article on Cohesion, which was later expanded for the *Encyclopaedia;* it contained one of the first estimates of the range of molecular forces and the size of molecules. His calculations yielded a molecular size a hundred times too large, but many years later Lord Rayleigh emphasized the importance of his analysis. From 1816 to 1823, Young contributed more than sixty articles on a wide range of subjects that reflected his dazzling virtuosity. His efforts, which filled 380 quarto pages, were often original dissertations. His article on Chromatics developed the wave theory of light, his essay on Carpentry dealt with the flexure of beams (Young's modulus), and his treatise on the Tides was based on fresh mathematical analysis and computation. Young's practical bent was expressed by his essays on the Bridge, Hydraulics and Steam Engines, while his historical interests found an outlet in forty-five biographies he wrote on leading men of science.

As a linguist, Young prepared a 33,000-word essay on Language, and his most celebrated piece was the article on Egypt, which appeared in 1818. It presented the first popular account in English of his attempt to decipher the Rosetta Stone, and virtually inaugurated the study of Egyptology. The *Edinburgh Review* called this article "the greatest effort of scholarship and ingenuity of which modern literature can boast," and the tablet erected to his memory in Westminster Abbey justly observes, "He first penetrated the obscurity which had veiled the hieroglyphics of Egypt."

Young was only one of a long line of celebrated contributors. Walter Scott furnished a memorable series of essays on Drama, Romance and Chivalry; Thomas DeQuincey wrote on Pope, Schiller and Shakespeare; Robert Malthus set forth his ideas on Population; and David Ricardo discussed his novel theories of Commerce and Political Economy. Such authors imparted a special distinction to the *Encyclopaedia*—so that the inhabitant of an isolated country house who secured a copy during the nineteenth century felt its twenty volumes would contain the essence of the 20,000 reference books lining the walls of the British Museum.

The elevation of the work into a supreme authority led to its abuse when readers employed it as a short cut in acquiring knowledge. This practice was parodied by Dickens in the *Pickwick Papers* when he described Mr. Pickwick's chance meeting with the ebullient editor of the Eatanswill Gazette one evening at the Saracen's Head Inn. The editor tells Mr. Pickwick he has instructed a critic to prepare an essay on Chinese Metaphysics for his Gazette by reading the article on China and the article on Metaphysics in the *Encyclopaedia Britannica* and combining the information obtained from these two sources. Unfortunately, Dickens does not describe the result of this unusual synthesis.

The *Britannica* became a significant forum for political ideas early in its history when it began to solicit material from leading intellectual figures. Its subscribers became familiar with the doctrines of the English Utilitarians when James Mill was commissioned to prepare a series of articles expounding the theories of the group. His contributions appeared in the same supplement as Young's famous article on Egypt—and included essays on Government, Jurisprudence, Education, Prisons and Liberty of the Press. When they were reprinted in a slim volume in 1828, the whole substance of radical thought was fully expounded between a pair of pasteboard covers. In March, 1829, Mill's essay on Government was subjected to a slashing assault by the youthful Macaulay in the conservative *Edinburgh Review*. In deriding Mill's ideas, he described him and his associates as "smatterers, whose attainments just suffice to elevate them from the insignificance of dunces to the dignity of bores." This attack was answered in the *Westminster Review,* and the resulting controversy was part of the political agitation culminating in the great English Reform Bill of 1832.

During the nineteenth century, many gifted writers were able to express their views in the *Encyclopaedia*. Thus it was natural that Macaulay, who began his literary career by attacking Mill's essays, should become a contributor to the eighth edition a generation later. His articles were not hasty exercises written for a fee, but elaborate essays prepared near the close of his life. His biography of Pitt filled more than seventy octavo pages; and his essays on Bunyan, Johnson and Goldsmith still appear in the set because of their literary brilliance. Macaulay's style is notable for its vividness and persuasive rhetoric. He did not feel it necessary to heap up a mass of biographical facts—rather he sought to capture the essential spirit of his subject in eloquent prose—it is understandable that editors should have retained his essays for four generations.

A century ago, educated readers were interested in extensive surveys of important subjects, rather than concise factual information. In satisfying this demand, the *Britannica* became a valuable record of the shifting interests and concerns of British intellectual life. This may be seen in the changing treatment of the Bible. When the first edition was published in 1768, there was no conflict between the sacred Scriptures and scientific inquiry. Scientists as well as theologians accepted the Biblical account of Creation and the Deluge because there was no evidence that would discredit the scriptural record. Therefore it was quite natural for the first edition to contain an engraving of Noah's Ark "floating on the waters of the deluge"—as well as a detailed plan and description of the Ark. The second edition a few years later was even more explicit. Its article on Chronology followed Archbishop Ussher's computations by giving the date of the world's creation as 4004 B.C. and stating that in 2348 B.C., "The old world is destroyed by a deluge which continued for 777 days." The editor of the second edition offered an elaborate theory of the Flood because he felt that to give up on this point "would utterly destroy the sacred writings." His theory was based on the supposed power of atmospheric electricity to raise a large quantity of water from the earth into the air, and it was reprinted for eighty years.

The attack against the literal belief in the Bible was launched from several directions. Skeptical thinkers questioned the miracles of Christianity by logical analysis, and geological discoveries demonstrated that the earth was much older than theological writers had assumed. As a result, the extreme position of fundamentalists became untenable and they were forced to retreat. Despite the mounting weight of scientific evidence, they continued to direct a stream of argument and invective at the "modernists." During the early part of the nineteenth century, the *Britannica* simply echoed orthodox opinion. The article on Christianity in the seventh edition in 1832 briefly discussed the controversy created by David Hume's celebrated "Essay on Miracles," which had sharply questioned the belief in supernatural events. The article cited authors who were said to have exposed the sophistry of Hume's arguments and concluded:

> Such a disputation, however, is but little calculated to promote edification, and seems to have originated rather in a love of paradox, or a desire to strike out something apparently new, than in any sound and comprehensive estimate of the evidences of Christianity.

The *Encyclopaedia*'s conservative point of view was accentuated because it was published in Edinburgh, a stronghold of religious orthodoxy. Consequently it avoided taking sides in the dispute about the relative claims of science and religion. The issue reached a climax when the theory of evolution was jointly presented by Darwin and Wallace in 1859. The theory was advanced too late to affect the eighth edition completed in 1860; and by the time the ninth edition was begun in 1875, evolution had been widely accepted. Nevertheless, the editor of the ninth edition cautiously announced in the preface to the first volume:

> This fresh outbreak of the inevitable contest between the old and the new is a fruitful source of exaggerated hopes and fears, and of excited denunciation and appeal. In this conflict a work like the Encyclopaedia is not called upon to take any direct part. It has to do with knowledge rather than opinion. . . .

The editor went on to explain that the work could not be an organ of any sect or party in science, religion or philosophy since its main duty was to give an impartial summary of the facts and results in every department of inquiry and research.

No one could quarrel with such a sober and judicious observation. But apparently the editors wished to reassure subscribers who might be disturbed by the prospect that advanced positions would be adopted on issues agitating English intellectual life. This was not the aim of the editors, for characteristically in the ninth edition, the essay on evolution as a philosophical idea was much longer than Huxley's article on the biological theory of evolution.

Despite its effort to avoid controversy, the *Encyclopaedia* became embroiled in the "religious question" because of its commitment to modern scholarship. Instead of repeating old dogmas, it became a vehicle for liberal ideas by allying itself with the new critical spirit in theology.

The editors selected William Robertson Smith, a brilliant young theologian, to deal with topics relating to Semitic studies. Smith had been elected to the Chair of Hebrew at the Free Church College at Aberdeen when he was only twenty-four years old, and he was widely regarded as one of the most promising young scholars in the British Isles. He became a controversial figure when his article on the Bible appeared. It expounded the ideas of the new school of higher criticism, interpreting the sacred text by the same methods used in studying other ancient works. This examination of the Scriptures as a human document composed by a number of authors aroused a storm of protest. Many elders of the Free Church in Scotland were distressed by his assertion that Moses did not write Deuteronomy and David was not the author of the Psalms. They raised a hue and cry that "Moses was in danger" and demanded that Robertson Smith be relieved of his academic position. After preliminary efforts to settle the matter had failed, a solemn assembly was convened to try Smith on a series of charges which, if sustained, would result in his ouster. The case dragged on for three years, and it was only in May, 1880 that the Elders voted by the narrow margin of 299 to 292 to dismiss the charges.

Despite this victory, the case was not over. Within ten days the question was reopened when the "H" volume was belatedly issued containing his article on Hebrew Language and Literature. It presented "unguarded statements" of the same kind that had previously been denounced. When Smith's opponents read the article they felt he had broken his promise to refrain from religious controversy. Therefore they brought new charges —and within a year he was removed from his post.

The ninth edition was a major monument of Victorian learning whose distinction was enhanced by an imposing array of contributors. They included such literary figures as Swinburne, Saintsbury, Matthew Arnold and Andrew Lang; the scientists Huxley, Kelvin, Rayleigh and Wallace; as well as a cross section of the intellectual elite of the British Isles drawn from the principal universities and learned societies. The editors were not content with native scholars; they called upon foreign authors to record advances being made abroad. Prince Kropotkin supplied articles on Russian subjects, and Julius Wellhausen summarized the results of the new school of German Biblical criticism in a long essay on ancient Israel. The ninth edition relied on comprehensive treatises rather than short articles, and these treatises were often reprinted to meet the demand for an authoritative treatment of certain topics. An example was Tait's seventy-four-page essay on Mechanics, which was used for many years as a standard text on the subject.

Outstanding advisors were secured in planning the ninth edition. High standards were insured when Huxley helped organize the coverage of the biological sciences, Maxwell assisted in physics, Cayley in mathematics, and Geike in geology. They prepared lists of articles that would be needed and suggested individuals who might be willing to act as contributors. Thus Huxley advised the editor in 1875:

> I think ——— is like enough to do the Coelenterata well if you can make sure of his doing it at all. He is a man of really great knowledge of the literature of Zoology and if it had not been for the accident of his being such a procrastinating ass, he could have been a distinguished man. But he is a sort of Baalam-Centaur with the asinine stronger than the prophetic moiety. I should be inclined to try him none the less.

The ninth edition reflected the learning and acumen of its editors. It was begun under the direction of its first editor, Thomas Spencer Baynes, who had formerly been a professor of logic at St. Andrews University. After he was forced to withdraw because of ill health, his place was taken by William Robertson Smith, whose Biblical articles had created such a furor. Smith in many ways was an ideal encyclopedia editor. The breadth of his intellectual interests coupled with his active participation provided the leadership required for this massive undertaking. Before becoming an editor, he contributed some twenty articles to the first eleven volumes; but after he joined the staff, he wrote more than two hundred articles—many of which were lengthy essays. The publisher made no effort to direct his editorial labor; and after the ninth edition was completed, Smith stated that while the work was in progress his principal communication with the publisher was a long slip of paper that would arrive every six months. At the top of the slip was printed THE BANK OF ENGLAND and on the bottom was the signature of the publisher, A. & C. Black.

As an editor, Smith was continually looking for new topics

that should be treated. This followed a long tradition of editorial pioneering, and therefore it was natural for him to write an editorial associate:

> Totemism is a subject of growing importance. . . . We must make room for it whatever else goes. Torture, though a nice paper, is not at all so necessary, for people can learn about torture elsewhere, and the subject is one of decaying and not rising interest.

To obtain something on the subject, Smith chose an unknown Cambridge don, James Frazer, and asked him to prepare articles on Totemism and Taboo. Frazer testified later that the searches made for these papers marked the beginning of his systematic application of anthropology that was to culminate in his monumental work, *The Golden Bough,* which he dedicated to William Robertson Smith.

The ninth edition was completed in 1889; its twenty-five volumes contained over 20,000 pages and nine thousand illustrations. Its 17,000 articles by 1,150 contributors represented a landmark of English scholarship; yet in covering the whole circle of learning there was room not only for weighty technical treatises, but for lighter diversions as well. The article on Angling began by describing the delightful sport of schoolboys who engage in bottom fishing for perch and carp with a bamboo rod, and then supplied detailed instructions on the art of fishing in streams and lakes. The article on Chess reminded readers:

> The cerebral organ, after being much occupied in business, or greatly worried by cares, finds in the absorbing and abstracting properties of chess that temporary relief which lighter pastimes do not always afford.

And then to prove its point, it offered a set of chess problems for the relaxation of its readers.

The ninth edition has often been known as the scholar's edition, because its planning and execution were in the hands of editors who did not attempt to simplify or popularize its contents. Its thorough coverage of the humanities and brilliant literary essays imparted a unique luster to the set and made it one of the jewels of British learning. Thus as the nineteenth century drew to a close, the *Britannica* was recognized throughout the world as a symbol of English learning—just as the Union Jack was acknowledged as a sign of British colonial power—and its supremacy, like that of the Empire, was accepted without question.

[4]

The Great EB

Until 1898, the *Encyclopaedia* was closely associated with the intellectual traditions of Edinburgh. This Scottish tradition was brought to a close when several enterprising Americans realized the work offered a good prospect for financial gain. Only five thousand copies of the ninth edition had been sold in the British Isles because of its prohibitively high price of £42. By 1898, nine years after its completion, sales had virtually ceased. Several American booksellers, led by Horace Hooper and Walter Jackson, believed there would be a large market for the set if it could be distributed at a low price. They secured reprint rights from A. & C. Black and decided to sell the work on the installment plan.

They required the assistance, however, of an established institution that would lend an air of respectability to their bold merchandising scheme. In searching for an ally, Hooper and Jackson turned their attention to the venerable London *Times,* which was in serious financial difficulty because of competition

from the new popular mass journalism. For more than a generation the *Times* had occupied a unique place in British life.
"Written to instruct the members of Parliament," it had become
an authorized spokesman of the English ruling class and a potent
force in molding public opinion. But by 1898, its daily circulation had declined to a mere 36,000 and its advertising revenue,
which was based on small classified ads, had failed to keep pace
with rising costs. Things were quite bleak in Printing House
Square when the American booksellers approached the editor
with their business proposition. They wished to advertise and
sell a reprint of the ninth edition through the *Times*. In return
for lending its name and prestige to the enterprise, the newspaper would receive the revenue from the *Encyclopaedia*'s advertisements and a royalty of one guinea on each set sold. At
first the editor was cautious—who after all were these confident
Americans, Hooper and Jackson, with their bold schemes and
generous promises of financial rewards? But economic conditions
were pressing—and after some hesitation, an agreement was
signed on March 14, 1898 between the American booksellers
and the *Times*. Under its terms, the newspaper agreed to accept
orders for the reprint which would be forwarded to the Americans in return for a commission of one guinea on each order.

The first advertisement for the new reprint announced that
the *Times* was offering the ninth edition for the low price of
£14. The public was told:

> The "ENCYCLOPAEDIA BRITANNICA" is not a mere
> aid to memory, to be hastily consulted in moments of emer-
> gency; it is not only the greatest of works of reference, it
> is A LIBRARY IN ITSELF. . . . The volumes are EMI-
> NENTLY READABLE.

The advertisement noted that the *Britannica* "gave no hospital-
ity to the sort of 'harmless drudges' who used to compile works
of reference when the world was younger"; and it concluded
with a series of testimonials that included Gladstone's observation: "To own a set of the *Encyclopaedia Britannica* is to acknowledge one's self as recognizing the best there is in literature."

An unusual feature of this campaign was that the entire set would be delivered after a down payment of only one guinea, and the rest of the purchase price could be paid in easy monthly installments. This was a striking innovation in the publishing field. Previously the full price had to be paid in advance, but now, thanks to "The Times Easy System of Payment," readers could enjoy the work while they were paying for it. Furthermore, since the reprint cost only one-third the price of the original, many people could now afford it.

The combination of a reduced price, heavy advertising and the installment plan made the reprint a great commercial success. Within two months 4,300 sets were sold, which almost equaled the number marketed in England during the previous two decades. Critics were irritated because in 1898 individual volumes of the *Times* reprint were from nine to twenty-three years old. Although nearly every advertisement stated that a reprint of the ninth edition was being offered for sale, this statement was overlooked by many people who were overwhelmed by persuasive advertising appeals. This led a witty journalist to remark: "The *Times* is behind the *Encyclopaedia,* and the *Encyclopaedia* is behind the times."

To bring the *Britannica* up to date, work was begun in 1899 on a ten-volume supplement known as the tenth edition. While this editorial labor was under way, Hooper and Jackson acquired complete ownership from A. & C. Black, and a famous British institution passed into American hands. This, however, had little effect on the contents of the set because the *Times* retained full editorial control, and as the newspaper later stated: "The *Times* is . . . fully conscious of its responsibility in using its absolute control of a work which is a national institution."

The first volume of the tenth edition was issued in May, 1902, and the remaining volumes reached the public during the following months. For business reasons, the ninth and tenth editions were combined to form a set of thirty-five volumes which was strenuously marketed. In addition to advertisements in the *Times,* announcements and pamphlets were distributed throughout the British Isles. Any innocent inquiry for information brought a shower of leaflets, illustrated brochures, and even prepaid telegrams which had merely to be signed and returned. To secure fresh leads, the *Times* launched a competition, with a scholarship to Oxford or Cambridge as a first prize. Contestants were required to answer questions using the *Britannica* as a source of information, and the publicity associated with this contest helped publicize the work.

Blaring ads proclaimed the unique features of the new edition:

> The *Encyclopaedia Britannica* can reveal all the kingdoms of the world in a moment of time. Railway communication, the telegraph, the motor car are slow vehicles in comparison with the rapid course of a thought that with the aid of these volumes can fly from Thibet to Korea, from Korea to the Congo!

The relatively subdued approach of 1898 was abandoned in favor of exaggerated claims that would catch the public eye. Readers were told they could avoid medical, legal and household expenses by purchasing the set because: "The doctor, the carpenter, the lawyer have all gone to the *Encyclopaedia Britannica* to learn. WHY NOT GO DIRECT and save the expense of an intermediary?"

As the insistent cry of "Going, Going, Gone" echoed through the advertising pages of the *Times,* readers were urged to place their orders before it was too late. Years later an editor of the newspaper recalled: "Flight was useless; the whole country from Land's End to John o'Groat's and from Yarmouth to Dunmore Head was pervaded by the *Encyclopaedia Britannica.* . . . There was no escape from the torrent of 'follow ups' save by the despatch of a firm order to purchase followed by an installment of one guinea."

Hapless consumers found it difficult to resist this whirlwind campaign, but occasionally there were protests. One prepaid telegram was returned to the *Times* with the message, "From my bath, I curse you!" A retired member of Parliament complained, "You have made a damnable hubbub, sir, and an assault on my privacy with your American tactics." Nevertheless, these methods produced results. When the books were closed in December, 1903 on the special offer for the tenth edition, the *Times* had sold a total of 30,000 copies of its reprint of the ninth edition and secured orders for an additional 32,000 copies of the tenth edition.

The driving force behind this flamboyant activity was Horace Hooper, the American bookseller, who had always believed a large untapped market existed for the set. He spoke of the work as "a thorough library of knowledge" which should be put within reach of every person who could read English—and he diligently sought to achieve this objective. Hooper, however, was more than a master promoter and a gifted salesman. His genuine interest in the *Britannica* helped lift it to new heights of scholarship, for as soon as the campaign for the tenth edition was completed, he was inspired by a vision of a new and greater work. He exclaimed to his associates: "Now we start from scratch, and have a completely new edition! Completely rewritten! Knowledge has moved too fast and we must catch up with it."

His infectious enthusiasm was responsible for the eleventh edition, which took nearly eight years to complete. The editor of this massive project was a journalist, Hugh Chisholm, who had previously served as an editor on the tenth edition. Under his regime, the *Times'* editorial offices were transformed into a veritable den of scholars, since many staff members were recruited from the ranks of the newspaper. Chisholm was a man with strong prejudices who obstinately clung to old-fashioned ideas on certain subjects. Once, it is said, he was shocked by some candid details in an article submitted on Obstetrics and demanded that they be modified or deleted. This led to a heated discussion with his subordinates, and in the ensuing argument, one of his sub-editors shouted, "Well, we ought to have something on the subject newer than what Adam did for Eve when he was alone with her in the Garden of Eden!"

The eleventh edition abandoned the monographic approach of the ninth edition by breaking comprehensive treatises into a series of shorter articles. As a result, it contained 40,000 entries compared with 17,000 in the ninth edition. Even more important, the text was increased from thirty million to forty-four million words, and this allowed the entire domain of knowledge to be covered far more thoroughly than had ever before been possible. Although many outstanding literary essays were retained from the ninth edition, there was room for a host of new articles on the humanities as well as on science and technology. Subjects connected with English life were treated in great detail, and major articles featured long, exhaustive bibliographies that were valuable to students and scholars.

The new edition was a notable achievement of co-operative labor and its success was largely due to Horace Hooper who proclaimed: "I'm determined that the eleventh edition must be the greatest book ever published. I mean that from an editorial and scholarly point of view. And I'm willing to pour as much money into it as I can lay my hands on."

Hooper's vision reached beyond the immediate goal of increased profits; he saw an opportunity to transform the *Britannica* into a unique instrument of education and culture. His partner, Walter Jackson, had little interest in these dreams. He was content to follow the economical methods of the past by retaining major portions of the ninth and tenth editions and issuing the work a volume at a time. This procedure would minimize expenses and maximize profits, but Hooper refused to accept the idea. As he later wrote, "We could easily have produced a book at half the cost by doing hack work and taking a large share of it from the tenth edition; but I felt that I should like to know that I had been instrumental in producing a great book, and in better form, than any other man."

This difference of opinion created a rift between the partners. When Jackson refused to discuss the matter and sailed for America where he had other business interests, Hooper notified him: "This action on your part . . . makes it necessary for us to go ahead without further consultation with you." Jackson promptly charged that his partner was "insincere and dishonest," and was plotting to deprive him of control by installing a board of "dummy directors." Inevitably, the dispute reached the law courts. In the midst of a series of charges and countercharges, Jackson issued a bill of particulars describing the role of the partners in arranging the sale of the London *Times* to the newspaper tycoon, Lord Northcliffe. Hooper replied in a long affidavit adding further details of how Northcliffe, who had made a fortune by introducing "yellow journalism" in England, had obtained control of the *Times*. These revelations created a sensation in Fleet Street; and Northcliffe, angered by the disclosure of such business secrets, ordered the *Times* to sever its connection with the *Britannica*. This precipitated a financial crisis because the costs of the eleventh edition, which had not yet been finished, were far greater than had been originally anticipated. A total of $700,000 had already been spent, and another $700,000 was needed to complete the work, but only $45,000 was on hand.

Outside financing was essential if the edition was to be completed on schedule, but without the name and prestige of the *Times,* banks would not lend the large sums required. Hooper was not discouraged by this unfavorable turn of events. Ignoring his partner's lawsuits, he cast about for another sponsor for the *Encyclopaedia.* When he learned that Oxford University might be interested, he told an intermediary, "As for now, offer a royalty of ten per cent on our sales. Tell them I'm sure it will bring them a great deal of money." When Oxford rejected these terms, Hooper replied, "They think I am trying to bribe them. I offered them too much . . . go to Cambridge now—and offer them just half."

Cambridge was interested, but desired further details. Hooper plunged into this task with enthusiasm:

> To me the *Encyclopaedia Britannica* is like the Bible. It's something holy! And who else but Cambridge should have it? It's got a great reputation, like Cambridge. And we're revising it completely. New articles! New plates! There's no financial risk, and I'll give the university a handsome commission on sales.

These persuasive arguments convinced the Syndics who managed the Cambridge University Press. They agreed to issue the *Encyclopaedia* under the University's imprimatur, even though it had taken no part in the planning or execution of the work.

The addition of Cambridge as a sponsor solved many pressing financial problems. Where Hooper had been able to obtain only $200,000 in bank loans, he could now raise five times that amount, thanks to the prestige of the University in banking circles. Despite this key role, royalties were calculated on a sliding scale that reached a maximum of ten shillings on each set sold— or only half as much as received by the *Times*.

Instead of issuing the eleventh edition piecemeal, as had been the practice in the past, an effort was made to publish the entire work at once. The first half was issued in December, 1910, and the second half six months later. The new edition was widely recognized as an outstanding achievement. Its 1,500 contributors included 168 Fellows of the Royal Society, fifty-six presidents and secretaries of learned societies, forty-seven members of the British Museum staff, as well as many other leaders of British intellectual life. When a banquet was held for the contributors at Claridge's in October, 1910, the American ambassador summed up the general view by describing the *Britannica* as "the Monarch of Encyclopaedias," and observing it was "the one encyclopedia in which we all look for the most comprehensive, the most thorough, and the most complete statement of facts on any particular subject."

Promotion of the new edition was necessarily subdued in England because advertising copy had to be cleared by Cambridge University, which was being criticized for lending its name to an enterprise it had neither supervised nor directed. But such modesty was abandoned in America where the connection between Cambridge and the *Britannica* was boldly exploited in advertisements issued in the name of the Cambridge University Press (Encyclopaedia Britannica Division). During the winter and spring of 1911, Americans were subjected to a massive sales campaign. During April and May, large ads appeared almost every Saturday and Sunday in the *New York Times*. On April ninth readers were told:

> The *Encyclopaedia Britannica,* 11th edition, is a clearing house of modern thought, knowledge and achievement through which the layman can pass his doubts and difficulties with the

certain assurance that no reasonable demand for knowledge and information that he may present will be dishonored.

The advertisements sought to strike a deeper emotional note by reminding readers, "Of all kinds of loneliness, a loneliness in a crowd is the most depressing; and of all kinds of ignorance, the ignorance of modern man . . . is the most humiliating." Those who wished to escape this painful condition were urged to obtain a copy of the eleventh edition.

Once again, intensive advertising, installment buying and reduced price offers yielded ample returns. With the advent of World War I, this elaborate system of advertising and installment buying trembled, and then collapsed. Hooper met this unfavorable turn of events in 1915 by issuing a photographic reprint of the eleventh edition which cut manufacturing costs by reducing the size of the printed page. The inexpensive reprint was marketed with the aid of the Chicago mail order house, Sears, Roebuck and Company; and more than 50,000 copies were sold. As a result of this association, Hooper was able to interest its president, Julius Rosenwald, in the financial potential of the *Britannica*—and in 1920 Sears, Roebuck acquired ownership of the work for $1,330,000. Sears made the purchase with optimistic expectations of profit, but these hopes were never realized. During two decades of ownership, Sears managed to lose several million dollars on what was to prove a costly white elephant.

In June, 1922, Horace Hooper died of a heart attack at the age of sixty-two. His career was eulogized in an editorial in the *New York Times,* which observed:

> In the view of the public, his success lay in the originality, boldness and brilliance of his operations. But that was merely the surface. The deeper source was his faith in the intelligence and the ambition of the great mass of citizens.

And the *Times* concluded that he had done more for popular enlightenment than many professional educators.

Hooper's death removed the driving force behind the *Britannica*'s editorial and financial achievements. His successors lacked the imagination, persistence and devotion to scholarship necessary to insure the *Encyclopaedia*'s continued growth as an intellectual force and a commercial enterprise. Before his death, Hooper attempted to bring the eleventh edition up to date by initiating work on the twelfth edition. It was issued in three volumes in 1922, and concentrated largely on the events of World War I. Four years later, another three-volume supplement, the thirteenth edition, was published containing articles by a number of celebrated figures including Henry Ford on Mass Production, Mencken on the American Language, Houdini on Conjuring, and Leon Trotsky on Lenin.

Soon after this supplement appeared, it became evident that the time was ripe for a completely new edition. Fifteen years had passed since the publication of the eleventh edition, and the march of events had made it increasingly inadequate for contemporary needs. To overcome this deficiency, work was begun in 1926 on the fourteenth edition, which was completed in two and a half years at a cost of $2,500,000. The new edition consisted of twenty-four volumes containing 35 million words, and its format, typography and physical layout have been retained to the present day. The *Encyclopaedia* lost much of its British character, since the fourteenth edition was freed from the restraining influence of the *Times*. This change was accentuated when separate editorial offices were established in London and New York. The new American influence was evident: nearly half of its 3,500 contributors were Americans—in contrast to the eleventh edition whose 1,500 contributors had included only 123 Americans.

Authors with a wide appeal were chosen and included many prominent personalities. Irene Castle wrote on Dancing, Helen Wills on Lawn Tennis, and Gene Tunney on Boxing; and the *EB*'s roster contained such stage and screen celebrities as Lillian Gish, Lon Chaney and Otis Skinner. These well-known names were deftly employed in publicizing the set and stimulating sales. The utility of the new edition was stressed in advertisements that announced, "It is unique in human interest and sheer practical value"; and its popular appeal was emphasized when readers were asked to "cast aside" their "old ideas of reference works and encyclopedias, for here is something new, different, tremendously vital, alive." Sales messages reported that the new edition was "Humanized, Modernized, Pictorialized"; and this slogan reflected the journalistic flavor of the work.

Despite the new American influence, British spelling and usage were retained to reduce editorial costs. This explains why thirty years later there is an entry on the Motor Car, and not the Automobile; one on the Gramophone, and not the Phonograph. Checkers is discussed in an article on Draughts, carbonated beverages under Aerated Waters, and pensions under Superannuation.

The fourteenth edition was not a financial success. Although 20,000 copies were sold within the first year, its publication coincided with the stock-market crash and the onset of the Depression. Sales fell precipitously and reached a low of 4,400 sets in 1933. With the passage of time, parts of the *Encyclopaedia* became obsolete, but economic conditions were so bad that it was impractical to issue a set of supplementary volumes. Therefore a plan of continuous revision was devised in which selected portions of the work were up-dated at periodic intervals. This permitted alterations to be adjusted to current income and allowed editorial expenses to be spread over a number of years. Because of this continuous revision, which is now carried out on an annual basis, the practice of numbering successive editions has been abandoned, and different editions are distinguished by their date of publication.

Sears, Roebuck was never able to exploit the *Britannica*'s commercial possibilities. Its acquisition had been due primarily to the personal interest of Julius Rosenwald, but its scholarly nature made its ownership by a mail order house rather incongruous. During World War II, Sears' president, General Robert Wood, decided to get rid of this unprofitable venture. In December, 1941, he offered the *Encyclopaedia* to the University of Chicago, but the University was unable to accept this gift because he asked for $300,000 to cover the *Britannica*'s inventory and accounts receivable. The trustees were reluctant to become involved in this venture, but William Benton, who was an academic vice-president, advocated accepting the offer because he felt the *Encyclopaedia* would be a valuable asset.

Benton, an astute businessman, had founded the advertising agency of Benton & Bowles with his friend Chester Bowles in 1929. Six years later, he decided to retire from the advertising world and devote himself to other pursuits. At the invitation of Robert Hutchins, president of the University of Chicago, he prepared a report on the school's public relations program and subsequently agreed to devote half his time to the University's affairs.

The *Britannica* was acquired by the University largely because of Benton's foresight and enthusiasm. For more than a year he attempted to raise the $300,000 required to cover its assets— but without success. The matter was brought to a head in January, 1943, when General Wood, despairing of the University's ability to secure money for this purpose, offered the entire enterprise including its inventory and receivables as an outright gift. Despite this generous gesture, the trustees still hesitated because working capital was needed. At this critical point, Benton agreed to advance the University $100,000. In return, he received a two-thirds interest in the *Encyclopaedia*, while the University retained an option to purchase back half of his interest after eighteen months for $50,000. Soon after Benton and the University gained control of the work, sales began to rise sharply as a result of wartime prosperity. Within eighteen months, the University earned over $300,000 in royalties. In view of this handsome return, the trustees decided against exercising their option to secure a larger interest, because, to quote the historian of the *EB*, "The University was doing so well through its affiliation and benefiting so handsomely from the company's prosperity that any change in the relationship was thought unwise."*

As early as 1941, concern was expressed in academic circles about the *Britannica*'s failure to reflect contemporary knowledge.

---

* Herman Kogan, *The Great EB; The Story of the Encyclopaedia Britannica*, Chicago, University of Chicago Press, 1958, p. 266.

A conference was called in New York by David Stevens, vice-president of the Rockefeller Foundation, and another was held in Chicago to discuss this problem. Professor Wilbur Jordan, general editor of the University of Chicago Press, reported the consensus at these meetings: the current edition "could not be regarded as scholarly in content nor an adequate delineation of the state of western learning in the year of its publication. This critical judgment," he said "was generally entertained among scholars" who believed it would be desirable to prepare a completely new edition.

When William Benton and the University of Chicago acquired the work in 1943, wartime conditions made it impossible to undertake such an ambitious program. Instead a temporary expedient was adopted; the Company established thirty fellowships for graduate students at the University of Chicago who were known as Britannica fellows. The fellows spent from one-third to one-half of their time checking articles and assisting faculty advisors and, in return, they received an annual stipend of $1,000 to $2,000. The use of graduate students, who could be hired at a minimum rate, was a temporary measure. Gradually they were replaced by a full-time editorial staff located in Chicago and a separate London editorial office, but no attempt was made to prepare a completely new edition. Instead, the program of continuous revision was expanded and several million words were changed each year. As a result, more than fifty million words have been altered since 1943.

Inevitably this has placed a premium on piecemeal changes, because it is much easier to patch up old entries than to prepare new material. This tendency has been accentuated by the inadequate sums allocated for editorial revision. *Business Week* reported on May 9, 1953 that although *Britannica* sales had reached $25 million in 1952, only $400,000 to $500,000—or two percent of the Company's income—was set aside for editorial work. During the last few years, this rate has increased to about four cents out of every dollar, but it is still much smaller than the *EB*'s annual advertising budget.

As far as possible, the *Encyclopaedia* seeks material that can be used for many years. This goal is expressed in its instructions to contributors:

> Such terms as "now," "at present" and "since 1950" should be avoided since they call attention to the immediate time of writing but will lose force by the time the article is in print. For the same reason, statistical material should be presented in general terms, contrasts or trends being shown by selected data, not with year-by-year figures.

This policy might be defended if dates were attached to individual entries so readers could tell when they were written and revised. This is a standard practice in scientific work, but it has not been adopted in the encyclopedia field because such frankness would result in a marked increase in editorial costs.

During the last decade, thanks to economic prosperity and the current emphasis on higher education, *EB* sales have risen at an astonishing rate. Dollar volume for the *Encyclopaedia* alone has risen from $12 million in 1949 to $55 million in 1959, and this growth has been shared by other reference works as well. It is one of the paradoxes of the encyclopedia field, however, that although a number of companies enjoy substantial sales in the United States, as far as the general public is concerned, one work —the *Britannica*—has become almost synonymous with the word "encyclopedia." This pre-eminence has been encouraged by a skillful program of public relations that has capitalized on the comprehensive coverage of the work and its illustrious contributors. During the 1930's, a popular radio show, "Information Please," featured a panel of experts who attempted to answer difficult questions sent in by listeners. Anyone who succeeded in stumping the experts received a free copy of the *Britannica* as a reward. This association helped fix the *EB*'s public image as a final authority in factual matters.

When the *Encyclopaedia*'s 190th anniversary occurred in 1958, the Company organized several events to commemorate the occasion. On June tenth, at a luncheon held in Chicago, Mr. Benton announced that the University of Chicago had already received more than five million dollars from the Company and he confidently predicted that by 1960 annual sales would exceed $100 million.

This optimistic spirit was reflected later in the year by the publication of a full-length history called *The Great EB,* which presented an exhaustive account of the *Encyclopaedia*'s growth and financial history. The author of this skillful exercise in public relations was Herman Kogan, a former Chicago newspaperman who was subsequently appointed Director of Company Relations for the *Britannica.* The early parts of his book were animated by a critical spirit, but the closing portion merely offered a glowing description of the Company's editorial and sales policies. Despite this defect, *The Great EB* is a useful historical work because it was compiled from the Company's private archives. It supplied a great deal of material for this chapter—and its quasi-official character was emphasized by its publication by the University of Chicago Press.

The *Britannica*'s history has acquired considerable status, and become a suitable subject for academic inquiry. In 1958 the University of Chicago awarded a Ph.D. in Library Science to a student who wrote a thesis on the *Encyclopaedia*'s history from 1768 to 1943.

[5]

The Britannica
under Attack

WHEN a work is as prominent as the *Britannica,* it is only natural that its real and imaginary faults should attract the attention of critics, cranks and querulous eccentrics who have been smitten by a desire to improve this familiar institution of scholarship. As an august symbol of authority, it is an attractive target for critics; and since it is continually cited as a source of information, its treatment of controversial questions has frequently provoked individuals whose ideas and beliefs have been slighted. Therefore it is instructive to examine various complaints that have been leveled against the *Encyclopaedia,* because they reveal some of its weaknesses and provide an opportunity to see how this institution has responded to hostile comment.

Critics have often recalled earlier editions with a sense of nostalgia. As early as 1861, Augustus De Morgan observed in reviewing the eighth edition:

> The *Encyclopaedia Britannica* is an old friend. Though it holds a proud place in our present literature, yet the time

was when it stood by itself, more complete and more clear than anything which was to be found elsewhere. There must be studious men alive in plenty who remember when they were studious boys, what a literary luxury it was to pass a few days in the house of a friend who had a copy of this work.

A generation later, the essay on American Literature in the ninth edition angered Southerners when it reported:

> Since the Revolution . . . the few thinkers of America born south of Mason and Dixon's line—outnumbered by those belonging to the single State of Massachusetts—have commonly migrated to New York or Boston in search of a university training. In the world of letters at least, the Southern States have shown by reflected light; nor is it too much to say, that mainly by their connection with the North the Carolinas have been saved from sinking to the level of Mexico or the Antilles.

Southern sensibilities were offended when the article went on to charge, "Like a Spartan marshalling his helots, the planter lounging among his slaves was made dead to Art by a paralyzing sense of his own superiority."

One journalist, Thaddeus Oglesby, was so incensed by this slur on Southern culture that he wrote a series of angry columns in the *Montgomery Advertiser* in 1891, to refute the "lies and calumnies" of the ninth edition. Oglesby cited a host of "celebrated" Southerners who, he claimed, had made notable contributions to American culture. When his columns were later gathered together in book form, they were called *Some Truths of History: A Vindication of the South against the Encyclopaedia Britannica and Other Maligners.* Although his book was an emotional indictment of the *Encyclopaedia,* it scored a few telling points by citing some factual errors and omissions. The essay on American Literature described the *Federalist* as a newspaper which was "the organ of the anti-Democratic party," whereas it actually was a series of essays on the Constitution by Hamilton, Madison and Jay. The article on Texas was seven columns long, but did not mention the Alamo, "that American Thermopylae": "room is found . . . for a special article on 'Concord' and the small skirmish there with small loss of life; no such room for the Alamo and its devoted band of immortals."

Oglesby was on solid ground when he pointed out one prominent defect in the ninth edition: "The fact that it contains no notice of any living person. History without our contemporaries is only half history; and it is simply ridiculous to claim completeness . . . when there are no biographies . . . of Bismarck, Gladstone, Huxley, Tyndall, Herbert Spencer, Tennyson, Swinburne or Browning."

The technical treatises were another legitimate source of complaint because they were intended for specialists, rather than laymen. Oglesby offered a wry comparison between the elaborate coverage of scientific topics and the meager treatment of American historical figures by recording:

> On Zachary Taylor . . . it has seventeen lines, but of "Tapeworms" it has thirteen solid columns, and on "Trematoda" it is full and thrilling in the extreme, as, for instance where it tells us that "all Trematoda have commonly been regarded as devoid of body cavity, and consisting of parenchymatous tissue, but that recent researches show that the intercellular space must be regarded as the homologue of coelum." This is highly important if true, as the papers used to say of news from the front during the war, and the clear, intelligible language in which it is expressed cannot fail of appreciation of any person in possession of the *Britannica*.

Subsequent critics have often avoided a sober analysis of the *Encyclopaedia*'s defects. Instead, they have become emotionally involved and treated its errors and omissions as a personal affront. This was illustrated by Willard Huntington Wright, who began his literary career as a cultural critic—and later became famous as S. S. Van Dine, the author of the Philo Vance mystery novels. In 1917, he launched a vitriolic attack on the eleventh edition in his book, *Misinforming a Nation*. He charged that the work was disfigured by a British bias which excessively inflated English art and culture: "The intellectual colonization of America by England has been going on for generations. . . . Too long has *bourgeois* British culture been forced on the United States; and we have been too gullible in our acceptance of it without question."

Wright complained because a host of second- and third-rate Englishmen appeared in the eleventh edition, but there were no entries on such major figures as Cézanne, Gauguin and Van Gogh; Santayana, Dreiser and Mahler. After citing a number of examples, Wright concluded that "a large fortune has been spent to make America pay handsomely for the adoption of English provincialism." The force of his critique was severely blunted, however, when he demanded that a number of minor Americans should be included in the *Encyclopaedia*—which would only have superimposed an American slant upon an existing British bias. At the end of his book, Wright supplied a list of two hundred figures who should be included in the set, but most of them have now been completely forgotten.

Misinforming a Nation stridently repeated a single point again and again, namely, "Taken as a whole, the *Britannica*'s divisions of culture are little more than a brief for British art and science." Wright made no effort to examine the content of different articles, but merely measured their length and complained when certain Englishmen were given too much space. This did not prevent him from boldly slashing away at the set:

> The truth is that the *Encyclopaedia Britannica,* in its main departments of culture, is characterized by misstatements, inexcusable omissions, rabid and patriotic prejudices, personal animosities, blatant errors of fact, scholastic ignorance, gross neglect of non-British culture, an astounding egotism, and an undisguised contempt for American progress.

Wright did not attempt to document these charges, but he was correct on one point. An excessive amount of space was devoted to minor British personalities. This was due largely to the English origin of the eleventh edition. When it appeared in 1910–11, the British Empire was at its height and the English image was being impressed on the colonial mind throughout the world. It was natural that the *Britannica* should reflect this buoyant national attitude by devoting considerable space to English achievements in art, music and literature. This nationalistic bias was encouraged by the ample dimensions of the eleventh edition—and its biographies of living celebrities enabled it to become a veritable Who's Who of British life.

Although the text was overhauled for the fourteenth edition and has been continuously revised since 1932, many articles on obscure British generals, scholars and aristocrats have been reprinted for fifty years. The 1958 edition contains long entries on such British "notables" as the statesman John Rutland, Roudell Selbourne and Stafford Iddesleigh; the divines Edward Benson, Henry Liddon and Alexander Duff; and the poets Charles Wells, William Sharp and Sydney Dobell. The biographies of many Americans have also been retained from earlier editions. They include the writers Josiah Holland, Esther Singleton and William Visscher; the artists Walter Gay, Alexander Proctor and Gari Melchers; and the poets Richard Gilder, Charles Leland and George Boker.

Despite this elaborate coverage, there are no entries in 1958 on such contemporary figures as Aaron Copland, Benjamin Britten, Georges Rouault or Fernand Léger. The article on Modern Poetry reports that "Yeats, Frost, Eliot, Stevens, Moore, Auden and Thomas are of almost unquestioned genius"; yet three of these poets—W. H. Auden, Marianne Moore and Wallace Stevens—do not receive separate notices.

Most entries from earlier editions are quite brief, but occasionally a minor figure receives an extended biography. An example is the Victorian painter George Watts. As a member of the Royal Academy and a recipient of many official commissions, he was highly favored as a portrait painter, and his biographical entry includes a long list of famous figures who served as his sitters. Despite this gallery of celebrated subjects, Watts is only a vague name in the history of art because he lacked creative vigor and artistic originality. Today the fact that he was once married to the actress Ellen Terry, who exchanged so many letters with Bernard Shaw, seems more interesting than his academically correct portraits. Despite the relative obscurity that now surrounds his name, he receives more space than Corot, Courbet or Seurat.

Biographies of minor British personalities were often flattering eulogies which reflected an insular pride in native achievement. Fortunately most of this excessive praise has been deleted, but there are some exceptions. The lengthy biography of Holman Hunt, one of the leaders of the pre-Raphaelite movement, cites his series of "great" religious paintings; and the article on William Etty, who specialized in pretty romantic nudes, states that he was probably a better painter than Delacroix although he lacked the force and intellectual flexibility of his French counterpart. Such reverential treatment of Victorian notables was once quite common, and it furnishes a humorous note in the 1958 edition. The entry on Sir Jonathan Hutchinson (1828–1913), a distinguished physician who served as president of the Royal College of Surgeons, describes one of his leading contributions in the following manner:

> His book, *Leprosy and Fisheating* (1906) exposed many popular errors, though his conclusion regarding a definite connection between this disease and the eating of salted fish has not been generally accepted.

This entry was reprinted for fifty years, but oddly enough it does not mention Hutchinson's Teeth, a malady found in children suffering from congenital syphilis, which has made his name familiar to medical students.

The publication of the fourteenth edition elicited considerable comment in newspapers and magazines, since it represented the first comprehensive revision since the famous eleventh edition. Most reviewers offered general remarks about the new edition without attempting to cite any specific errors or defects. Allan Nevins, however, declared in the *Saturday Review of Literature* (October 12, 1929): ". . . it is dismaying to find in Richard Garnett's old article on Washington Irving—in the face of the discoveries by Mr. Hellman and others—that Irving never married because he remained 'true to the memory of an early attachment blighted by death.'" This article has been replaced by another contribution, but instead of dismissing this romantic attachment, it states:

> Yet, even as Irving was finishing his comic book, he suffered tragedy in the death of his fiancée, Matilda Hoffman, the daughter of his employer. Partly by reason of his intense grief—he never married—his life during the following six years was empty and aimless.

This passage is particularly mystifying because it was written by Stanley T. Williams, who rejected this story in his book *The Life of Washington Irving,* which is cited in the bibliography as the definitive work on the subject. In his book he records: "Concerning these events posterity has been sentimental. That Irving always cherished Matilda's Bible; that he wept over a miniature of her; that years later he left the room in agony at the mention of her name; that out of loyalty to her memory he never married—these are but a few of the legends canonizing Matilda Hoffman and her lover." Despite these critical remarks, however, Professor Williams accepts this sentimental tradition in his article on Washington Irving.

A good deal of material appeared in the fourteenth edition that should have been replaced. The *New York Times* reported on October 25, 1929 that the entry on South Bend, Indiana recorded that the chief industry of that city was the manufacture of "wagons and carriages" by the Studebaker Brothers. When this story appeared, the *Britannica* issued a statement claiming that this was the only complaint received in the midst of hundreds of enthusiastic letters praising the new edition.

A few months later, however, a more serious objection was raised by Edwin Franden Dakin, whose critical biography of Mary Baker Eddy was creating a lively controversy in literary circles. He charged in a lecture that the article on Christian Science was seriously biased because it was written by Clifford P. Smith, chief of Christian Science publications. Dakin asserted that the article was designed to prevent the true facts about Mrs. Eddy's life from becoming public. When the *New York Times* reported on his criticism on February 18, 1930, the *Britannica* declined comment. But the following day it issued a statement describing the editors' efforts to obtain impartiality in doctrinal and religious matters by having articles on Catholic subjects written by Catholics, and Protestant topics by Protestants. After explaining how the *Encyclopaedia* endeavors to avoid religious controversy, the Company reminded the public:

> However, when a question of fact is brought to our attention by a responsible person, regardless of whether or not he is seeking personal publicity, we are more than glad to give consideration to the evidence. Indeed, we are always glad of the cooperation of the public in maintaining the traditional accuracy of the work.

Despite this willingness to accept constructive criticism, the 1929 articles on Christian Science and Mary Baker Eddy still appear in the 1958 edition. The entry on Christian Science is a rather colorless account that says nothing about the astonishing personality of the woman who founded this movement when she was fifty-seven years old and guided it for more than three decades.

The biography of Mary Baker Eddy is much more revealing. Its official character is emphasized when it declares that "one of her pastors . . . predicted for Mrs. Eddy a great future and spoke of her as 'an intellectual and spiritual genius.' " It then observes:

> Naturally Mrs. Eddy was the first practitioner and the first teacher of her religion. As a practitioner, she demonstrated her religion by healings in many cases, until duties which could not be left to others required her time.

No details are furnished about these "healings," and the article accepts without question Mrs. Eddy's statements about her early life even though they were made when she was a very old woman. Thus it reports: "At the age of 12 she had the courage and independence to dispute a point in theology when she was examined for church membership"; and it states: "The beginning of Mrs. Eddy's interest in religious or spiritual healing can be traced to an incident which occurred when she was 12 years old, immediately before her examination for admission to the

Congregational Church." But the official record of the Tilton Congregational Church shows that she was not admitted to membership until she was seventeen.

The article on Mary Baker Eddy was retained either because of editorial oversight, or in deference to certain readers who might be disturbed by an accurate account of the founding of Christian Science. The *Britannica*'s misleading treatment reflects the tendency of the fourteenth edition to court public favor by accepting the claims and beliefs of various religious sects. A generation earlier, the eleventh edition did not consult with religious groups in preparing its articles. Consequently it was attacked in *America* and the *Tablet* when it offered an independent analysis of the history and doctrines of the Catholic Church. This criticism, which has been voiced a number of times in the last fifty years, was renewed in 1956 when an editorial in the April issue of *Catholic Library World* asked:

> Wouldn't you think that the editors of the *Encyclopaedia Britannica* would revise the article on the Blessed Virgin Mary? Like other encyclopedias, *Britannica* boasts of a policy of continuous revision. Failure to rewrite this pseudo-scientific, scurrilous piece can be nothing less than deliberate.

Returning to the subject in the November issue, the author of the editorial noted that the article on Mary had been reprinted for more than six decades and that it referred to a book written seventy years ago by an Englishman trying to stem the Oxford Movement. The editors of the *Britannica* replied that a new article was being prepared, but maintained that the decision to undertake this revision had nothing to do with the attack.

One reason why the article on Mary aroused displeasure in Catholic circles was its discussion of the doctrine of her Perpetual Virginity. The article asserted: "This doctrine was, to say the least, of no importance in the eyes of the evangelists, and so far as extant writings go there is no evidence of its having been anywhere taught within the pale of the Catholic Church of the first three centuries." When a new article on Mary appeared in the 1958 edition, it was much more circumspect. It summarized the contradictory conclusions of Catholic and Protestant historians, but did not take sides on the issue.

The practice of rewriting religious material to meet the approval of different groups was sharply criticized by the Watch Tower Society, the official spokesman of Jehovah's Witnesses. It declared in its magazine *Awake!* (November 22, 1962) that in the conflict between Truth and "Tolerance" the *Britannica* has sacrificed the truth to avoid making enemies. To support this charge, it compared a number of entries in the eleventh and 1959 editions. In 1910 the essay on Celibacy frankly discussed the difficulty of enforcing celibacy among the clergy during the Middle Ages. The modern entry, written by a Jesuit priest in Japan, says nothing about these difficulties; instead it offers the *Catholic Encyclopedia* as an authority on this controversial subject.

The article on the Eunuch was cited as another example. The eleventh edition reported:

> Even more vile, as being practiced among a civilized European nation, has been the Italian practice of castrating boys to prevent the natural development of the voice, in order to train them as adult soprano singers such as might formerly be heard in the Sistine chapel. . . . Driven long ago from the Italian stage by public opinion, they remained the musical glory and the moral shame of the papal choir till the accession of the Pope Leo XIII one of whose first acts was to get rid of them.

The present entry, however, merely observes:

> The Italian practice of castrating boys in order to train them as adult soprano singers ended with the accession of Pope Leo XIII.

While some groups have accused the *Britannica* of being pro-Catholic, others have claimed it is hostile to the Church. Its chief competitor, the *Encyclopedia Americana,* bluntly declared that the *EB* was animated by an anti-Catholic bias, and it repeated this provocative charge until it was restrained by the Federal Trade Commission in July, 1948. According to the FTC, the *Americana* asserted in its promotional material:

> The *Americana* is published in America by Americans for Americans. It has an American viewpoint and looks at the world through American eyes.
>
> What impresses a Catholic most in the new *Americana* is the evident intention of the editorial staff to play fair. . . . In this the *Americana* is a striking contrast to the *Britannica*. The editors of that encyclopedia impress one as having of set purpose picked out foes of the Church, to misrepresent her. They are as accurate in this misrepresentation as we might expect Benedict Arnold to have been, had he written on the separation of the American Colonies from England. Not so the *Americana*. It chooses loyal Catholics to write on Catholic subjects. The Jesuits are assigned to a Jesuit; and not, as in the *Britannica*, to their avowed enemy.

This broadside was not a defense of Catholic ideas, but an appeal to religious prejudice for commercial gain. It has no foundation in fact. Since 1936 the *Britannica* has carried an article on the Society of Jesus written, not by an enemy of the Jesuits, but by a member of the Society. It is such a favorable and flattering account of the order that it will be discussed in a later chapter as an example of clerical apologetics. The principle that religious subjects should be governed by the canons of historical scholarship, rather than religious dogma, was one of the great triumphs of the ninth edition—and it is distressing to find this principle impugned by a rival encyclopedia seeking to increase its sales.

Critics have occasionally discussed the *Britannica*'s defects in recent years, but their comments have had little effect on its contents. A barbed, caustic critique was presented by Wilhelm Herzog, a European literary figure who was best known for his dramatization of the Dreyfus trial. His article appeared in the Swiss trade publication, *Der Schweizer Buchhandel* (November 15, 1947), under the picturesque title, "Concerning the Misery of the Most Famous Encyclopedists." He pointed out that the 1946 edition contained no biographies of General Marshall or General Eisenhower, who had been continuously in the news since 1941. Furthermore, there were no biographical entries on Ernest Hemingway, William Faulkner, Ignazio Silone or Aldous Huxley, although they had possessed an international reputation for many years. "How," Herzog asked, "are such omissions to be explained? Great care and conscientiousness are among the chief virtues of an encyclopedist. How can the management of the *Encyclopaedia Britannica*, which boasts of the contributions of the most outstanding scholars, account for such a lack of conscientiousness and care? What excuse does it have?"

After noting that the biography of Göring was only carried as far as 1933 and the entry on Stalin stopped with the year 1928, Herzog observed:

> It is to be regretted that the undertaking founded in 1768 seems to have lost in the last decade all power of differentiation. The ability to select and grade has apparently been lost. With tremendous expense a jumble of 37 million words is produced, newly published each year, so that every purchaser of the latest edition erroneously accepts it as up to date. But random tests show that the articles, being twenty and thirty years old, are out of date like refurbished bargain hats.

Herzog sharply disagreed with a statement in the *Encyclopaedia*'s preface that most of its material needed revision only at long intervals, saying, "This claim, put forward to avoid the reproach of being obsolete, is as presumptuous as it is incorrect." To prove his point, he cited a mass of ancient bibliographies on major literary figures, and declared:

> No automobile factory, no department store, not even Sears and Roebuck Co. would sell old sets as new ones in any field. The mechanization of the scholarly profession, the industrialization and commercialization of intellectual research, has had this result: out of the realization of Diderot and D'Alembert's splendid idea . . . the arsenal of intellectual weapons for the French Revolution . . . has come . . . this Information Catalogue in the United States that pretends to be a successor to the *Encyclopaedia Britannica,* which was once justly esteemed so highly.

A library of fundamental knowledge, serious research and

independent criticism has been transformed into a giant
Department Store, whose owners bought up the original stock
with all rights, copyrights, records and manuscripts, according
to recognized commercial principles. They invested a capital
of several million and sold the articles produced years and
decades ago as if they were goods, without being aware of the
spirit that breathed in this encyclopedic work.

Herzog concluded that he had "been able to give only a fleet-
ing indication of the defects and omissions of a very famous
work. For a friend and admirer of encyclopedia research it is
almost a physical pain to see how the critical spirit of the eighteenth century, that creates and determines values, has been extinguished in the advancing twentieth century."

When this critical onslaught was brought to the attention of
the editor-in-chief, Walter Yust, in the spring of 1948, he replied:
"When [Herzog] states that *Britannica* is not up to date in every
respect, he is quite correct. But his conclusion that this is evidence
of incompetence, lack of scholarly integrity on the part of the
editors is, to say the least, impertinent." Mr. Yust went on to
explain that because of the war, the *Encyclopaedia*'s plan of
annual revision had been interrupted, but once its ten-year cycle
was completed, "nothing will appear in the *Britannica* older than
five years." Although Mr. Yust claimed that about two and one-
half million words were changed annually, he did not explain
why some articles have been reprinted for decades.

His optimistic forecast was contradicted a few years later when
a critical essay announced that the 1950 edition contained serious
defects. This lucid piece, which appeared in the *New Republic*
(February 19, 1951), was unusual in several respects. Unlike
other critiques that concentrated on the humanities, it discussed
the inadequate treatment of the physical and social sciences. Its
author, Paul Nemenyi, an expert in fluid dynamics, provided an
impressive demonstration of the *Encyclopaedia*'s antiquated state
without indulging in the inflated rhetoric and sarcasm employed
by other critics. He reported that many entries in such rapidly
changing fields as anthropology, sociology, physics and medicine
were taken from the 1929 edition. Such obsolete material included

the entries on Child Psychology, Cosmology, Aerodynamics, and X-rays and Crystal Structure. Consequently there was nothing in the set on supersonic aerodynamics, and the term "shockwave" was used with reference to geology, not physics. Dr. Nemenyi asked, "What is the average age of material contained in this 'New Survey of Universal Knowledge'?" And he replied, "From a varied, though admittedly small, sample I conclude that the average may be anywhere from 15 to 30 years."

In addition to criticizing individual entries, Dr. Nemenyi offered some positive suggestions. In the first place, he urged that "misleading or ill-conceived articles, whatever their subject and age, should have first priority for complete replacement." He then advocated, *Each article, excepting very minor ones, should be dated,* stating both the year it was written and when it was revised." Needless to say, the *Britannica* did not accept this simple but revolutionary proposal, presumably because if its texts were dated readers would soon discover the true age of its material.

Although Dr. Nemenyi listed many entries in the 1950 edition that were twenty years old, the Company paid no attention to his criticism. He specifically cited the articles on Vision, Viscosity, Surface Tension and Brownian Motion; yet eight years later, these articles were still being reprinted.

I presented a critical account of the 1959 edition in the *Columbia University Forum* (Winter, 1960). Its contents were summarized in a two-column story in *Newsweek* and several newspapers reported on my critique. The Spring issue of the *Forum* carried an extended reply by Dr. Robert Hutchins, chairman of the *Encyclopaedia*'s Board of Editors. He made little effort to dispute my factual findings, but complained that I had singled out only ninety of the *EB*'s 42,000 entries. After describing the influential role of the Board of Editors, he closed on a plaintive note:

> If Dr. Einbinder had taken a less superficial, and somewhat straighter, look at the *Britannica,* he would have been impressed by the work that is being done to maintain and to raise, if possible, the standards of a great institution.

The *Encyclopaedia* takes a dim view of anyone who suggests that this "great institution" is inadequate. When the Book Editor of the *Houston Post,* Diana Hobby, devoted a column to my criticism on January 24, 1960, she received a long and blustery letter from the *Britannica* implying that only her age, sex and innocence could have let her take seriously so villainous an article. Later, when she informed her readers about the subsequent exchange of views in the *Forum,* she stated that this letter "sounded like a wounded dragon lashing its tail."

The *New York Times* reported on my debate with Dr. Hutchins, and the editor of *Encounter* invited me to contribute an essay on the *Encyclopaedia*'s "British-style" errors. Before its publication in May, 1961, the editor sent an advance proof to the *Britannica*'s London editorial office, and announced that he hoped to print a rebuttal in the near future. The Company, however, did not seek to refute my criticism; instead it ran a large advertisement in the London *Times* (April 21, 1961) explaining why the set could not be "wholly up to date." This advertisement was placed in a number of English newspapers and literary weeklies, and it was followed by another cycle of ads a month later listing an imposing array of *EB* contributors.

Academic circles have known for some time that a large gap exists between the *Encyclopaedia*'s advertising image and its actual contents. Some teachers and professors believe it is not a reliable source of information and caution their students against blindly reproducing its material in their reports and term papers. This warning, however, has not been widely publicized. As a result, some students who obtain the set may be disappointed when they discover it does not live up to their expectations. Since no one seems to have undertaken a comprehensive survey of the *Britannica*'s contents, the true distance between its lofty claims and its actual performance may not be appreciated, even by those who are disenchanted with the set.

Although a number of critical observations have been published in recent years, the Company has not curbed the enthusiasm of copywriters who announce in sales messages:

Through generation after generation, *Britannica* has been the most important single source of authoritative, up-to-date information. And, as the world has changed and accumulated knowledge has expanded, *Britannica* has grown to keep pace with the times. Now, continuing a great tradition, *Encyclopaedia Britannica* stands ready to provide readers of today with knowledge, inspiration, success and power.

[6]

Outmoded Critical Views

Wɪᴛʜ the passage of time, many authors who were famous
during their lifetimes pass into oblivion, while others who were
once neglected are heaped with posthumous honors. This process
is vividly conveyed in Max Beerbohm's whimsical story "Enoch
Soames." It relates how an obscure writer barters his soul to the
Devil so he can return to the Reading Room of the British
Museum, a century after his death, to learn what posterity has
written about him. After concluding this bargain, Enoch Soames
is transported by a time machine into the future. He arrives at
the British Museum on June 3, 1997, and vainly searches
through standard reference works for his name. Finally, in the
History of Inglish Littracher 1890–1900 he discovers his name.
But as he unravels the phonetic dialect in which the book is written, he is dismayed to find that it merely describes a story written
by Max Beerbohm about an imaginary character called "Enoch
Soames," a third-rate poet who believes himself a great genius

and makes a bargain with the Devil to know what posterity will think of him!

To put this story in a contemporary setting, we might imagine that Baudelaire is able to visit this world again for a few hours to learn what the twentieth century thinks of his poetry. By chance, he is deposited on Fifth Avenue and 42nd Street in front of the New York Public Library. As he is in a hurry, he asks the attendant inside for help. The latter directs him to the volumes of the *Encyclopaedia Britannica*. On reaching his name in the set, Baudelaire discovers an anonymous notice that fails to discuss the poetic qualities of *Les Fleurs du mal,* but merely reports:

> The consummate art displayed in these verses was appreciated by a limited public, but general attention was caught by the perverse selection of morbid subjects, and the book became a byword for unwholesomeness among conventional critics.

Ruffled and upset, Baudelaire searches through the entry to learn if his poems are still being read a century after their publication. Frustrated in his quest for information, the flustered dandy leaves the library before anyone can tell him that this article was written fifty years ago—long before there was any comprehension in English-speaking countries of his attempt "to extract *beauty* from *Evil*."

Baudelaire's discomfort would be shared by many readers who do not realize that many articles in the *Encyclopaedia* were prepared several generations ago. This policy is defended by the editor in the introduction that appears in the first volume of the 1958 edition:

> Experience down the years indicates that 75% of the material in an encyclopaedia needs changing only at long intervals. The other 25% requires continuous revision, some every year, some every two years, some every three years and so on. With the plan of annual printings, all the material in the Britannica, both the 75% and the 25%, is scheduled in yearly classifications for more extensive revisions than have ever been possible in the history of encyclopaedias.

Unfortunately, such revisions are often inadequate. Gustav Mahler is described in a short entry primarily as a conductor, and not as a composer. The article on Music states that "five years after his death, Béla Bartók was generally regarded as superior in many ways to almost every other composer of his time"; but his biography consists of only sixteen lines. A section on the Music of the 20th Century praises "Alban Berg's amazing feat of composing a full length opera, *Lulu,* on one tone row," but he is not given a separate entry—an honor reserved for the English composers Stanford and Parry, who produced dreary cantatas in the 1890's.*

Such lapses are not confined to modern music. Heinrich Schütz is considered one of the most important German composers before Bach. He is described as a "giant" in the article on Music, but he does not receive an entry. The biography of Mozart discusses only his vocal music—and ignores his symphonies, concertos and chamber music, which include some of his greatest compositions. The essays on Programme Music and the Symphonic Poem stop with Richard Strauss; and the article on Gounod quotes a judgment of Saint-Saëns written sixty years ago:

> Gounod did not cease all his life to write for the church, to accumulate masses and motets; but it was at the commencement of his career, in the *Messe de Sainte Cécile,* and at the end, in the oratorios *The Redemption* and *Mors et vita,* that he rose highest.

The article adds, "Saint-Saëns held that the three works he mentions will survive all the master's operas." But today Gounod is remembered largely because of his opera *Faust,* while his masses are rarely performed.

* The *EB*'s negligence in dealing with modern music was confirmed by Paul R. Farnsworth in the *Journal of Psychology* in 1957. He examined the *Encyclopaedia*'s biographical coverage of 250 composers born since 1870. Although forty-nine of them appeared in the 1929 edition, not a single additional name was added between 1929 and 1950! And in the 1957 edition, only four new composers were included: Converse, Lekeu, Weill and Shostakovich.

Sometimes views are expressed that seem to belong to a dated novel of the 1920's, rather than to a contemporary reference work. The entry on Chamber Music tartly remarks:

> The trombone and side drums in the chamber music of Stravinsky will do well enough in a very smart house-party where all the conversation is carried on in an esoteric family slang and the guests are expected to enjoy the booby-traps.

This odd passage was written by Donald Francis Tovey, who served as a music editor on the eleventh and fourteenth editions. As a contributor, Tovey could write eloquently about the operatic art of Gluck and offer profound observations on the classical masters, but he was bewildered by modern music and could only employ a caustic wit to hide his confusion and uncertainty.

Tovey's difficulty is quite common. Again and again, we observe a young critic gradually becoming an aged conservative unable to keep up with artistic innovation. Change is a law of art as well as life. That is why it is necessary for an encyclopedia to revise its articles frequently in dealing with contemporary trends; for what was once controversial soon becomes an accepted mode, as the daring of one generation becomes the cliché of the next. Eighty years ago, music critics were baffled by the complexity of Wagnerian opera with its leitmotivs and mystical philosophy; today they argue about the atonal innovation of Arnold Schönberg and Anton Webern. Behind this relentless change is the creative energy of artists whose experiments often bewilder critics accustomed to the ways of the past.

The characteristic discord between critics and creators is illustrated by Tovey's inability to deal with atonal music. Saturated in the rich orchestration and sumptuous harmony of Wagnerian music drama, Tovey and his contemporaries saw the future of music in terms of the further development of Wagnerian ideas. This belief was strengthened by Strauss' tone poems and Schönberg's ultra-romantic *Gurrelieder* with its enormous orchestral and choral forces. When Schönberg abandoned romanticism and began his harmonic experiments, Tovey was startled by this unexpected development. He curtly expressed his displeasure in his essay on Harmony in the *Britannica*:

> Arnold Schönberg's harmonic theory is often masterly in its analysis of classical music; but it is extremely disappointing in its constructive aspect. . . . Schönberg's theory rests on no observation at all, for the piling up of 4ths has no origin in classical harmony and only a quickly exhausted melodic value. . . . To find the composer of the *Gurrelieder* fathering such theories is as disconcerting as to discover Einstein telling fortunes in Bond Street.

Despite these acid remarks, Schönberg continued to father such theories until he arrived at the austere art of composition with twelve tones. Thirty years ago when Tovey wrote this article, such querulous criticism might have been understandable, but it is hardly sensible after leading contemporary composers have been employing these theories of harmony and composition for a generation.

It is difficult to excuse such outmoded judgments when long-playing records and FM broadcasting have made an enormous range of music available to the general public. Many people with the aid of their own listening experience can question the opinions expressed fifty years ago by critics who were limited to concert performances and printed scores. The *Encyclopaedia* neglects this growth in musical taste and sophistication by retaining articles from an earlier era. For example, Tovey's essay on Monteverdi maintains:

> . . . the student finds that the historian whom Palestrina and Bach paralyze into hagiology writes as if Monteverdi were the Wagner of a 17th century more glorious than the 19th. And this is difficult to reconcile with the fact that if all the music of the 17th century were destroyed, not a single concert-goer would miss it.

This cavalier attitude would consign to oblivion not only the operas and madrigals of Monteverdi, but also the cantatas and organ music of Dietrich Buxtehude, the concerti grossi of Arcangelo Corelli, and the stage works of Henry Purcell. Inconsistently, however, the *Britannica* warmly praises Purcell's opera *Dido and Aeneas* by observing, "Dido's exquisite song of farewell is one of the flawless things in music, classical in form and in its dignified restraint, and yet of rare emotional quality."

Time exposes many mistaken judgments. It reveals the uncertainty of fame and demonstrates that belated recognition may come to an author. Stendhal had to wait for half a century before his genius was acknowledged; and in music, Bach was rescued from obscurity by the youthful enthusiasm of Felix Mendelssohn. In our own time, the reputation of John Donne has been rehabilitated through the efforts of modern critics, led by T. S. Eliot, who have initiated a shift in taste from the Victorian verse of Browning and Tennyson to the more taxing idiom of late Elizabethan poetry. Oblivious to this change in critical opinion, the 1958 edition records:

> The influence of Donne upon the literature of England was singularly wide and deep, although almost wholly malign. . . . The first impression of an unbiased reader who dips into the poems of Donne is unfavorable. He is repulsed by the intolerably harsh and crabbed versification, by the recondite choice of theme and expression, and by the oddity of the thought.

This judgment, first presented fifty years ago, follows the line laid down by Dr. Johnson in the *Lives of the Poets* when he branded Donne and his contemporaries as metaphysical poets in whose verse "the most heterogeneous ideas are yoked together." In the past, critics were repelled by the complexity of Donne's language and imagery, but he no longer seems formidable after the intricate images of *The Waste Land* and the obscure symbolism of *Ulysses*.

During his youth, Donne was a passionate poet for whom "all Divinity is love or wonder." He portrayed the gamut of erotic emotion from stark disillusion to sexual celebration, but in his later years he became a brooding preacher who expressed dark, deep thoughts on man's rapid and inevitable journey to the grave. The article on Donne does not describe this profound transformation which enabled him to pass from the sensual delights of his youth to the somber meditations of his closing years. It neglects his *Sermons* and *Devotions,* although they are inspired by a profound Christian vision of the human soul on its passage through life. One quotation in particular has become widely known because of its use by Hemingway: "No man is an *Iland, intire* of it selfe . . . therefore never send to know for whom the *bell* tolls; It tolls for *thee.*"

Although the *Encyclopaedia* disparages Donne, it praises Thackeray: "The grace and apparent spontaneity of Thackeray's verses are beyond question. Some of the more serious efforts, such as 'The Chronicle of the Drum' (1841), are full of power and instinct with true poetic feeling." An excerpt from this poem may suggest why Thackeray is remembered today as a novelist, and not as a poet.

> I think I see my poor mammy
> > With me in her hand as she waits,
> And our regiment, slowly retreating,
> > Pours back through the citadel gates.
> Dear mammy she looks in their faces,
> > And asks if her husband has come?—
> He is lying all cold on the glacis
> > And will never more beat on the drum.

The entries on Donne and Thackeray were prepared by Edmund Gosse, who served as chief literary editor of the eleventh edition. A number of his contributions have been reprinted, despite their limitations. Thus he expresses a Victorian prejudice when he cites Swinburne as "the poet of youth insurgent against all the restraints of conventionality and custom"—and refuses to acquit his poetry "of an animalism sometimes of love, sometimes of hatred." Today young men no longer look to Swinburne to justify their revolt against conventionality and custom, while if they seek animalism in literature, they are likely to turn to the prose of Henry Miller or D. H. Lawrence rather than the verse of Swinburne.

Since many Victorian evaluations are retained, it is hardly surprising that Tennyson's poetry should be lauded in extravagant terms:

We still look to earlier masters for supreme excellence in particular directions; to Wordsworth for sublime philosophy, to Coleridge for ethereal magic; to Byron for passion, to Shelley for lyric intensity, to Keats for richness.

Tennyson does not excel each of these in his own special field, but he is often nearer to the particular man in his particular mastery than any one else can be said to be, and he has in addition his own special field of supremacy.

This opinion reflects Tennyson's enormous popularity in the nineteenth century. For more than fifty years he was the dominant figure in English poetry, and among his countrymen, his literary fame was surpassed only by that of Dickens. But in the intervening years, his reputation has shrunk to more modest proportions.

Although many critical judgments are derived from earlier editions, there are occasional exceptions that demonstrate the utility of commissioning fresh articles. The essay on Herman Melville is a splendid example of contemporary criticism that offers a delightful contrast to the antiquated entries on Tennyson, Thackeray and Donne. It discusses Melville's stature as a novelist and explains the symbolism that animates *Moby Dick* by means of extensive quotations. It reports that Melville was virtually forgotten until the first biography of his life was published in 1919, a century after his birth, and specifically notes that this "recovery" was strikingly paralleled by a similar elevation of Donne and other metaphysical poets. Yet while Melville receives an excellent modern treatment, Donne is represented by an old entry.

It would be misleading, however, to create an impression that most of the critical and esthetic views in the *Encyclopaedia* are outmoded or erroneous. This is not true, even in entries that are several generations old. Edmund Gosse justly praises Flaubert's style, Tovey skillfully captures Bach's musical genius, and Swinburne aptly conveys the dramatic qualities that make Marlowe a major Elizabethan figure. But difficulties arise in other cases.

The article on Zola acknowledges that "he became the most discussed, the most read, the most bought novelist in France";

but it fails to discuss his theory of naturalism. This theory sought to apply the scientific method to literature by portraying modern life with photographic realism. According to Zola, the novel was a vehicle of scientific experimentation, and he announced in his preface to *Thérèse Raquin*, "I have tried to study temperaments rather than characters. . . . If one reads the novel with care he will see that each chapter is the study of a curious psychological case."

Zola's daring realism and bold subject matter made him a center of controversy, and his literary ideas exerted a deep influence, particularly in the United States where writers such as Dreiser, Norris and Farrell elevated naturalism into one of the dominant modes in American fiction. This development has enhanced Zola's importance, but his position and subsequent influence cannot be registered in a meager biography prepared in 1910.

While artistic reputations may be created with dramatic swiftness, eminence is difficult to achieve in philosophy; but once attained, it persists for many years. Consequently, although many articles on philosophy are fifty and seventy-five years old, they rarely suffer from outlandish views. But there are occasional exceptions. The biography of Johann Herbart provides a detailed account of his metaphysics and concludes:

> Among the post-Kantians Herbart doubtless ranks next to Hegel in importance. His criticisms are worth more than his constructions; indeed for exactness and penetration of thought he is on a level with Hume and Kant.

Although Herbart may once have been fashionable, he is no longer regarded as a major figure in philosophy. Unlike Herbart, the intellectual stature of Sören Kierkegaard has steadily grown since his death, and his posthumous fame has been accelerated by the rise of existentialism, of which he is regarded as a spiritual founder. Although the 1958 edition devotes two pages to Herbart, the entry on Kierkegaard consists of only thirteen lines. The bibliography accompanying this entry lists only three titles, none of which is in English; and the most recent one was published in 1896!

The case of Kierkegaard is instructive because he was almost completely ignored during his lifetime. The Danish moralist wrote in his journal, "Denmark has need of a dead man," and in the same vein he recorded, "My life will cry out after my death." Although he began to attract attention on the Continent two generations ago, he was virtually unknown in English-speaking countries until the 1930's when translations of his works began to appear. Kierkegaard's startling modernity, his acute diagnosis of the spiritual sickness of our time, and his penetrating analysis of the weaknesses of conventional Christian faith have evoked a powerful contemporary response. Today, when men no longer believe in the inevitability of moral progress, the reputation of the Danish iconoclast has steadily increased until he is now recognized as one of the most incisive thinkers of the last century.

The *Britannica*'s failure to deal with Kierkegaard is matched by other critical aberrations. The essay on Milton is eight pages long, but does not discuss his poetry. As far as *Paradise Lost, Paradise Regained* and *Samson Agonistes* are concerned:

> Of these three poems and what they reveal of Milton, no need here to speak at length. *Paradise Lost* is one of the few monumental works of the world. . . .

The essay then vainly attempts to summarize the action of this great epic in a single sentence.

Some may believe that an encyclopedia should not contain literary criticism, but confine itself to biographical facts. If this were true, there would be no entry on Homer whose life is lost in legend, and none on Lucretius whose personal history is limited to a few notices—one of which records for the year 94 B.C.:

> Titus Lucretius the poet is born. Afterwards he was rendered insane by a love potion and after writing, in intervals of insanity, some books, which Cicero afterwards amended, he killed himself by his own hand in the 43rd year of his age.

Despite this scarcity of biographical information, the *Britannica* provides a two-page analysis of *De Rerum Natura,* as well as a ten-page critique of the *Iliad* and the *Odyssey,* because these poetic compositions are major literary landmarks that cannot be ignored. Similarly, other figures are given extended notices because of their creative work, even though little is known about their personal lives.

Sometimes, however, the task of evaluating major figures is avoided by concentrating on biographical details, because it is easier to heap up factual information than to explain original contributions. This may explain why Pascal, whose sentences reverberate in the memory, is treated in a dreary essay that leaves his spiritual depths unfathomed. In a similar fashion, the biography of Dostoevski acknowledges that in his last novels he "gave his full measure as one of the greatest novelists of all time," but says nothing about the imposing characters who dominate these novels. Yet the visions and obsessions of Stavrogin, Raskolnikov and the Karamazovs are of paramount importance in understanding Dostoevski.

Although the article on Shakespeare is twenty pages long, it fails to discuss his individual plays, or to quote a single line from his dramatic work. Instead, it devotes four and a half pages to an account of his life, five pages to the publication dates of his plays, and another four pages to portraits that claim to represent the dramatist. The worship of his personality is carried so far that it overshadows his literary achievement. The great tragedies of his maturity are noted only in passing, yet an elaborate history is presented of the discredited theory that Francis Bacon is the author of these plays.

In the past, authors used Shakespeare's works as a splendid pretext for writing about themselves. Romantics like Hazlitt, Lamb and Swinburne related the stories of his plays and shed pious tears over the death of his heroes and heroines. They adopted an attitude toward "The Bard" of well-meaning friends and disciples who doled out emotion in essays filled with literary prestige and respectful opinion. Modern critics such as Caroline Spurgeon and J. Dover Wilson have dismissed these effusive displays because they wish to define the essential features of Shakespearean drama by means of rational analysis and research. Their efforts have established a picture of his art that differs sharply from the sentimental portraits of the past. Their work is clearly acknowledged in the entry on Dramatic Criticism which states, "The chief contribution of the 20th century is the remarkable advance in Shakespearian criticism." But these advances are ignored in the article on Shakespeare which repeats the outmoded conceits of an earlier age:

> The Shakespearian drama is magnificent and incoherent; it belongs to the adolescence of literature, to a period before the instrument had been sharpened and polished, and made unerring in its touch upon the sources of laughter and tears. Obviously nobody has such power over our laughter and tears as Shakespeare. But it is the power of temperament rather than of art. . . .

The article presents an extended catalogue of his faults, which include his want of finish, the imperfect fusing of the literary ore, the issues obscured by a careless generosity, and the emotional confusions of tragi-comedy. It calls attention to "the jest and bombast lightly thrown in to suit the taste of the groundlings," which it cites as one of the "flecks that to an instructed modern criticism are all too apparent on the Shakespearian sun." But these supposed flecks on the Shakespearean sun have nothing to do with modern scholarship; they spring from a much more venerable source—the snobbery of the Restoration, which freely altered and adapted Shakespeare's plays to suit the popular taste of the Court.

This attitude was forcefully expressed in Dryden's preface to his version of *Troilus and Cressida,* which attempted to justify the changes he had made in "the divine Shakespear":

> Yet it must be allowed to the present age, that the tongue in general is so much refined since Shakespear's time, that many of his words, and more of his phrases, are scarce intelligible. And of those we understand, some are ungrammatical, others coarse; and his whole style is so pestered with figurative expressions, that it is as affected as it is obscure.

These ideas, advanced in 1679, are quite similar to those presented by the *Britannica* in 1958.

Few writers have had as much nonsense written about them as Shakespeare. Alexander Pope, who edited his plays, believed he was an erratic genius and claimed that the more "disgusting" passages in his plays had been interpolated by actors. Dr. Johnson stated, "Shakespeare wanted art"; and Voltaire reported that his plays contained "pearls in a dung heap." Coleridge was the first critic to provide an informed judgment of his dramatic achievement by emphasizing his role as a conscious artist. In 1815 he critically observed, "Among us it is current, I might say, an established opinion, that Shakespeare is justly praised when he is pronounced to be a 'wild irregular genius, in whom great faults are compensated by great beauties.' " Modern critics have seconded Coleridge's attack on this view. A number of important studies in the last generation have discussed Shakespeare's extraordinary use of language, his searching psychological insight and the poetic symbolism that enriches his work, but they are not employed in the article on Shakespeare. T. S. Eliot has tersely explained why intelligent and informed criticism is essential in this case:

> When a poet is as great as Shakespeare is, we cannot judge his greatness unaided; we need both the opinion of other poets, and the diverse views of critics who were not poets in order to understand.

The struggle over Shakespeare took place after his death, so he was spared the excesses of admirers and the censure of critics. French painters in the nineteenth century were not so fortunate. They were forced to endure sarcasm and ridicule in a painful struggle for recognition. The attacks launched against the realistic art of Gustave Courbet are quite instructive because virtually the same arguments were used later against the naturalism of Zola and Maupassant. Courbet offended official critics of the Second Empire because his art was based on contemporary reality, rather than heroic scenes from classical mythology. His paintings depicted masons, peasants and washerwomen—instead of idealized visions of gods and goddesses, or flattering portraits of wealthy aristocrats. This was a disturbing innovation in a country where art had always been associated with the personal taste of the monarchy or the refined luxury of the aristocracy.

Courbet refused to paint gods and goddesses because he could not see them. The nude bathers in his canvases were real women, not idealized models. They shocked conservative critics with their fleshy torsos, their fat thighs and heavy breasts. Journalists labeled them *"ignoble, grotesque, monstrueuse,"* and they condemned their creator as a *"virtuose de la bestialité."* Courbet, however, was defended by Zola, who praised his friend as a member of "the family of flesh makers" that included Veronese, Rembrandt and Titian. His art marked a shift from the tired conventions of classicism to realistic scenes drawn from contemporary life. The antagonism created by his paintings may be traced in cartoons that appeared in the popular press. One caricature showed Courbet at a salon watching a placid bourgeois examining one of his pictures. The caption reported: "A bourgeois has stopped before my picture. He is not having a nervous attack. Therefore my show is a failure."

The *Encyclopaedia* fails to deal with this controversy and offers an erroneous prediction instead:

> Though Courbet's realistic work is not devoid of importance, it is as a landscape painter and a sea painter . . . that he will be most honored by posterity.

In a similar vein, the article on Corot praises his figure painting whose "simplified classical conception of form with a Rembrandtesque rendering of planes is remarkable for its strength and purity," but does not discuss his landscapes, which are an essential facet of his art. Thus by a curious inversion of taste, Courbet is honored as a landscape painter, while Corot is lauded as a master of the human figure.

Such misrepresentations would not be important if they did not undermine our confidence in other judgments contained in the set. Such doubts are justified in the field of painting. A vivid case is the meager entry on Piero della Francesca, which fails to reflect his contemporary position as one of the great masters of Renaissance art. During the last sixty years, he has gradually but surely come to be recognized as one of the foremost painters of the fifteenth century, and therefore as one of the foremost painters of all time. His elevation has made the journey to Arezzo to view his monumental cycle of frescoes an esthetic necessity for art lovers visiting Italy. But this critical change is not recorded in the 1958 edition. Instead, it mistakenly lists the artist as Piero De'Franceschi and notes:

> Though Piero was for some time neglected and forgotten, he has of late come into his own again, for his art, which so happily combines the decorative element of two-dimensional design with the representation of three-dimensional space, seems to contain much that certain modernists are striving after.

These "modernists" are not the abstract painters of today—they are Cézanne and the post-Impressionists whose work stimulated a fresh appreciation of the architectural qualities of his art.

It was natural that discerning connoisseurs should recognize Piero's mastery once they had grasped the visual solidity imbedded in Cézanne's canvases. This recognition would have bewildered nineteenth-century critics like Ruskin and Pater, who explored the Quattrocento for confirmation of their artistic ideals. They had discovered the genius of Botticelli and Bellini, but ignored Piero because they were seeking the mysterious smile, the graceful gesture and the romantic sentiment—attributes that could be embroidered into charming essays. This literary approach has been discredited by the classicism of Cézanne which has encouraged critics to examine a painting as a visual experience rather than as an opportunity for verbal display. The twentieth-century approach has raised Piero della Francesca into the select circle of true masters, but this change cannot be recorded in an antiquated article taken from the eleventh edition.

Occasionally, views are presented that merely seem eccentric. The current essay on Michelangelo states: "The fresco of the 'Last Judgement' in the Sistine Chapel is probably the most famous single painting in the world." These words were written seventy-five years ago, before Walter Pater had set down his ecstatic hymn to "La Gioconda" whose beauty reveals "strange thoughts and fantastic reveries and exquisite passions." If there is a more famous painting than the "Mona Lisa," it is probably

"The Last Supper." Yet it is an ironic commentary on artistic fame that both "The Last Judgement" and "The Last Supper" are ruined paintings—the first by the draperies painted over Michelangelo's nude figures, and the second by Leonardo's reckless use of an oil medium on a plaster wall.

During the nineteenth century, it was popular to relate the "story" behind the paintings of Burne-Jones, Rossetti and Millais. The literary gifts of Ruskin and Pater encouraged a subjective response to a work of art, and frequently the objective description of a painting or statue was abandoned in favor of a magic metaphor, an incisive phrase or the verbal rendering of light and shade. The article on Velazquez is taken from the ninth edition and originally contained a vigorous description of his art:

> A realist of the realists, he painted only what he saw, consequently his imagination seems limited. His religious conceptions are of the earth earthy, although some of his works such as the Crucifixion and the Scourging, are characterized by an intensity of pathos in which he ranks second to no painter. His men and women seem to breathe; his horses are full of action and his dogs of life; so quick and close is his grasp of his subject.

The deletion of such critical judgments and impressions may explain why the *Britannica* often fails to furnish a definite image of an artist's work or creative personality, despite its wealth of biographical detail. This concentration on factual matters may reflect the British reluctance to regard art as an esthetic experience, since many of these entries were prepared several generations ago when the *Encyclopaedia* was published in England. Therefore they may be regarded as a legacy of the Puritan spirit which views an infatuation with beauty as a dangerous heresy. Art in Victorian England roused mixed feelings; the public admired the masterpieces exhibited in the National Gallery, but was embarrassed by realistic representations of the female nude. One method of dealing with this problem was to clothe the visual arts with a thick layer of factual material that would effectively attenuate their sensual and esthetic attraction. This practice was widely adopted in the eleventh edition. In 1929, when the work shifted to America, little effort was made to rewrite the biographies of major artists that were a product of Victorian criticism, and during the intervening years, many of these arid notices have been retained without change. Consequently it is not surprising that recent artistic developments should be neglected.

Brancusi's famous abstract "Bird in Space" is shown as an example of Sculpture Technique, but is accompanied by a startling caption:

> A simple form so subjective that it has no aesthetic meaning except to the artist.

Brancusi himself does not receive a biographical entry, although this honor is accorded to a number of academic sculptors including George Barnard, Lorado Taft and Paul Manship.

As noted previously, literary questions, as well as artistic matters, are often slighted. The essay on Satire does not mention the name of Swift, although he is the greatest satirist in the English language. His biography fails to examine his style or position in the development of English prose; yet he played an important role in transforming English from the involved Renaissance style of Donne and Milton to the supple simplicity of modern prose. Before Swift, English was modeled after the ornate style of Latin; but after Swift, Dryden and Defoe, the language assumed its modern form. This historical development is neglected in the entry on Swift, which concentrates on biographical facts; yet the article has been abstracted from an earlier essay that justly praised his style:

> His own prose is the acme of incisive force and directness. He uses the vernacular with an economy which no other English writer has rivalled. There is a masculinity about his phrases which makes him as clear to the humblest capacity as they are capable of being made to anyone. Ironist as he is, there is no writer that ever wrote whose meaning is more absolutely unmistakable. He is the grand master of the order of plain speech.

This passage has been dropped even though the present entry on Swift is almost two and a half pages long.

A similar lack of judgment is found in dealing with literary works that embody a profound philosophy of life. The article on Goethe reports that the crowning achievement of his life was the completion of the second part of *Faust*, but allots only a few sentences to a summary of its contents:

> It is a phantasmagory; a drama the actors in which are not creatures of flesh and blood, but shadows in an unreal world of allegory. . . . Yet behind the elusive allegories . . . there lies a philosophy of life, a ripe wisdom born of experience, such as no other modern European poet has given us. *Faust* has well been called the "divine comedy of 18th-century humanism."

The article, however, does not explain this philosophy or illuminate the ripe wisdom that infuses the second part of *Faust*; consequently readers are unable to learn why it should be called the "divine comedy of 18th-century humanism."

Another example is the *Paradiso,* the final part of *The Divine Comedy,* where Dante attempts to convey the ineffable presence of God by a spiritual voyage through the heavenly spheres. Only three sentences are devoted to this remarkable voyage, although the entry on Dante is four pages long. Such cursory treatment recalls the scene in the Inferno where Virgil and Dante encounter the lost souls of those who have lived without blame or praise, and Virgil says: "Let us not speak of them, but look, and pass."

Not a single line is quoted from the *Paradiso,* although many critics have emphasized the utility of quotations. The selection of brief passages was elevated into a serious method of criticism by Matthew Arnold who noted: "There can be no more useful help for discovering what poetry belongs to the class of the truly excellent . . . than to have always in one's mind lines and expressions of the great masters, and to apply them as a touchstone to other poetry." One of Arnold's famous touchstones is the line from the *Paradiso: "E la sua volontate è nostra pace*—In his will is our peace," a line that may be familiar even to those who do not know its origin.

Quotations rarely appear in modern articles because their emphasis is on brevity and factual matter, but they were often used in the past when entries were cast in the form of long essays which attempted to deal with literary works on an emotional as well as an intellectual plane. The essay on Milton in the ninth edition skillfully captured the triumph and elation produced when the blind poet published *Paradise Lost* by quoting his description from *Samson Agonistes* of Samson's victory over the Philistines:

> But he, though blind of sight,
> Despised, and thought extinguished quite,
> With inward eyes illuminated,
> His fiery virtue roused
> . . . as an eagle
> His cloudless thunder bolted on their heads.

Here quotation goes beyond the function of recalling an author's words; it becomes a means of recapturing his spirit. But characteristically, this passage has been removed in condensing the article to its present length.

An encyclopedia should portray the salient aspects of the classics by summarizing their action and ideas, and it should encourage readers to explore these works by distilling the insights of modern scholarship. It should supply a consensus of informed critical opinion, and departures from this standard should be made quite clear. In recording the views of various critics, there is no guarantee of critical infallibility since artistic judgments do not tend toward some absolute truth, but are conditioned by their time and place. Criticism is an art—not a science. Its practice depends on the sensitivity and acumen of its practitioners, for as Cézanne observed, "Taste is the best of judges."

In fulfilling its intellectual responsibilities, an encyclopedia might heed the words of T. S. Eliot:

> No poet, no artist of any art has his complete meaning alone. His significance, his appreciation is the appreciation of his relation to the dead poets and artists. You cannot value him alone; you must set him, for contrast and comparison, among the dead.

[7]

Sexual Prudery and Victorian Attitudes

Every age has a characteristic way of looking at reality and organizing its experience of the external world, and every era has its limitations, blind spots and taboos in examining human affairs. An example is the prudery of the Victorian age which made "the facts of life" a forbidden subject. Thackeray was forced to bow to a "society that will not tolerate the Natural in our Art," while Trollope reluctantly acknowledged, "it behooves an English novelist to be pure." Sometimes facts were knowingly disregarded, but in most cases they were merely adjusted to fit prevailing taboos. When evasion did not suffice, writers simply ignored distasteful topics in the belief they were serving the best interests of society. The resulting suppression of sexual matters was so consistent and effective that the term "Victorian" has become a synonym for prudery and sexual censorship.

During the last generation, an enormous expansion has occurred in the freedom with which sexual topics can be discussed in print. A century ago, English authors could only hint at the existence of physical relations between men and women; today writers can analyze the varied course of love in intimate detail. Since the *Britannica* has been built up by accretion over the last three generations, some of its entries in the 1958 edition reflect the prudery of the past rather than current ideas. The article on Aristophanes was written eighty years ago by the classical scholar Richard Jebb. He states:

> The *Lysistrata* expresses the popular desire for peace at any cost. As the men can do nothing, the women take the question into their own hands, occupy the citadel, and bring the citizens to surrender.

The central point of the comedy—that the women refuse to have sexual relations with their husbands and lovers until the war is brought to an end—is not mentioned.

Jebb summarizes the plot of the *Ecclesiazusae* ("Women in Parliament") in a single sentence:

> The women, disguised as men, steal into the ecclesia, and succeed in decreeing a new constitution.

This is hardly adequate. The women, after seizing power and establishing a social utopia, place sexual relations on a new basis to assure themselves ample gratification at all times. They decree that if a young man is attracted to a girl, he can only possess her after satisfying an old woman first. If he refuses and continues to pursue the girl, the old women are authorized to seize him and insist that he do their bidding. This regulation leads to a hilarious moment in the play when an ardent youth inflamed by the beauty of a young girl vainly attempts to capture her. As he loudly proclaims his passion in front of her house, the youth is accosted by an old woman who demands that she be satisfied first. No sooner does he elude the woman, then he is seized by an ugly old crone desiring his youthful body. As he struggles to escape, a third hag appears on the scene who looks more like an ape than a human being. She snatches his free arm, and the two women impatiently drag him off the stage.

If Aristophanes is not condemned for his coarseness, it is probably because of his great prestige as a classical author. But while Aristophanes is spared, Rabelais is not so fortunate. He is treated in an essay originally prepared for the ninth edition by George Saintsbury who examines certain questions raised by his work:

> The first is connected with the great blemish of **Gargantua** and **Pantagruel**—their extreme coarseness of language and imagery. Rabelais's errors in this way are of course, looked at from an absolute standard, unpardonable. . . . Rabelais's coarseness, disgusting as it is, has nothing of the corruption of refined voluptuousness about it, has nothing of the sniggering indecency which disgraces men like Pope, like Voltaire, and like Sterne. The general taste having become considerably refined since, Rabelais has in parts become nearly unreadable— the worst and most appropriate punishment for his faults.

Perhaps the most famous of these coarse scenes occurs when Gargantua mounts to the top of Notre-Dame, unbuttons his codpiece and releases a deluge of urine on the populace below who rush to escape from the yellow flood. Another striking chapter describes Gargantua's search for an ideal "rump-wiper." After trying many diverse objects including a kerchief, a pillow, a slipper, a purse, assorted hats, a hen, a rooster, a hare, a pigeon and a decoy-bird, Gargantua concludes: "There is no rump-wiper like a good downy goose, provided you hold its head between your legs."

During the Victorian age, religious controversies as well as sexual topics were banished from polite society. Since the foundations of orthodox Christianity were being undermined by Darwin's scientific discoveries and Huxley's polemics, it was impossible to avoid religious dispute completely. Sometimes, however, critics were able to shelter readers from the heresies and blasphemies of Renaissance writers. Saintsbury follows this course in his article on Rabelais. After summarizing a number of theories about his religious beliefs, he concludes:

> There is absolutely nothing within the covers of Rabelais's works incompatible with an orthodoxy which would be recognized as sufficient by Christendom at large, leaving out

of the question those points of doctrine and practice on which Christians differ.

This statement may reassure readers, but Rabelais' language will hardly lull the orthodox to sleep. In the famous scene where Parisians flee from Gargantua's flood of urine, their curses include:

> By the wounds of God! I deny God! Did you see that! . . . Christ's power, or Our Lady's Muff! St. Quenet's belly! God's holy name! . . . Crucified Christ! Holy Sunday! May the devil take me! . . . By St. Foutin, the fornicating apostle! . . . By St. Mamie, but we are done for from laughing (*par rys*).

From which Rabelais derives the name for the city of Paris. This long string of oaths was not translated by Urquhart and Motteux, whose translation was used during the Victorian period. Consequently most people had no idea of this blasphemous material, and it was easy for Saintsbury to conceal Rabelais' irreligious sentiments. But this is hardly feasible today when more accurate translations are available.

Readers are still being deceived by antiquated versions that conceal Rabelais' blasphemy and Aristophanes' earthy humor. Such defective translations are employed in the *Great Books of the Western World,* published by the *Britannica,* and their effect can be easily demonstrated. In *The Birds* by Aristophanes, Iris, a female herald, is sent by Zeus with a message from the gods. The hero impudently defies Zeus' power and threatens to put his messenger to sexual use. His threat is translated by Dudley Fitts (1957) as follows:

> And if *you* get in my way,
> Iris or no Iris, messenger or what ever you are,
> I'll just hoist up your legs and get in between:
> then, by God, you can tell your wondering friends
> how you met an old battleship with a triple prow!

Bickley Rogers, whose prim translation of 1907 is used by the *Great Books,* conceals Aristophanes' coarse humor by rendering this passage in the following way:

> As for you, his waiting maid, if you
> Keep troubling me, with your outrageous ways,
> I'll outrage *you*, and you'll be surprised
> To find the Strength of an old man like me.

Aristophanes and Rabelais are major literary figures who employed humor as a means of expressing their ideals. Aristophanes is more than a purveyor of phallic jokes. He is an ardent advocate of peace and a brilliant lyricist whose epitaph was inscribed by Plato: "The Graces seeking an imperishable sanctuary, found the soul of Aristophanes." Rabelais is more than an exponent of the earthy aspects of life; he personifies the spirit of humanism and the revival of learning. His world encompasses not only drinking, swearing and whoring, but also the radiant dream of the Abbey of Thélème whose motto, *"Fay ce que vouldras*—Do What Thou Wouldst," seeks to liberate men from the narrow constraints of mysticism and asceticism.

Aristophanes and Rabelais require no apologies, no distressed explanations, no discreet silences—they can be presented as they really are.

In Victorian times, silence or severity might be the rule in dealing with the loose morality exhibited by foreign writers, but the sexual levity of English authors was universally condemned. A favorite object of censure was the dramatic art of the Restoration whose aim was to amuse the licentious court of Charles II. More than a century ago, Walter Scott forcefully expressed this attitude in an essay on the Drama, which appeared in the supplement to the fifth edition. He charged:

> In one heinous article, however, the poets of this age sinned against virtue, good taste and decorum; and endangered, by the most profligate and shameless indecency, the cause of morality, which has often been considered as nearly allied with that of the legitimate Drama. . . . What had been merely coarse was, under his influence [Charles II] rendered vicious and systematic impurity. Scenes, both passionate and humorous, were written in such a style, as if the author had studied whether the grave seduction of the heroic, or the broad

infamy of the comic scenes, should contain the grossest insult to public decency.

Scott concluded his attack on the authors of the Restoration by declaring that their dramas were "fitter for a brothel than for the library of a man of letters." His outburst was provoked by the free speech and amorous behavior of these writers as well as by their "shameless" dramatic works. Their cynicism is aptly illustrated in one of Dryden's letters to a fellow dramatist who was in exile: "Ask me not of Love, for every man hates every man perfectly, and women are still the same bitches."

Scott's essay was replaced long ago, but the harsh views he expressed can still be found in the *Encyclopaedia*. The notice on Congreve was written eighty years ago by Swinburne. It asserts:

> Art itself, more than anything else, had been outraged and degraded by the recent school of the Restoration, and the comic work of Congreve, though different rather in kind than in degree from the bestial and blatant licence of his immediate precursors, was inevitably for a time involved in the sentence passed upon the comic work of men in all ways alike his inferiors.

Swinburne's words may seem strange, since his own poetry was attacked for its erotic and animal exuberance, but this merely confirms the pervasive influence of Victorian ideals. They permeated the consciousness of writers and critics until their stifling restrictions became an accepted part of the intellectual climate. Swinburne's harsh judgment of the Restoration merely follows the lead of earlier critics like Macaulay, who categorically condemned one of Congreve's predecessors by observing: "Wycherley's indecency is protected as a skunk against hunters. It is safe because it is too filthy to handle. . . ."

One of Wycherley's amusing comedies is *The Country Wife*. Its hero pretends he has been castrated so he can call on the wives of his friends when they are alone without arousing suspicion. His friends encourage these visits because they mistakenly believe that his presence will prevent their wives from forming alliances with unknown lovers. Such plots, which emphasized sexual dalliance rather than moral virtue, could only offend Victorian critics. Yet the language and spirit of these plays are bright and witty, and no more obscene than the dialogue of a modern Broadway comedy. A search for pornography in the drama of the Restoration can only lead to disappointment. This may be demonstrated by two quotations from *The Country Wife* which have been selected because of their "lewdness."

> A mistress should be like a little country retreat near the town; not to dwell in constantly, but only for a night and then away, to taste the town better when a man returns.

> Why, 'tis as hard to find an old whore-master without jealousy and the gout, as a young one without fear or the pox.

If Congreve is spared by Swinburne, it is probably because he is the author of an undoubted comic masterpiece, *The Way of the World*. Yet he is as free as his predecessors in *Love for Love*, when Scandal remarks:

> I know Trapland has been a whore-master, and loves a wench still. You never knew a whore-master that was not an honest fellow.

Later in the play when a young sailor sees a "well-rigged" widow he cries: "I should like such a handsome gentlewoman for a bedfellow hugely; what say you mistress, would you like to go to sea . . . ?"

Often the effect of sexual prudery is obvious, but in other cases its presence may pass unnoticed. The entry on the Earl of Rochester, one of the most dissolute of King Charles' courtiers, reports that "as a poet he was a follower of Abraham Cowley," but says nothing about the licentious wit and erotic strain that made his verses popular in court circles. A short ditty describing maidenhood may be quoted as an example:

> Have you not in a Chimney seen
> A sullen Faggot, wet and green,
> How coyly it receives the Heat
> And at both Ends does fume and sweat?

> So fares it with the harmless Maid
> When upon her Back she's laid;
> But the kind experienced Dame
> Cracks, and rejoices in the Flame.

A passing reference in the *Britannica*'s bibliography to an expurgated collection of his poems is the only hint that some of Rochester's poems cannot be read aloud in polite society.

The article on Thomas DeQuincey is another instance where a reader may be led astray. It relates that "in 1816 he married Margaret Simpson, 'the dear M———' of whom a charming glimpse is offered in the *Confessions*," but fails to reveal the true cause and significance of his marriage.

The register of the parish church in the village of Grasmere, where DeQuincey was sojourning with his friends the Wordsworths, records that an illegitimate son, born to Margaret Simpson, was baptized on November 15, 1816. Three months later she married DeQuincey. The delay was caused by the essayist's indecision and obsessive procrastination which prevented him from taking the step required to legitimize his son. Since Margaret was only the daughter of a local farmer, while DeQuincey was a gentleman, the Wordsworths strongly opposed his match with a member of the lower classes.

These facts, which were first published by M. L. Armitt in 1916, are ignored in the entry on DeQuincey, which explains:

> It was impossible to deal with or judge him by ordinary standards—not even his publishers did so. Much no doubt was forgiven him, but all that needed forgiveness is lowered by the kindly veil of time, while his merits as a master of English literature are still gratefully acknowledged.

DeQuincey's marriage was of decisive importance because it forced him to support a growing family by his literary efforts. The large number of children that resulted from his marriage drove him into debt, and this difficulty plagued him until his death. To escape his creditors, he was forced into hiding where he managed to eke out a meager existence by writing for periodicals. As a result, his major works, including his celebrated essays and the *Confessions of an English Opium Eater*, first appeared in magazines. In dealing with this side of his life, the *Britannica* merely reports:

> During nearly 50 years DeQuincey lived mainly by the pen. His patrimony seems never to have been entirely exhausted, and his tastes and habits were simple and inexpensive; but he was reckless in the use of money, and had debts and pecuniary difficulties of all sorts.

The true depth of his "pecuniary difficulties" can be appreciated from two excerpts from his letters:

> For as things now are, I spend months after months in literary labour: I endure the extremities of personal privations; some of which it would be humiliating to describe; (by way of illustration I may mention—that having in a moment of pinching difficulty for my children about 10 months since pawned every article of my dress which could produce a shilling. I have since that time had no stockings, no shoes, no neck-hankerchief, coat, waist-coat or hat. I have sat constantly barefoot. . . .

> . . . my difficulties have increased to a horr'd degree, considering that young children are obliged to have their part in them. Already in September my household, now of 9 persons, had been reduced to a single meal a day—usually at night. Even then my youngest daughter, 5 years old, besieged the ears of all about her with clamors for something to eat from morning till night.

The article on DeQuincey was written three generations ago, at a time when poverty was a distasteful subject. Therefore it disregards his painful struggle to feed his family and stay out of debtor's prison. Such mundane matters were of only limited interest to affluent readers during the nineteenth century. To most middle-class Victorians, poverty was almost as repulsive a subject as sexual passion. They were living through an ugly phase of the Industrial Revolution, when child labor was the rule and coal-burning factories were blackening the English countryside. Indigence was suspect because of its intimate association with the harsh reality of lower class life, and prosperous Englishmen did not wish to be reminded of this fact. The article on DeQuincey still reflects this attitude by glossing over the extreme poverty that embittered the essayist's life, and in doing so, it seriously misrepresents his life.*

Long before the Victorians had elevated respectability into a supreme virtue, Dr. Johnson protested: "We have had too many honeysuckle lives of Milton. . . . If a man is to write *A Panegyrick* he may Keep Vices out of sight; but if he proposes to write *A Life* he must represent it as it really was." This demand could not be satisfied a century ago when Englishmen expected spotless virtue from poets, authors and statesmen, since honesty would have destroyed many reputations and called into question the very basis of Victorian morality.

Robert Burns is an obvious case. The beloved Scottish poet is represented by an essay reprinted from the ninth edition. It avoids a candid examination of the poet's life because this would reveal his promiscuity—something that could only shock Victorian sensibilities and make Burns the object of a puritanical attack. The author of "Auld Lang Syne" is spared this indignity; his life is described with great tact and discretion:

---

*Oddly enough, DeQuincey became a contributor to the *Britannica* in 1838, because he was destitute in Edinburgh. The publisher at that time was Adam Black, a shrewd Scotsman. One day Black saw DeQuincey being conveyed to prison by the sheriff's officers. When Black discovered that the essayist was being taken to jail because of a debt of less than £30, he agreed to pay the debt if DeQuincey would furnish him with articles on Pope and Shakespeare for the seventh edition of the *Encyclopaedia*. This bargain was faithfully fulfilled by the essayist.

His article on Shakespeare concentrates on the life and personality of the dramatist, and neglects his plays and poetry—a practice which has been followed in subsequent editions. An interesting aspect of this essay is the tender way in which DeQuincey analyzes Shakespeare's marriage to Anne Hathaway, six months before the birth of their first child. This situation must have touched DeQuincey's own experience because he devotes a good deal of space to the match. He notes that since Anne was considerably older than her husband, "it was easy enough for a mature woman, armed with such inevitable advantages of experience and self-possession, to draw onward a blushing novice"; and making Anne the active agent in the affair, he quotes Shakespeare's lines to explain her success:

> And, when a woman woos, what woman's son
> Will sourly leave her till she hath prevailed?

> . . . His nervous constitution received a fatal strain. . . . From these hard tasks and his fiery temperament, craving in vain for sympathy in a frigid air, grew a thirst for stimulants and revolt against restraint. . . . The poet was jilted, went through the usual despairs, and resorted to the not unusual sources of consolation.

By suppressing the facts about Burns' active sex life, the *Encyclopaedia* manages to preserve both the poet's reputation and middle-class English decorum. It observes that the poet was "intimate with his future wife, Jean Armour," but fails to disclose that she bore him two sets of twins before they were married. During his escapades, Burns impregnated a number of girls who bore him illegitimate children. He acknowledged their paternity and boasted that he was called a fornicator. Chafing at the necessity for repeated public repentance for his transgressions, he complained:

> Often at weddings my mouth has watered deliciously to see a young fellow, after a few commonplace stories from a gentleman in black [the Minister], strip and go to bed with a young girl—whilst I, for just the same thing—only wanting the ceremony—am abused like a pickpocket.

Once when he was considering marriage, he wrote a friend of its advantages:

> And then to have a woman to lye with when one pleases without running any risk of the cursed expense of bastards and all the other concomitants of that species of smuggling— these are solid views of matrimony.

The *Britannica* does not examine Burns' private life, but concentrates on his literary work to present a flattering image of one of Scotland's famous figures. It offers a pleasing picture of a rustic poet who wrote many charming songs and lyrics, but seriously misrepresents the range and nature of his creative activity by neglecting the erotic verse he both wrote and collected, whose outspoken language has few equals in English literature. When this treatment originally appeared, it was attacked on the ground that patriotism had been allowed to take the place of criticism.

The essay had been prepared by J. N. Nichol to replace a contribution by Robert Louis Stevenson, who at the time was an unknown writer of twenty-five. Stevenson received slightly more than five pounds for his effort, but it was never printed because the Edinburgh publishers of the *Britannica* felt that its critical spirit did not agree with accepted Scottish tradition. Some time later, Stevenson discussed the problem raised by an honest account of Burns' life. He noted that the treatment of the poet as a man is "broken, apologetic and confused"—and added: "If you are so sensibly pained by the misconduct of your subject, and so paternally delighted with his virtues, you will be an excellent gentleman, but a somewhat questionable biographer."

Behind the façade of propriety and respectability erected by the Victorians, life continued in strange and devious ways. Sexual topics and marital scandals might be hidden from curious eyes and banished from public print, but they could not be eliminated so easily from life itself.*

When Walter Scott condemned the drama of the Restoration in 1816, he was forced to argue a thesis that later critics would have taken for granted. The same sentiments led Thomas Bowdler in 1818 to issue *The Family Shakespeare,* omitting those words and expressions "which cannot with propriety be read aloud in a family." This innovation led to the practice of "bowdlerizing" literary works in subsequent decades when prudery was triumphantly installed in England. The fate of the *Britannica*'s essay on Love vividly illustrates the progress of Victorian ideals. When the essay first appeared in the third edition in 1797, it anticipated several strands of thought that were to become widely accepted in British life. One was the strict separation of love and sexual desire; another was the firm belief that members of the lower classes had few human attributes. The essay declared:

> Savages feel the influence of the sensual appetite, and it is extremely probable that they have some ideas of beauty, but among savages love is seldom known. Even amongst the lower

* See Note I, p. 351, for the case of Charles Parnell.

orders of civil society it seems to be a very gross passion, and
to have in it more of the selfishness of appetite than the generosity of esteem. To these observations many exceptions will
no doubt be found; but we speak of savages in general, and of
the great body of the labouring poor, who, in the choice of
their mates, do not study, and indeed are incapable of studying,
that rectitude of mind and those delicacies of sentiment, without which neither man nor woman can deserve to be esteemed.

The factory system created by the Industrial Revolution supplied a major stimulus for equating the erotic life of the lower
classes with that of savages since it created a great mass of impov-
erished, illiterate workers who were housed in wretched slums.
As industrialism spread, the number of workers increased, but
their existence was scarcely noticed by authors who catered to
the interests and preoccupations of the middle class.

The concept that love should be considered one of "those delicacies of sentiment" was carried so far that it became very difficult to speak openly about erotic matters in polite society. However, when the article on Love was originally prepared, things
had not gone so far: in 1797 it was still possible to enumerate
the diverse symptoms produced by sexual passion in a manner
that would have been distasteful to Victorians. Thus the article
on Love depicted its effect in an extravagant clinical manner
reminiscent of Burton's *Anatomy of Melancholy* when it recorded:

> In some instances, the person is sad and watchful; in
> others, the person, not being conscious of his state, pines away,
> is slothful, and regardless of food; though the wiser, when
> they find themselves in love, seek pleasant company and active
> entertainments. As the force of love prevails, sighs grow deeper,
> a tremor affects the heart and pulse; the countenance is al-
> ternately pale and red; the voice is suppressed in the fauces;
> the eyes grow dim; cold sweats break out; sleep absents itself,
> at least until morning; the secretions become disturbed; a
> loss of appetite, a hectic fever, melancholy, or perhaps mad-
> ness, if not death, constitutes the sad catastrophe.

Later moralists did not recognize that love is a powerful emotion which sometimes produces clinical consequences: they converted passion into a private sentiment hidden from public view. The condensation and disappearance of the article on Love reflects their successful depreciation of love as an important human experience. Although an abridged version of this article appeared in the seventh edition in 1842, by the time the eighth edition was issued, a decade later, the rising tide of Victorian prudery had gained so much strength that it swept the essay out of the *Encyclopaedia*. From that time until the present, there has been no article on Love in the *Britannica*, although it is discussed in a number of other entries.

The treatment of sex and scandal has been influenced by the personal views of contributors and changing mores of society. The shifting attitude toward provocative material can be traced in successive editions. The ninth edition of 1875–89 faithfully reflected the prudery of the Victorian age, and entries reprinted from this work are a primary source of many of the narrow opinions expressed in the current set. When the eleventh edition was published in 1910–11, Queen Victoria had been dead for a decade and the oppressive restraints associated with her reign had diminished, so it was possible to discuss the private lives of historical figures frankly. This freedom was encouraged by the imposing scholarship of the eleventh edition and its editorial ties with Cambridge University which shielded it from puritanical attack. A generation later, when the fourteenth edition was issued in 1929, brevity and discretion became the rule. Old entries were condensed, and in the process, juicy bits of scandal were deleted, as well as vivid portraits of vice and violence.

The shifting attitude of successive editions is illustrated by the treatment of Admiral Nelson and Lady Hamilton. Their open liaison was one of the celebrated scandals of the nineteenth century. It involved double adultery because both partners were already married; and since Nelson was a great naval hero, this extramarital relationship could hardly be concealed even by zealous Victorians. The ninth edition commented briefly on the affair in its article on Lord Nelson:

He was singularly susceptible to female influences; and he formed for some years an erring attachment for Emma, the wife of Sir William Hamilton, ambassador at Naples in 1798. She was an adventuress of great beauty and parts; and, though his conduct at Naples does not seem to have been due to her evil counsels, he became almost a slave in his wild passion; and this not only led to a separation from his wife, but had given him many wretched moments, and had caused much pain to his aged sovereign.

Patriotism was upheld by exonerating the heroic Nelson—and morality was sustained by blaming Emma for instigating the affair. This satisfied the Victorian code which demanded unquestioned purity and fidelity for wives, while it overlooked masculine adventures. The editorial policy of the ninth edition was consistent with this double standard; Emma Hamilton did not receive an entry despite her enormous notoriety because she was regarded as a "wicked woman," but her insignificant husband was given a biographical article that carefully outlined his diplomatic career and antiquarian interests.

When the eleventh edition appeared a generation later, a freer atmosphere prevailed. Even more important, the letters secretly exchanged between Nelson and Lady Hamilton had been published, and they revealed for the first time the facts behind their liaison and the illegitimate daughter that resulted from their alliance. These revelations excited the interest of the British public, and their curiosity was gratified by a detailed account in the eleventh edition. The article on Emma Hamilton described her successive lovers and the existence of her two illegitimate children. A fresh biography of Nelson traced the course of their turbulent romance and discredited the foolish notion that it was caused by an evil adventuress who had seduced the Admiral. It related how Nelson's behavior on his return to England offended and alienated fashionable court circles:

> . . . Nelson insisted on forcing Lady Hamilton on them and would go nowhere where she was not received. When it was discovered that he insisted on making his wife live in the same house as his mistress, he was considered to have infringed the

accepted standard of good manners. After enduring insult at once cruel and cowardly to the verge of poorness of spirit, Lady Nelson rebelled. A complete separation took place, and husband and wife never met again.

The final version of the Nelson-Hamilton affair was supplied by the fourteenth edition which suppressed most of the information contained in the earlier edition. The article on Lady Hamilton was shortened by eliminating the account of her early amours and her first illegitimate child. The detailed review of Nelson's romantic entanglement was dropped from his biography and only a few lines were allotted to the subject:

> The whole question of Nelson's conduct at Naples is of course bound up with his friendship with Lady Hamilton. No one denies that it was now that Nelson's friendship for this woman ripened into the intimacy that was eventually to separate him from his wife. But that a private attachment, culpable as it may have been, warped his judgment in public matters no one has shown, nor has anyone explained why it should.

This version, which appears in the 1958 *Encyclopaedia*, devotes three pages to the Admiral's naval and diplomatic activities, but assigns only three sentences to his romance with Lady Hamilton. Its conclusions are contradicted by the article on his mistress which states: "Lady Hamilton subjected, and drew him into a most unhappy participation in the domestic troubles of Naples. . . ." Consequently a reader is unable to gain a clear idea of this famous liaison.

Certain facts have always caused difficulty. Fifty years ago, it was impossible in English-speaking countries to discuss homosexuality openly. The word "homosexual" could not appear in a book intended for the general public. Therefore, the eleventh edition could deal only obliquely with the celebrated trial of Oscar Wilde, although it was the great literary scandal of the 1890's. Its biographical entry on Wilde observed that at Oxford, "he adopted what to undergraduates appeared the effeminate pose of casting scorn on manly sports, wearing his hair long, decorating his rooms with peacock's feathers, lilies, sunflowers, blue china and other *objets d'art.* . . ." It noted that his success as a dramatist disabused hostile critics of suspicions about "his personal character which had been excited by the apparent looseness of morals which . . . it had always pleased him to affect"; but the article could not describe the reality behind this elegant pose. It could only report, "Wilde was sentenced to two years' imprisonment with hard labour for offences under the Criminal Law Amendment Act." The nature of his crime and the "fatal revelations" that led to his downfall could not be explained.

Similarly, in the eleventh edition, Arthur Symons was forced to portray Paul Verlaine's personal life in cryptic terms by relating: "In 1871, the strange young poet Jean Arthur Rimbaud came somewhat troublingly into his life, in which drink had already brought a lasting disturbance." Edmund Gosse in his article on Rimbaud simply observed that their relation was "extravagant," but could not expose the homosexual nature of their attachment, although it led Verlaine to shoot his youthful friend—a crime for which he was sentenced to two years in prison.

This reluctance to discuss homosexuality in reference books would be of only historical interest today, if these entries were not reprinted in the current edition. A similar reticence is exhibited in the biography of Alexander von Humboldt, which describes his final emotional attachment in the following terms: "In his later years the sway of an old and faithful servant held him in more than matrimonial bondage, and four years before his death he executed a deed of gift transferring to this man Seifert the absolute possession of his entire property."

The article on Tschaikovsky states:

> Tschaikovsky married Antonia Ivanovna Milyukova on July 6, 1877, but the union proved an impossible one through no fault of hers but simply through his own abnormality of temperament; and it resulted in separation in October.

The article, however, does not mention the nature of the composer's abnormality or note that his unfortunate attempt at marriage produced a nervous breakdown which forced him to flee in terror from his bride. This silence is consistent with the *Britannica*'s failure to treat homosexuality. The index in the 1958 edition lists only two direct references to the subject; one deals with the homosexual behavior of animals, and the other with its prevalence among female prostitutes. There is no separate entry on homosexuality; and a reader will not find a single reference to the Kinsey Report, despite its important revelation that one-third of its male sample reported some kind of homosexual experience.

The Victorian desire to make artists and poets respectable members of society is sometimes carried to amusing extremes. The article on Robert Browning records:

> He frequented literary and artistic circles, and was passionately fond of the theater; but he was entirely free from a coarse Bohemianism, and never went to bed, we are told, without kissing his mother.

The entry on castrati observes that "the abominable practice to which they owed their existence has now been entirely abandoned"—but it neglects to describe the nature of this "abominable practice." Indeed, a reader who consults this entry might think that they owed their existence to an operation on the vocal cords because they are defined in the following way:

> CASTRATO, an adult male soprano who has been operated on in his youth to prevent his voice from changing in the ordinary way to the normal masculine pitch.*

The *Encyclopaedia* does not provide material that would be useful in the sexual instruction of youngsters. Information on such topics as Menstruation, Gynecology and Sexual Reproduction is couched in the Latin terminology and technical language used in medical texts. A typical example is the article on Gynecology which supplies an elaborate account of the cause and cure of female disorders. Its characteristic tone may be suggested by a brief excerpt:

---

* Their origin is explained in the article on the Eunuch, but this information is not indexed under Castrato.

The vaginal walls are kept moist by a thin opalescent fluid containing desquamated epithelium and cervical mucus; its acid reaction is caused by the vaginal bacilli (Döderlein). When the secretion is excessive it is called leucorrhoea or "the whites."

There is no discussion of the psychological or physiological changes accompanying adolescence; indeed, there is no article on Adolescence, and no reference in the index to Masturbation or Enuresis ("bed-wetting"). Consequently this work, which is supposed to be a storehouse of knowledge on almost every conceivable subject, does not provide useful information in the area of sex education—despite the importance of the subject to parents with teen-age children.

Fortunately censorship and Victorian ideas have operated on only a small percentage of the *Britannica*'s text, but whenever their influence has been felt, severe distortions have occurred. As far as the entire set is concerned, prudery is like a rare disease that strikes infrequently but leaves serious consequences in its wake. It seals off important areas of human experience from mature examination and perpetuates taboos which are no longer accepted by educated readers. Such defects suggest the possibility that Victorian sentiments have exerted a subtle influence on a wide class of entries retained from earlier editions, and their continued presence is a disturbing sign of editorial neglect. In a large and diverse reference work, the lack of effective editorial control is a serious matter because it allows strange inconsistencies to accumulate.

A few examples may suffice. The article on Masks contains a lively mural which portrays a group of men wearing grotesque masks dancing around a lovely young woman. Her nude figure is adorned with a single piece of clothing—a sweeping crescent that serves as a headdress. Her pink flesh is silhouetted against a gold background, and her breasts and supple thighs are richly reproduced in the best traditions of an academic calendar art that revels in the romantic representation of the female figure.

The prudery exhibited by literary entries taken from the ninth edition is flatly contradicted by the current article on Sexual

Behaviour which portrays copulation with photographic realism. Although it does not discuss human sex practices explicitly, the article furnishes a bold, realistic description of love among the primates:

> The investigatory responses with which the female chimpanzee greets the male sometimes include handling the penis and scrotum, and the resultant sexual excitement often culminates in coition. Almost every region of the partner's body is explored and stimulated in the course of precopulatory activities of apes, but the male's attention is focused particularly upon the female genitalia. The female's vagina is thoroughly investigated with the male's fingers and often with his tongue and lips, and the excitatory value of such stimulation is revealed by the fact that it often produces erection and pulsation of the clitoris.

This passage is much more explicit than anything in the pages of Rabelais—yet the *Encyclopaedia* condemns Rabelais for his "extreme coarseness of language" while offering an intimate view of the sexual behavior of chimpanzees, birds, fishes and reptiles. Lest it be thought that the passage just quoted applies merely to apes, its connection with human sex practices is stressed in the next paragraph:

> The sexually-exciting function of certain forms of stimulation in humans is indicated by the almost universal occurrence of particular types of bodily contact before coition. . . . Mutual masturbation and mouth-genital contact appear regularly in the sexual behaviour of some cultures, and the stimulation of specific erotic zones such as the female breast is practiced in many societies. The similarity of the precoital activities of humans and other primates suggests the existence of an underlying pattern common to the order, and the belief that such widely distributed responses as mouth-genital contact are "abnormal" or "perverted" is probably incorrect from the strictly zoological point of view.

To say the least, the editorial canons operating in the *Britannica* are rather obscure. It conceals Aristophanes' earthy humor and criticizes the drama of the Restoration, while presenting a survey of sexual behavior (seen from a zoological point of view) that leaves nothing to the imagination. Any attempt to reconcile such discordant passages seems quite hopeless since they are drawn from completely different worlds of discourse. Yet it is obvious that an encyclopedia must maintain some degree of consistency if it is not to degenerate into a compilation of contradictory opinions expressed by different contributors.

[8]

The Changing Face
of Biography

Biography is not a static or fixed art, but is constantly changing in response to contemporary knowledge and interests. During the Victorian era, multi-volume biographies were often commissioned to commemorate recently deceased personalities. They were usually prepared under the watchful eye of a close relative to insure that they would contain nothing that might impair the dignity of their subject. When *The Life and Letters of* ———— was published, *The Life* always referred to the public life, and *The Letters* omitted any personal correspondence that might reveal intimate family secrets. As a result, these imposing volumes never revealed the inner life of their subjects, but merely served to embalm their memory in flattering literary portraits. Lytton Strachey, whose *Eminent Victorians* helped destroy this ponderous, reverential mode of biography, trenchantly described its essential features:

> Those two fat volumes, with which it is our custom to commemorate the dead—who does not know them, with their

ill-digested masses of material, their slipshod style, their tone of tedious panegyric, their lamentable lack of selection, of detachment, of design? They are as familiar as the cortege of the undertaker, and wear the same air of slow, funereal barbarism.

Whenever these works depicted living persons in an unfavorable way, their names would invariably be deleted. This genteel practice led Carlyle to observe, "How delicate, how decent is English biography, bless its mealy mouth."

Today it is common to examine an individual's behavior for a secret motivation, a hidden compulsion or an infantile fixation that may be a key to his personality. In earlier times, character was frequently explained in terms of heredity or social environment—and such explanations can still be found in articles retained from earlier editions. The entry on Coleridge states:

> . . . In the light of the biographical study of the last generation, he can be seen as a victim of heredity and malady, his rare powers and inefficiencies being alike innate, and the opium-eating a fatal consequence.

Since this appraisal is taken from the ninth edition of the 1880's, "the biographical study of the last generation" does not refer to modern psychoanalytic interpretations, but rather to nineteenth-century notions of heredity and degeneration popularized by Galton and Lombroso. These ideas led biographers to explore the genealogy of their subjects for the cause of the intellectual and emotional tendencies which, they believed, were inherited like physical traits. The *Britannica* follows this approach by claiming that "the best elements of Goethe's genius came from his mother's side," and that he inherited from his father "an unamiable stiffness of manner" and a "stability of character which brought him unscathed through temptations and passions." In a similar vein, the entry on Emily Dickinson seeks to follow her family tree over a span of five hundred years by observing: "In all her heredity, according to her biographer, traced back nine generations in America and 13 in England, there is nothing to explain her genius—nor to confute it."

The *Encyclopaedia*'s biographical coverage has undergone a number of changes in the last eighty years. Until 1902 there were no articles on living persons, and during the nineteenth century, biographical entries were often lengthy essays that offered stylists like Macaulay and Symonds an opportunity for impressive literary performances. Their spacious manner may still be seen in old entries on English notables. An example is John Morley's essay on Edmund Burke taken from the ninth edition. Although it moves at a leisurely pace and suffers from some dull patches in dealing with Burke's parliamentary career, it contains a number of vivid passages. It relates his dispute with a friend who had complained that his stirring defense of Marie Antoinette was "a mere bit of foppery; for was she not a Messalina and a jade?" Burke indignantly replied, "Are not high rank, great splendour of descent, great personal elegance and outward accomplishments ingredients of moment in forming the interest we take in the misfortunes of men?" Such lively quotations were frequently employed in the past, and it was natural for Morley to quote Dr. Johnson's celebrated description of the statesman:

> Burke, sir, is such a man that if you met him for the first time in the street, where you were stopped by a drove of oxen, and you and he stepped aside to take shelter but for five minutes, he'd talk to you in such a manner that when you parted you would say, "This is an extraordinary man."

The length of Victorian biographies was a major asset, but they often concealed important facts about their subjects. This attitude was carried to its logical extreme by Thackeray who instructed his children not to allow the publication of his personal papers. After his death, his daughter reported, "Papa said when I drop there is to be no life written of me, mind this & consider it my last testament & desire." His injunction was effective in curbing the curiosity of biographers since it delayed the publication of his letters for many years and kept his private life shrouded in mystery. This ignorance impairs the current article on Thackeray, which does not explain the connection between his personal life and his literary activity. It states: "Mrs.

Thackeray, to quote Trollope, 'became ill and her mind failed her' in 1840, and he 'became as it were a widower to the end of his days.' . . ." Nothing more is said about this painful experience, although the novelist exploited it in *Vanity Fair,* whose heroine, Amelia Sedley, is modeled after his wife. George Osborne neglects Amelia after their marriage, just as Thackeray had neglected his own wife—and Amelia, like his wife, is threatened by insanity. Fortunately in the novel she recovers, but her trials illustrate the theme of the book: "Which of us is happy in this world? Which of us has his desire, or having it, is satisfied?"

Although the article on Thackeray cites works published as late as 1941, it fails to discuss the great emotional experience of his adult life which was successfully concealed for many years. This emotional upheaval came to light when certain private letters were made public. The magazine section of the *New York Times* announced this discovery on February 8, 1914, in a bold headline:

SECRET OF THACKERAY'S HOPELESS LOVE NOW REVEALED: His Lifelong Passion for Mrs. Brookfield, Hitherto Supposed to Be Only His Friend, Discovered Through Heretofore Unpublished Letters. . . .

These letters disclosed that the novelist had been passionately in love with the neglected wife of a close friend. A warm intimacy had developed as a result of their mutual troubles; and after *Vanity Fair* was published, an emotional tie was formed that lasted for three years. Thackeray called this relation the great passion of his life, and wrote to a common friend: "I don't see how any woman should not love a man who had loved her as I did J.: I don't see how any man shd. not love a woman so beautiful, so unhappy, so tender; I don't see how any husband, however he might have treated his treasure, should be indifferent at the idea of losing it. . . . We must part in peace. I have loved his wife too much to be able to see her belong even to her husband any more—that's the truth."

Mrs. Brookfield asked her son to burn the personal letters she had received from Thackeray, but instead he sold them to a

London dealer. Some of Thackeray's private papers also went astray, until the letters exchanged by the couple were finally acquired by an American collector who revealed their contents. The affair with Mrs. Brookfield is a significant element in understanding Thackeray's literary career, because he used the relationship in his novel *Henry Esmond*. However, he inverted the situation in the novel by having Lady Castlewood fall in love with the hero, which allowed the novelist to soothe his wounded vanity and ambivalent feelings.

The effort made by nineteenth-century biographers to conceal matters that might shock the public is graphically illustrated by the life of Dickens, whose final years were darkened by a painful marital scandal. A few details reached the public, but the true facts were suppressed by his friends in deference to his literary reputation.

After more than twenty years of marriage, Dickens forced his wife out of his home, although she had borne him ten children and suffered through several miscarriages. When his wife was sent away, only the eldest child was permitted to accompany her. Dickens retained custody of the rest of the children, and their care was entrusted to his wife's sister, who had lived for some years in the Dickens household. This callous action might have remained a secret if the novelist had not felt an urgent need to justify himself. In May, 1858, under a column labeled PERSONAL in his magazine *Household Words*, Dickens announced to an astonished public that he and his wife had separated for "strictly private" reasons. He branded any rumors that might be circulating about the matter as "abominably false." He righteously proclaimed, "Whosoever repeats one of them, after this denial, will lie as wilfully and as foully as it is possible for any false witness to lie, before heaven and earth." Not content with this outspoken denial, Dickens wrote a letter to a friend containing further details. A few months later the letter was made public by the *New York Herald Tribune*. Dickens falsely stated that his wife desired the separation because of an estrangement "caused by the mental disorder under which she sometimes labors." He attempted to play the part of a hero by claiming that he had previously refused to accept the idea because "the children were the first consideration." This letter created quite a stir, but its effects were hardly favorable. The *Herald Tribune* remarked in an editorial, "One more uncalled-for letter from Mr. D. will finish him."

Despite the publicity and notoriety surrounding the separation, the *Britannica* hardly mentions the matter. Its biography of Dickens merely notes:

> . . . Returning at last to his beloved Rochester district on the great road of Kent, he set up his house at Gads Hill. It is sad to realize that this material domestic settlement had followed on a moral unsettlement and the separation of Dickens and his wife, by agreement (of which the little that needs saying has already been said) had already taken place in 1856.* But indeed, apart from that tragedy, it is typical of Dickens that his repose could never be final.

These words were written by G. K. Chesterton some thirty years ago. Since he was born in 1874, Chesterton grew up under the influence of Victorian ideals which demanded moral perfection from its heroes. As an admirer of Dickens, he was reluctant to diminish the reputation of his hero, so he hurried over the separation, despite Dickens' public pronouncements on this "strictly private" matter. Earlier editions did not even mention the existence of this unpleasant subject. Indeed, the ninth edition smugly declared, "There is not much room for variety of incident in the life of a novelist securely established in public favour, working hard, and happy in the exercise of his art."

Yet behind the separation was an even darker scandal, one which was first revealed by Thomas Wright in *The Life of Charles Dickens* (1935). When Dickens first left his wife, a rumor spread that he had done so because he preferred his wife's sister, Georgina, who had remained behind to care for the children. When Thackeray heard of this supposed affair at the Garrick Club, he replied, "No such thing, it's with an actress." Dickens repaid Thackeray for this bit of frankness by refusing to speak to him. The actress in question was Ellen Ternan, a fair-

* This date is incorrect; the separation occurred in 1858.

haired, blue-eyed creature whom Dickens had met in 1857, a year before he thrust his wife aside. At the time she was only eighteen years old, the same age as the novelist's daughter, Kate.

After the separation, Dickens set Ellen up in a cottage near his home and visited her several times a week. She remained his mistress for twelve years, until his death in 1870. Ellen was the first person to be mentioned in his will, in which she was left a legacy of £1000. Although this liaison was well known in Dickens' circle, it was carefully suppressed by his official biographer, and its existence was made public only in 1934, more than sixty years after the novelist's death.

The actual cause of the separation was unknown when Chesterton wrote his celebrated essay on Dickens, so he cannot be blamed for not discussing it. However, he felt it was necessary to exonerate Dickens for the failure of his marriage:

> As Pickwick was the foundation of his public life, his marriage was naturally the foundation of his private life; and in this also he has been the object of criticism as he was certainly an object of sympathy. Very little good is done by making guesses about a story of which the spiritual balance and proportion were probably never known to more than three or four people. It is significant that those who were nearest to it, and who survive to speak or rather to be silent, agree in laying no great blame upon anyone involved.

Unfortunately for Chesterton's remarks, the first information about the scandal came from those who were intimately involved. Thomas Wright reported that Ellen Ternan had told the story of the affair to Canon Benham, the Vicar of Margate, who said, "I had it from her own lips, that she loathed the very thought of the intimacy." The story was confirmed by Dickens' daughter, Kate, who informed Gladys Storey: "My father was like a madman when my mother left home. The affair brought out all that was worst—all that was weakest in him. He did not care a damn what happened to any of us. Nothing could surpass the misery and unhappiness of our home."

These revelations upset Dickens' faithful disciples, who found it difficult to accept the sordid tale. Bernard Shaw wryly commented on the matter in a letter in the London *Times*: "The facts of the case may be in bad taste. Facts often are." Nevertheless, one need not possess a morbid curiosity to be interested in the affair, since it sheds considerable light on Dickens' development as a novelist. His romantic attachment to Ellen Ternan may well explain why he was able to provide a much more realistic portrait of women in his late novels, like *Great Expectations*, than in his earlier ones, like *David Copperfield*. It is understandable that Chesterton's biography should be reprinted because of its vigor; but this does not excuse the failure to correct its errors and omissions, particularly when they impede an appreciation of Dickens' artistic growth.

Biographical "facts" often continue to appear long after they have been corrected by later research. An example is the current notice on Ruskin, which has been reprinted from the eleventh edition. It states:

> On April 10, 1848 . . . Ruskin was married at Perth to Euphemia Chalmers Gray, a lady of great beauty, of a family long intimate with the Ruskins. The marriage, we are told, was arranged by the parents of the pair, and was a somewhat hurried act. It was evidently ill-assorted, and brought no happiness to either. . . . No particulars of their life have been made public.

This is not true. In 1949, the veil cast over Ruskin's married life by his parents and his faithful followers was removed by the publication of Euphemia Gray's letters. These letters reveal that Ruskin's passion for Effie Gray was "rampant and unmanageable"; and that he ardently pressed his suit in his correspondence, addressing her as "my mistress—my friend—my queen—my darling—my only love." Far from arranging the marriage, his parents did what they could to prevent it from taking place, but Ruskin was adamant. After the ceremony, Ruskin never consummated the marriage. The painful facts were set forth in Effie Gray's letter to her parents written on the eve of her flight from Ruskin:

> The reason he did not make me his wife was because he was disgusted with my person the first evening on 10th April.

. . . Then he said that after six years, he would marry me [her euphemism] when I was 25. This last year we spoke about it. He then said as I professed quite a dislike to him that it would be SINFUL to enter into such a connexion, as if I was not very *wicked,* I was at least insane and that the responsibility that I might have children was too great, as I was quite unfit to bring them up.

This letter sheds a vivid light on obscure portions of Ruskin's private life, but its contents are not recorded by the *Britannica.*

Dr. Johnson once remarked to Mrs. Thrale, "A story is a specimen of human manners, and derives its sole value from its truth." He repeated this thought in a letter written near the close of his life: "Whether to see life as it is will give us much consolation, I know not; but the consolation which is drawn from truth, if any there be, is solid and durable; but that which may be derived from error must be, like its original, fallacious and fugitive."

Dr. Johnson's remark is almost a truism, but the quest for truth is often hampered by a desire to romanticize famous figures. To meet this demand, biographers frequently invent picturesque adventures or colorful incidents to enliven their narrative, and these fictional additions sometimes become confused with actual events. Creative artists are particularly susceptible to such distortions because the public believes the beauty and turbulence of their art reflect their tumultuous personal life. Goya is an instructive example: many writers have embellished his biography with romantic legends in an effort to mirror the excitement of his art. The *Britannica* follows this tradition by reporting:

> Goya was a true son of Aragon; he took part in street scuffles between the youths of rival parishes; after one of these fights, in which three of the combatants were killed, he was compelled, at the age of 19, to flee from Madrid.

One might think from the definite nature of this story—with its three combatants killed—that it is based on an eyewitness account, but this is not the case. Little is known about Goya's early life, yet the *Encyclopaedia* article records:

In consequence of his riotous and dissolute life he found it convenient to leave Madrid also, and he made his way to the coast as one of a traveling troupe of bull-fighters, and finally reached Rome, broken in health and destitute.

No documentary evidence exists describing this trip, but the idea that Goya joined a group of bull-fighters fits the popular image of the artist. Such a fanciful tale may be useful in a Hollywood scenario, but it hardly belongs in a standard reference work.

Since none of Goya's letters or personal papers has survived, few facts can be ascertained about his early life. Stories about this period did not begin to circulate until fifty years later, when he was a famous old master; therefore they cannot be taken seriously. More information is available about the artist's maturity. But writers usually prefer to proceed in a fictional vein by presenting a throbbing account of his friendship with the Duchess of Alba. Some authors have even attempted to identify the Duchess as the model for his portraits of the naked and clothed maja—although her slim, aristocratic figure does not resemble the fleshy torso and sensuous features of the maja. Oddly enough, although the *Encyclopaedia* supplies legendary material about Goya's early life, it neglects his relation with the Duchess of Alba, which has been the subject of endless comment.

Sometimes biographical entries are marred by obvious omissions. The celebrated liaison of Duse and D'Annunzio was the talk of European society. Eleonora Duse at the time was the reigning actress of the Continent, and her decision to champion the plays of the young Italian poet who had captured her heart helped make D'Annunzio an international figure. Although the entry on Duse is more than a page long, it merely notes her "life-consuming friendship" with the poet, but offers no details on this crucial experience. Instead of portraying how she eagerly advanced his career until he cast her aside, the article attempts to inflate her mental powers by cataloguing her intellectual interests. It asserts that she steeped herself in the writings of Pascal, Keats and Thomas à Kempis, as well as *The Confessions of St. Augustine,* but neglects her private life. In doing so, it transforms the consummate artist who excited the critical admiration of George Bernard Shaw into a pale pseudo-intellectual who flits from one theatrical triumph to another. Thus the passionate woman of forty who told a friend after she had fallen in love with the youthful D'Annunzio—"You're probably right. . . . I must choose between the head and the heart. I choose the heart"—becomes a colorless personality of a bygone era.

A similar reticence is exhibited by the article on D'Annunzio which disregards his private life, although it is an essential element in understanding this "Mediterranean superman." D'Annunzio exclaimed, "I live voluptuously with long intervals of sadness"; and his life was a long series of abandoned love affairs, punctuated by numerous brief encounters. His licentious temperament was expressed in his literary work. In describing his *Book of the Virgins,* he boasted: "Side by side with very mild pages there are others of great boldness. The scene unfolds between a brothel and a church, between the smell of incense and the stench of corruption." People who came in contact with the poet soon became disenchanted with his restless nature which was continually seeking sexual adventures. Duse remarked, "His life is like an inn. Everybody goes through it." And his wife said, "When I married my husband I thought I was marrying poetry itself. I would have done better to buy, at three francs-fifty, each volume of poetry he published."

D'Annunzio's work can hardly be explained without referring to his erotic life. Freud's observation is quite apt in this regard:

> If a biographical effort really endeavors to penetrate the understanding of the psychic life of its hero, it must not, as happens in most biographies through discretion or prudery, pass over in silence the sexual activity or the sexual peculiarity of the one examined.

D'Annunzio's literary productions were almost always a direct transcription of his personal experience. A celebrated example of this tendency is his novel *Il fuoco,* which created an international sensation in 1900 because it offered an intimate portrayal of his affair with Duse. Certainly, there is little point to a catalogue of his works which fails to explain their autobiographical origin or their peculiar mixture of sexuality and cruelty, estheticism and decadence.

The psychological analysis of intellectual activity is now a common practice. The *Britannica* reflects this vogue in some of its articles, but its comments frequently fail to match the sophistication of the public. The entry on Edgar Allan Poe records that he suffered from "platonic erotomania," but does not explain the meaning of this apparently contradictory term. The biography of Nietzsche dismisses his final mental illness by declaring:

> We may take him at his word when, on July 8, 1886, he writes to his sister:—"My health is really quite normal—only my soul is so sensitive and so longing for good friends of my own kind. Get me a circle of men who will listen to me and understand me—and I shall be cured."

The original copy of this letter has never been found. Since it is known that Nietzsche's sister frequently altered the text of her brother's correspondence to increase her importance in his life, the authenticity of this letter is rather doubtful. To attribute his psychosis to extreme solitude and spiritual sensitivity is hardly convincing. Even Nietzsche's sister, who made every effort to minimize the importance of his mental illness, admitted that his addiction to chloral might be a possible cause for his breakdown. The loss of his faculties occurred in January, 1889, only a few years after some of his most important works were written, including *Beyond Good and Evil, The Genealogy of Morals,* and *Ecce Homo.* The nature of the philosopher's mental derangement is particularly significant because his ideas were expressed in aphorisms and flashing insights that sprang from the depths of his mind with a dramatic swiftness. His ecstatic, almost hypnotic, manner of speaking has affinities with the startling insight occasionally displayed by certain psychotic patients who are able to interpret intuitively the products of the unconscious mind.

Ten days before his collapse, Nietzsche addressed a letter to the playwright Strindberg who had sent him a copy of his *Strings of Conscience:*

My dear Sir! You will soon hear an answer to your short story—it sounds like a rifle-shot. I have summoned a Council of Princes to Rome, I shall have the young Kaiser shot—*au revoir!* for we shall see one another. *Une seule condition.* Divorçons.

Nietzsche-Caesar

Nietzsche suffered a complete breakdown when he saw a tired old horse being brutally beaten by a cabman in Turin. Sobbing, the philosopher flung his arms about the animal's neck. Speechless and momentarily paralyzed, he had to be carried to his lodgings. Shortly thereafter, he dispatched a series of letters to the ruling princes of Europe, as well as to the Pope, notifying them that as the Crucified One he was going to unite and govern Europe. He admonished the German princes in a fatherly tone:

My children, it is a great mistake to have anything to do with the mad Hohenzollerns, even for those who are of my race through Stephanie. . . . Withdraw modestly into private life. I give Bavaria the same advice.

The Crucified One

After his collapse, Nietzsche was confined to a mental asylum in Jena for more than a year. Although he was finally released in the care of his mother, he never regained his sanity.

Kierkegaard has observed that many philosophers build imposing, spacious palaces of pure thought, while they continue to live in some hastily erected hovel nearby. A philosopher's circumscribed life often furnishes an illuminating contrast to his bold, far-reaching ideas. Thus Nietzsche's psychosis sheds an eerie light on the productions of his later years; just as Schopenhauer's final decades, when he was an irritable and unproductive recluse, offer a thoughtful commentary on his ascetic philosophy. By dismissing the psychosis that overwhelmed Nietzsche in the midst of his creative activity, the *Britannica* ignores the unconscious elements that molded his thought, or as Nietzsche himself might have said, the imperative demands of the Dionysian spirit are hidden behind a false portrait of an Apollonian thinker who calmly constructs a philosophical system according to the dictates of logic and reason.

One of the simplest reasons why biographical articles become inadequate is the discovery of new documents that throw light on previously unknown matters. This is illustrated by the recent recovery and publication of a mass of personal papers belonging to James Boswell that provide an intimate description of his private life. These papers are particularly valuable because his personality has puzzled biographers who have tried to explain how such a "foolish" person could have written so great a book as the *Life of Johnson*. Macaulay put the matter rather bluntly when, as a young man in 1831, he wrote:

> Many of the greatest men that have ever lived have written biography. Boswell was one of the smallest men that have ever lived and he has beaten them all. He was a man of the feeblest intellect. Servile and impertinent, . . . a bigot and a sot, an eavesdropper and a common butt in the taverns of London.

Twenty years later, when Macaulay prepared his celebrated essay on Johnson for the *Britannica*, he found no reason to soften this opinion. He reported that Boswell "could not reason, that he had no wit, no humour, no eloquence is apparent from his writings. . . . Nature had made him a slave and an idolator. His mind resembled these creepers . . . which can subsist only by clinging round the stems and imbibing the juices of stronger plants." The article on Boswell rejects this biased opinion in favor of a more judicious view, but is unable to penetrate the recesses of his personal life because it neglects the private papers unearthed during the last generation. An astonishing cache has been recovered from Fettercairn House and Malahide Castle; it includes more than four thousand separate items, many of which are several hundred pages long. The publication of these papers during the last decade has attracted wide interest because they offer a remarkably frank account of his personal life.

Boswell's *London Journal* describes his arrival in the city from the provinces, an impetuous young man of twenty-one, who spent his time hunting for pretty women and literary celebrities. The *Journal* opens with the penetrating observation that "the ancient precept to 'Know thyself' . . . cannot be so perfectly obeyed without the assistance of a register of one's life." It then records Boswell's intellectual experiences, and his sexual adventures when he went whoring "in a rich flow of animal spirits and burning with fierce desire." Once, after a particularly prolonged debauch, he wrote: "This is an exact state of my mind at the time. It shocks me to review it"; and he added, "In whatever way it is to be explained, I have mentioned the fact." This relentless frankness is one of the great virtues of his personal papers and makes them a unique source of information about his strange, complex character.

The *London Journal* clarifies in many ways Boswell's role as the biographer of Dr. Johnson. It furnishes a contemporary account of their first meeting which is far more restrained than the colorful description given in the *Life of Johnson* many years later. By comparing parallel passages in the private papers and the biography, it is possible to demonstrate that Boswell did not transcribe verbatim his conversations with Dr. Johnson and transfer them to his biography; rather he took copious notes, which he later reworked to increase their effectiveness. The journals and private papers rescue Boswell from his shadowy existence as the biographer of Johnson; they depict his personal foibles and reveal his role as a conscious literary artist. They relate that he met and argued the existence of God with Voltaire, interviewed Hume on his deathbed, and asked Rousseau if he could keep a seraglio of thirty women for his pleasure. Since this rich and varied treasure of private papers is ignored, it is hardly surprising that the article on Boswell in the 1958 edition should be a thin, superficial review of his literary activity and personal traits.

The great drama of some men's lives is expressed by their deeds. In others, the words uttered during hours of distress preserve their memory. The eleventh edition faithfully portrayed the eloquent resistance of the martyr John Huss. At his first arraignment when Huss attempted to defend himself, the outcry of his opponents was so loud and insistent that he could not be heard. He was forced to bring his speech to an abrupt close with a few words, saying, "In such a council as this I expected to find more propriety, piety and order." Later in a letter to his friends in Prague he expressed his thoughts: "I write this in prison and in chains, expecting tomorrow to receive the sentence of death, full of hope in God that I shall not swerve from truth, nor abjure error imputed to me by false witnesses." After his condemnation, when he had been tied to the stake and the fagots were about to be lit, he was urged for the last time to recant. His only reply was:

> God is my witness that I have never taught or preached that which false witnesses have testified against me. He knows that the great object of all my preaching and writing was to convert men from sin. In the truth of that gospel which hitherto I have written, taught and preached, I now joyfully die.

Chanting the prayer *Kyrie eleison—Lord, have mercy on us—* he perished in the flames. His brave words, which once appeared in the *Encyclopaedia,* were deleted when Huss' biography was condensed to its present length.

The Sacco-Vanzetti case is another instance in which the words of the accused have assumed a special significance. Without reference to the character of the defendants and the spirit of the times, it would be difficult to explain why a murder trial in Massachusetts should have aroused international agitation and protest. The *Britannica* presents a dry factual summary that neglects the wider issues raised by the case. But if the fate of the defendants has continued to exercise a hold on the American imagination long after their execution, it is largely because of their passionate plea of innocence. Vanzetti's words became a rallying cry for an entire generation of liberals: "What we have suffered during these seven years no human tongue can say, and yet you see me before you, not trembling, not changing color, you see me looking in your eyes straight; not blushing or in fear." His bold speech helped to elevate the "good shoemaker" and the "poor fish-peddler" into symbols of radical protest:

> If it had not been for this thing, I might have lived out my life talking at street corners to scorning men. I might have

died, unmarked, unknown, a failure. Now we are not a failure. . . . This is our career, and our triumph. Never in our full life could we hope to do such work for tolerance, for justice, for man's understanding of men as we do now by accident.

These words have become part of the American tradition; they go beyond the immediate question of the guilt or innocence of the defendants to the larger issue of justice and the legal process. They raise the deeper question of whether men who hold unpopular or subversive opinions can secure a fair trial in times of emotional or political tension.

Although Vanzetti's words are not quoted by the *Britannica*, the utility of quotations is clearly recognized in other articles. The biography of Napoleon is a stirring account of his meteoric rise from the obscurity of Corsica to the domination of Europe. It describes his invasion of Italy by repeating his famous declaration made at the beginning of the campaign:

You are badly fed and all but naked. . . . I am about to lead you into the most fertile plains in the world. Before you are great cities and rich provinces; there we shall find honour, glory, and riches.

Quotations are also featured in the essay on Ikhnaton, the heretical Pharaoh, to explain the convictions and revolutionary ideals that make him one of the remarkable figures of the ancient world. During his brief reign, he sought to overthrow the religion of his ancestors and establish a new religion dedicated to Aton, the Sun God. The essay quotes from the "Hymn to Aton" to illuminate the creed of this Pharaoh who believed in "living in truth"; and it concludes by observing that we must look back on him today as the earliest monotheist and the first prophet of internationalism.

Such excellent articles indicate that biographies need not be dreary factual accounts; they can be stimulating portraits of historical figures that may be read with interest and excitement. Their diversity and individuality must be emphasized to dispel the idea that there is a simple way of insuring superior biographical coverage. Each life presents its own problems and must be treated accordingly. The essay on Alexander Hamilton contains a comprehensive survey of his philosophical ideas and traces the impact of these ideas on the course of American constitutional law and government. The splendid article on Gandhi goes beyond a chronology of his life to present a lucid discussion of his philosophy of non-violence which animated the struggle for Indian independence. Such treatments recognize that a man's ideas may be as significant as his deeds and achievements, and it demonstrates how an encyclopedia can supply a vivid portrait of a man's life that can satisfy the needs of a wide class of readers.

[9]

Lives of the Famous
and the Infamous

In presenting a picture of earlier ages, it is necessary to consider the lives of those who have passed through the world and left their mark upon it. An encyclopedia singles out a few of the army of the deceased—good or bad, famous or infamous— and assigns them individual articles because their deeds have endowed them with an interest and importance that transcends their own generation. The emotion that attracts us to the celebrated personalities of the past was eloquently expressed by D'Alembert when he wrote in the preface of the *Encyclopédie*:

> Man is not contented to live and reign among his contemporaries alone, but drawn by curiosity and self-love, eagerly and naturally endeavors to embrace the past, the present and future times. We desire at once to live with both our successors and predecessors. This shows us the origin and design of history, which unites us with Ages past by representing their Vices, Virtues, Knowledge and Errors, and transmitting our own to posterity. It is by history we learn to esteem men

only for the good they do and not for the seducing pomp that surrounds them.

Inevitably, many entries are devoted to men who are discussed because of their worldly power, rather than their moral or spiritual qualities. The leaders of any institution with a long history are a varied lot whose lives contain bright and dark chapters, and it is sometimes difficult to separate their virtues from their vices. This is particularly true in dealing with the darkness of the medieval papacy for which existing documents are limited, and their reliability uncertain. An example is John XII, who ruled from 955 to 964. He was elevated to the papal throne when he was only seventeen years old, and he proved unfit for this high office. The article on Rome reported in the eleventh edition:

> His palace was the scene of the most scandalous licence, while his public acts were those of a baby tyrant. He conferred a bishopric on a child of ten, consecrated a deacon in a stable, invoked Venus and Jupiter in his games, and drank to the devil's health. He desired to be both pope and prince, but utterly failed to be either.

This brief account of John's vices has been condensed in the current edition:

> His palace was the scene of scandalous licence, while his public acts were those of a tyrant. He desired to be both pope and prince, but utterly failed to be either.

Thus the blasphemous deeds of the Pope are now discreetly omitted; and the same policy is followed in treating Alexander VI. The eleventh edition was outspoken in condemning his vice and greed. It narrated his sins with a fervor and concreteness reminiscent of Dante's catalogue of human frailty in the *Inferno*, demonstrating that Alexander's ruling passions were a love of women and a lust for gold. It related that he sired four children by his mistress Vanozza dei Cattanei, including the notorious Cesare Borgia and the beautiful Lucrezia Borgia. Cesare became the ruthless instrument of the Pope's crimes, while Lucrezia was bartered to a succession of husbands for wealth and power. After Alexander grew tired of Vanozza, he brought the dazzling young Giulia Farnese, the wife of an Orsini, into the papal palace as his mistress. The eleventh edition faithfully traced the dark record of Alexander VI by portraying his reign in somber colors:

> But in spite of the splendours of the Court, the condition of Rome became every day more deplorable. The city swarmed with Spanish adventurers, assassins, prostitutes and informers; murder and robbery were committed with impunity, heretics and Jews were admitted to the city on payment of bribes, and the pope himself shamelessly cast aside all show of decorum, living a purely secular and immoral life, and indulging in the chase, dancing, stage plays and indecent orgies.

The 1958 entry sharply tones down the vice and violence of his reign and concludes on an almost apologetic note:

> Alexander VI is one of the most disputed figures in papal history. . . . His private life was, no doubt, indefensible and recent attempts to rehabilitate his character do not carry conviction. Nevertheless, many of the depravities attributed to him must be regarded as legendary.

The practice of retouching history to agree with clerical views may lead to dull, listless entries, but it has one great advantage— it protects the *Britannica* from the troublesome charge that the work is "anti-Catholic."

During the nineteenth century, articles often contained ethical evaluations of leading figures. This approach appealed to prevailing English sentiment which viewed history as a form of moral justice in which the innocent should be praised and the wicked condemned. It led historians to act as judges who passed sentence on the great men of the past, and the practice survived in the twentieth century, long after the restrictions of the Victorian era had passed away. As a result, corruption and sexual license were openly discussed in the eleventh edition, and its consequences were delineated by a scholarship that cast a harsh and sometimes lurid light on historical figures. Such an approach occasionally exaggerated the depravity of a ruler's personal life, but seldom left its character in doubt. A colorful example is Frederick II, Emperor of the Holy Roman Empire, who spent most of his life battling Moslems in the East and the Pope in the West. His biography, prepared fifty years ago, reports: "Licentious and luxurious in his manners, cultured and catholic in his tastes, he united in his person the most diverse qualities." After relating that his varied interests led him to establish a menagerie of strange animals and write an outstanding treatise on falconry, the article candidly explains: "His wives were kept secluded in oriental fashion; a harem was maintained at Lucera, and eunuchs were a prominent feature of his household."

The unconventional tastes and licentious manner of many royal personages create a problem for an encyclopedia, whose readers may be disturbed by the parade of mistresses and illegitimate offspring that are an intimate part of many European dynasties. This difficulty is particularly acute in dealing with British monarchs whose lives contain scandalous episodes. In such cases, there is a conflict between the demand for historical accuracy and the desire to please the public. This conflict may be accentuated because the *Britannica* is dedicated to Queen Elizabeth and sold to Englishmen who might be shocked by the license of some of the Queen's ancestors. Consequently patriotic motives and commercial considerations may be responsible for a wavering, inconsistent standard of honesty. The *Encyclopaedia* itemizes the illegitimate children and "notorious lasciviousness" of Charles II, and describes George IV as a "notorious profligate" and a "worn-out debauchee." But modesty prevails in other instances. The biography of George II concentrates on his official acts, but says nothing about his German mistresses who conducted a brisk, profitable trade in Royal patents. The Victorian entry on William IV, the "Sailor-King," who preceded Queen Victoria on the throne, is extremely cautious. It portrays his romantic attachment with an actress, when he was Duke of Clarence, in the following manner:

> Meanwhile he formed a connection with Mrs. Jordan, the actress, with whom he lived on terms of mutual affection and

fidelity for nearly twenty years. The death of Princess Charlotte in 1817 compelled him to break with Mrs. Jordan, and to marry (1818) Adelaide of Saxe-Meiningen. . . .

The article does not mention that as a result of this "connection," Mrs. Jordan bore the prince ten illegitimate children who were given the name and title of FitzClarence. It neglects these irregular domestic arrangements, and the fact that Mrs. Jordan had four other illegitimate children before she met the prince. Instead it piously concludes that the king died "leaving behind him the memory of a genial, frank, warm-hearted man, but a blundering though well-intentioned prince."

In the past when complete editions were prepared about once every generation, it was often necessary to discuss events that occurred near the date of publication. The pressure to include such "last-minute" developments was very strong because a new edition would not be issued for many years; but the necessity for haste prevented a thoughtful, judicious treatment. In such cases, the demands of scholarship were sacrificed to meet a publication deadline.

When the *Britannica*'s biography of Edward VII was being prepared, he was still alive; and it was impossible to explore his private life without embarrassing the throne. His sudden death in 1910 only magnified the necessity for a respectful account. Therefore an extended eulogy was presented that concentrated on his travels and official life. In deference to the Crown, it dutifully described his participation in royal receptions and court ceremonials, and carefully avoided anything that might detract from this imperial image. This article, which was reprinted for fifty years, cautiously observes, "He was a keen patron of the theatre, and his thoroughly British taste for sport was as pronounced as his inclination for most of the contemporary amusements of society." Due to this reticence, the figure of Edward VII remains shadowy and insubstantial; yet his private life is quite instructive because it supplements the familiar picture of the Victorian age that stresses the moral values and material aspirations of the middle class.

Edward's luxurious habits as Prince of Wales dispel the illusion that the principles of prudery and propriety were universally accepted. While the bourgeoisie was industriously increasing its material possessions and the working class was struggling to survive under the yoke of the factory system, young aristocrats were happily dissipating the wealth accumulated by their forefathers. As gentlemen, they concentrated on the pursuit of pleasure, following in the footsteps of their grandfathers who had enjoyed the sexual laxity of the Regency. Middle-class ideals with their emphasis on thrift, industry and moral rectitude were alien to these "young bloods" who preferred to ignore the factories, mills and railroads that marked the rising tide of the Industrial Revolution. They avoided useful labor, devoting themselves to a sporting life; their principal interests were hunting, horse racing and pretty women—and their greatest enemies were boredom and solitude. At the center of this society of pleasure-seeking artistocrats was a group of rich young men known as "heavy swells," whose social leader was the Prince of Wales. One of their favorite activities was to make alliances with fashionable demi-mondaines—attractive women who were ready to make themselves agreeable to gentlemen who could satisfy their expensive tastes. In the curious language of the period, these popular young women were known as "houris" or "soiled doves." Wealthy noblemen seeking a more exciting round of sexual pleasure than was possible within the confines of a conventional marriage would furnish these "soiled doves" with pleasant love nests where they could enjoy their favors. Although the standards of Victorian society did not permit aristocrats to marry such women, they were able to savor discreetly the pleasure of their company.

This gay and luxurious way of life suited the temperament of the Prince of Wales. He enjoyed his role as an elegant fashion plate, although it forced him to change his clothes six times a day. His allowance on the Civil List was £100,000, yet his personal expenditures were so large he could not make ends meet. This extravagance forced him to spend part of each year visiting the country homes of wealthy aristocrats, bankers and businessmen who could house and entertain the prince and his elaborate entourage.

Edward's adult life was largely devoted to an energetic flight from the rigid, narrow upbringing of his childhood. His social contacts were varied and diverse; only one group was taboo: writers, poets and intellectuals—all those who had anything to do with the mind, for as one of his confidants related, "As a class we do not like brains."

The prince's passion for dissipation led to a series of affairs with some of the famous beauties of the day. Not content with aristocratic society, he often traveled incognito to Paris accompanied only by his equerry. Despite his marriage to the Princess Alexandra, his amorous intrigues continued; the Victorian double standard was faithfully maintained in the royal household. The princess treated her husband's love affairs as his private hobby, while Edward regarded them as a royal prerogative sanctioned by the example of his promiscuous predecessors, George II and George IV.*

The *Encyclopaedia* does not depict this side of his personality. It simply states: "The king won the genuine affection and confidence of the people; and in Queen Alexandra he had an ideal consort to whom all hearts went out." Yet after he ascended the throne, Edward persisted in a compulsive hunt for erotic adventure, although he was no longer an impetuous youth, but a roué in his fifties. Surprisingly enough, British society was not shocked by Edward's extravagant way of life, his mistresses, or his heavy losses at the race track. As Lord Granville remarked, "The Prince of Wales is loved because he has all the faults of which the Englishman is accused." Fifty years ago, his private life could not be examined or discussed, but now that the king and his social circle have disappeared, there is no reason why the true nature of his life should be concealed, particularly when it had important social consequences. His flamboyant manner counteracted the depressing influence of the evangelical puritan movement which had introduced the dreary Sunday Blue Laws into

* In 1818 Leigh Hunt described the Prince Regent (George IV) as an *Adonis in loveliness,* a corpulent gentleman of fifty who was the violator of his word, a libertine in disgrace, a despiser of domestic ties, and the companion of gamblers and demireps.

English life, and his ostentatious elegance coupled with his popularity near the close of his life helped replace the rigid standards of the Victorian era with a more relaxed moral code.

Rudyard Kipling once tartly described the prince as "a corpulent voluptuary"; but his life is a useful reminder of the complexity of the past. It illustrates the danger of representing a period by a simple slogan that imposes a uniformity that may not actually exist. Thus the prudery of the Victorian age should be supplemented by the activity of a small but significant group of aristocrats who managed to escape its rigid standards by secretly indulging in an active round of pleasure and promiscuity. An intimate biography of Edward VII would reveal the gulf separating his exuberant private life from the sober industry of his middle-class subjects, and it could offer an illuminating commentary on the diversity of Victorian life.

Our image of certain historical figures has been influenced by the way in which they have been described by later writers. Some have been elevated, others degraded, to serve partisan interests. A notable case is Richard III. His career was recorded in somber colors by Sir Thomas More in a biography written during the Tudor reign. It portrayed Richard as a brutal, ambitious usurper who seized the throne by guile and violence—and it contrasted his wickedness with the virtue of Henry Tudor, who had reunited the Houses of Lancaster and York by defeating Richard at Bosworth Field. More's hostile account depicted the usurper as "little of stature, ill-featured of limbs, crook backed, his left shoulder higher than his right . . . he was malicious, wrathful, envious . . . lowly of countenance, arrogant of heart . . . dispiteous and cruel." His forceful prose helped to fix the image of Richard as an absolute villain devoid of human sympathy, whose brief reign was stained with crime and intrigue. This lurid picture was repeated in Shakespeare's melodrama which presents Richard as a monster with a hunched back, whose evil spirit is symbolized by his withered arm and twisted countenance. When Richard appears on the stage, he tells us in his opening soliloquy that he is:

Deform'd, unfinish'd, sent before my time
Into this breathing world, scarce half made up,
And that so lamely and unfashionable
That dogs bark as I halt by them;

and then he announces,

I am determined to prove a villain
And hate the idle pleasures of these days.

Shakespeare's play was written in 1593, more than a century after Richard's death. It was based on the grim chronicle created by Tudor historians, yet contemporary documents fail to verify this image of Richard as a misshapen monster. They merely report that he was a frail, thin person of less than average height, but do not mention any physical deformity. The *Britannica*'s treatment of Richard III is torn between the conventional Tudor description and authentic documents when it relates:

Tradition represents Richard as deformed. It seems clear that he had some physical defect, though not so great as has been alleged. Extant portraits show an intellectual face characteristic of the early Renaissance, but do not indicate any deformity.

This description comes at the close of the entry; but such judicious caution is neglected in an earlier passage which repeats the Tudor version of the tumultuous events of 1483:

On June 13 came the famous scene when Richard appeared suddenly in the council baring his withered arm and accusing Jane Shore and the queen of sorcery; Hastings, Morton and Stanley were arrested and the first-named at once beheaded.

Thus Richard suddenly appears in the article as a monster with a withered arm! Shakespeare employs this incident to create an exciting scene in which Richard cries:

Look how I am bewitch'd; behold, mine arm
Is like a blasted sapling, wither'd up.
And this Edward's wife, that monstrous witch,

Consorted with that harlot strumpet Shore,
That by their witchcraft thus have marked me.

This striking scene was invented by More and copied by Shakespeare. Actually, Richard had Hastings seized and beheaded for treason, not witchcraft, yet the story is zealously repeated as though it were unquestionably true. This assurance extends to the greatest mystery of English history—the fate of the "little Princes," the young sons of Edward IV who were the rightful heirs to the throne. According to the *Britannica,* "There seems no reasonable doubt that early in August Edward V and his brother Richard . . . were murdered by their uncle's orders"; but this statement is contradicted by the entry on Edward V which states that "there is no actual evidence of Richard's guilt."

The only support for this charge is contained in two fragmentary reports, neither of which says anything about the manner in which the princes died. Once again, More's biography fills the breach—it claims that James Tyrell was engaged to commit the deed, and that he smothered them with the aid of an accomplice, "by means of featherbed pillows stuffed hard in their mouths." More asserted that his account was based on Tyrell's confession, secured nineteen years after the act was supposedly committed and which was only announced after Tyrell had been executed for another crime. No effort was made to exhibit the assassin before his death. Indeed, it is significant that when Henry Tudor ascended the throne, he did not charge Richard with the murder of the little princes, although he had every reason to do so if the charge were true. All that can be said now with certainty is that the princes disappeared from sight while they were in Richard's custody.

The article on Richard III is defective because it confuses a popular tradition with the results of modern scholarship. When it was written fifty years ago, the Tudor portrait was still accepted, but this is no longer true. A sound treatment should explore the familiar story supplied by More and Shakespeare, as well as the modern view, so both accounts can be clearly distinguished. Similarly, a biography of Henry V should compare the idealized figure created by Shakespeare with the portrait that emerges from existing documentary records, because in such instances a king has two faces perpetuating his memory—one offered by literature and the other by history. They may be compared with his public and his private life—one is familiar to laymen, while the other is known to scholars. Both views should be presented whenever historical fact and literary fiction have become intimately associated with a monarch's name, since each is necessary to explain his subsequent influence and reputation.

The place occupied by particular historical figures is governed by a number of factors. One pervasive influence has been the patriotic spirit which seeks to elevate individuals who symbolize a nation's ideals and aspirations. The search for heroes has been particularly strong in America where citizens, lacking a hereditary monarchy or an entrenched aristocracy, have elevated the Founding Fathers to a heroic pantheon. A mood of reverence surrounds the saga of the American Revolution with its stirring tales of Lexington, Concord and Valley Forge. This emotional fervor was echoed by Edward Everett, the most famous orator of his day, when he contributed a 40,000-word eulogy on George Washington for the eighth edition in 1860. Everett, who is now remembered because he spoke with Lincoln at Gettysburg, concluded his essay on a lofty note:

> In the final contemplation of his character, we shall not hesitate to pronounce Washington, of all men that have ever lived, the greatest of good men, and the best of great men. . . .
> In the possession of that mysterious quality of character manifested in a long life of unambitious service, which . . . inspires confidence, commands the respect and wins the affection of contemporaries . . . and a living proof that pure patriotism is not a delusion; nor virtue an empty name, no one of the sons of men has equaled George Washington.

Such exuberant exhibitions were common in the past—and one can discover the bombast of an earlier era in the modern *Encyclopaedia* which prides itself on objectivity and sober restraint. The article on Ulysses Grant in the 1958 edition was written by John Fiske, who died in 1901. He presents an enthusiastic eulogy that minimizes Grant's failure as President and passes over the widespread corruption that flourished during his administration. His archaic essay describes in quaint language how Grant was victimized by his associates:

> The scandals, indeed, were rife in Washington, and affected persons in close relations with the President. Grant was ill-fitted for coping with the difficulties of such a situation. Along with certain high intellectual powers he had a simplicity of nature charming in itself but often calculated to render him the easy prey of sharpers.

Despite the Civil Service Act, Grant continued to appoint old cronies to public office. One of his most disastrous choices was an illiterate acquaintance, General John McDonald, as Collector of Internal Revenue for the Federal District of St. Louis. After his appointment, General McDonald organized a giant conspiracy among whiskey distillers to circumvent Federal excise taxes. False receipts were issued and counterfeit revenue stamps were employed to defraud the government. Distillers who refused to join the conspiracy were threatened with prosecution for minor infractions of the revenue statutes. Soon hundreds of thousands of dollars were flowing into the coffers of the Whiskey Ring. The Ring was finally uncovered through the efforts of the Secretary of the Treasury, who discovered that railroad freight receipts showed that more whiskey was being shipped out of St. Louis than distillers had reported was manufactured in the city.

Among those implicated in the conspiracy was Orville Babcock, Grant's personal secretary, who had been lavishly entertained by members of the Whiskey Ring. Babcock received a check for $25,000 from General McDonald when the collector visited Washington, and in return he tried to warn his accomplices that the Secretary of the Treasury was investigating their activities. Despite overwhelming evidence, Grant refused to believe his secretary was involved in the scandals. He eagerly accepted Babcock's flimsy explanations for his conduct, and his faith remained unshaken throughout his term of office, despite his secretary's intimate and continued contact with many of the most corrupt men of a corrupt decade.

When Grant became President, the nation hoped he would

press forward with the vital work of Reconstruction, but by the time he left the White House eight years later, hope had vanished. The Gilded Age had come to American politics and with it the reign of the robber barons and the influence peddlers. Corruption was rife in Washington and the Presidency had sunk to a new low. Yet Fiske concludes his article with a glowing tribute:

> Grant showed many admirable and lovable traits. There was a charming side to his trustful simplicity. . . . His good sense was strong, as well as his sense of justice and these qualities stood him in good service as president, especially in his triumphant fight againt the greenback monster. Altogether, in spite of some shortcomings, Grant was a massive, noble and lovable personality, well fit to be remembered as one of the heroes of a great nation.

It may be natural that Grant's successes during the Civil War should obscure his subsequent failure as President, but sometimes the propensity to elevate military leaders is carried to extreme lengths. The *Encyclopaedia* presents a very flattering portrait of the German general, Erich Ludendorff, who served under Hindenburg during World War I. Readers are told how he took the offensive in 1918 so armies under his command could exchange the role of an anvil for that of a hammer, and they are informed:

> General Ludendorff was above all a man of action. . . . His resolution, his almost superhuman and invincible powers of work and action, his understanding of the moral factors in warfare, inspired the German army with boundless confidence in his leadership and qualified it for mighty exploits.

This reverential report was prepared by a lieutenant colonel in the German army. But a later section notes that Ludendorff abandoned his country when the armistice was concluded, and fled to Sweden. After returning to Germany in 1919, he became a "focus of all extreme reactionary conspiracies." He helped organize and instigate the "Kapp Putsch" of 1920, and then openly joined Adolf Hitler in his attempted coup of 1923. Later he ran for president of the Reich on the National Socialist ticket—yet he is described by the *Britannica* as a man whose "brain, heart and will were all unsparingly enlisted in the service of one aim, the honour of his country."

This naïve defense of Prussian militarism is surprising in an American reference work. It is contradicted by the article on Hindenburg which critically discusses the myths and legends surrounding his career. Unlike the glowing entry on Ludendorff, it relates that Hindenburg and Ludendorff frustrated the effort of the Reichstag to sue for peace in July, 1917, and notes that "the supreme command exercised dictatorial power." It records how the generals guided the war—and observes that after the armistice Hindenburg "prepared his memoirs, *Out of My Life* (1920), in which he declared that the German army had not been truly beaten but had been betrayed by the revolution, thus creating the legend of the 'stab in the back.'" Finally it concludes, "Perhaps the best description of this massive personality is the title of an English biography, 'Wooden Titan.'"

The *Britannica* is often more patriotic than scholarly in its treatment of American Presidents. The 1958 article on Grover Cleveland omits the details of the heated campaign of 1884 which is now remembered because of the charge that the Democrats' antecedents were "rum, Romanism and rebellion." The article simply notes:

> The campaign that followed was one of the bitterest political campaigns in American history. Cleveland was accused of favoring the South because he avoided war service and his private life was attacked. . . .

No reasons are given for the attack on Cleveland's private life, yet his response sheds considerable light on his personal character.

On July 21, 1884, the *Buffalo Evening Telegraph* published a sensational story under the headline, "A Terrible Tale." The newspaper reported that ten years earlier Cleveland had had an affair with a widow, Maria Halprin, which resulted in an illegitimate child. Cleveland agreed to support the child, who was later separated from his mother and sent to an orphanage. When he was asked about the matter, Cleveland made no effort to deny the story; instead he told his friend Goodyear, "Tell the truth," and the truth was told. Since the story was made public ten days after he was nominated, its effects were overcome because voters decided they preferred Cleveland, who was blameless in public office though delinquent in private life, to James G. Blaine, who was guilty in public office although possibly blameless in private life.

Had the scandal been revealed during the Democratic convention, Cleveland probably would not have been nominated— and had it been disclosed during the close of the campaign, he might not have been elected. The Maria Halprin affair is thus of considerable interest because it illustrates Cleveland's courage under fire; and neglecting this episode only succeeds in diminishing his stature as a man and as a political leader.

It is perhaps fitting that Theodore Roosevelt, one of the most colorful personalities in American history, should receive a long and enthusiastic article whose purple prose matches the purple sage of his beloved West:

> It can be said of Washington that he founded the American nation, and of Lincoln that he preserved it; it can be said of Roosevelt that he revitalized it. Twice, at critical times, through his vision, his ardour, his effective anger, his faith in American institutions and his peculiar understanding of all sections of the American people, he cleansed the body of the nation of treacherous poisons, and set its soul to work on labours higher than the acquisition of physical comforts. He dreamed nobly for his country and impelled millions of his countrymen to dream nobly.

This strain of hero worship obscures the true nature of the first Roosevelt's administration. One reason for this fervent enthusiasm is that Roosevelt's varied life offered a glorious wish fulfillment to sedentary Americans of an earlier age. He was a leader of the Rough Riders, a naturalist, a big game hunter, a New York Police Commissioner, and President of the United States—so he held, at one time or another, many positions youngsters like to dream about. The *Britannica* documents in great detail his adventurous life and public career, but fails to evaluate his actual achievements as President, or record his famous advice, "Speak softly and carry a big stick. . . ."

One would hardly guess from the heroic tone employed that Roosevelt had close ties with the business community, which contributed large sums to his political war chest. One would never suspect that his attack on the trusts had only a limited effect and that more anti-trust suits were successfully initiated and completed during the four years of Taft's administration than during Roosevelt's seven years in office. Yet because of TR's bellicose speech and aggressive personality, he has been identified in the popular mind as the great "trust-buster." Such misconceptions arise whenever a flamboyant figure captures the imagination of the public; and it is only years later that scholars succeed in dispelling the fiction surrounding his career.

The eulogies and hero worship favored by nineteenth-century American historians are no longer fashionable. Scholars now recognize that such emotional displays merely obscure their subjects by making them objects of national reverence rather than topics for serious study. The articles on Grant, Cleveland and Theodore Roosevelt are instructive examples of how inflated rhetoric and patriotic sentiments can produce a misleading or distorted picture of the past. Such inadequate entries can be found in the *Encyclopaedia* because its editors have relied on existing articles instead of securing fresh contributions.

The effect of retaining old material can be easily traced in the respectful treatment of certain American presidents. The portraits of Warren Harding and Calvin Coolidge were prepared some thirty years ago and attempt to gild their rather tarnished images. Although the article on Harding is one and a half pages long, only two sentences are devoted to the corruption and scandals that disfigured his administration. It notes that "government investigations later . . . revealed an extent of political immorality in Washington such as had no parallel in recent times." But it fails to provide any details about these scandals, even though they involved the Secretary of the Interior who received $400,000 for leasing federal oil lands to private operators.* Instead the biography of the President observes:

> Harding himself enjoyed personal popularity; his nature was kindly and genial, and there was general confidence in his honesty and devotion to his duties; but he was regarded as easy-going in his relations with friends and disinclined to scrutinize their activities critically.

The *EB*'s indulgent attitude reaches its acme in the treatment of Calvin Coolidge who left the White House only a few months before the fourteenth edition appeared. His biographical entry strives to magnify the importance of his colorless administration:

> Although his name is not connected with any positive policy, except perhaps that of thrift, Coolidge's prestige among the American people increased each year. . . . Lacking many of the conventional traits of an orator, President Coolidge proved himself a political preacher second only to Roosevelt, and the public addresses in which he set forth his views systematically, made a strong personal appeal.

When these words were published in 1929, they were merely a bit of conventional political flattery in deference to a recent Chief Executive; but it is rather surprising to come across this judgment thirty years later. Indeed, the average reader may be astonished to discover that more space is devoted in the 1958 edition to Coolidge's uneventful career than to Franklin Delano Roosevelt's dramatic life—a balance that reflects the *EB*'s haphazard editorial standards.

It would be a mistake to leave the impression that historical

* There is some information about these scandals in the *Britannica,* although it is not indexed under Harding's name. The article on the Secret Service states: "The intensive efforts of the government resulted in the conviction in 1929 of Albert B. Fall, former Secretary of the Interior, and Harry F. Sinclair of the Sinclair Oil Company. . . ." But the entry on the Oil Reserve Scandals reports: "In criminal actions Doheny and Sinclair were acquitted of charges of bribery and conspiracy, but Fall was convicted and served a prison term."

investigation inevitably impairs personal reputations and destroys popular idols. This is not always the case. A notable example is Abraham Lincoln, who has come to occupy a major position in the American tradition. His figure as a wartime President has been etched by the eloquence, vision and scholarship of modern historians, led by Carl Sandburg, J. G. Randall and Allan Nevins, who have traced his role in the bloody conflict to preserve the Union. They have created a moving portrait replacing the older image of the frontier lawyer, the rural scholar and melancholy lover of Ann Rutledge. This change occurred during the last generation and was largely inspired by the publication in 1939 of Carl Sandburg's monumental four-volume study, *Lincoln: The War Years*. The wartime leader that emerges from his work is not recognized by the 1958 *Britannica* because its article on Lincoln was written in 1929. It concentrates on his early years and brusquely passes over his occupancy of the White House by stating, "His story thenceforward is the story of his country." For further information, readers are directed to the entry on the United States. This failure to discuss Lincoln's Presidential career was understandable a generation ago, but it can hardly be justified three decades later.

In dealing with historical figures, an encyclopedia should endeavor to assess their lives in the light of contemporary scholarship. There is no need for empty eulogies or fretful silence. Evil need not be condoned nor virtue magnified to serve the interests of a narrow nationalism or a partisan spirit. What may be fitting and proper, of course, is a matter of personal judgment—and each entry must be considered on its individual merits. Inevitably, authors and editors are influenced by existing biographical evidence and prevailing standards of society. Nevertheless, the fundamental principle should be a fidelity to historical truth, rather than a desire to flatter popular preconceptions, for the checkered lives of the great are memorable in so far as they offer a view of the diversity of human experience and insight into the shifting tides of fame and fortune. Such knowledge can only be supplied when an encyclopedia fearlessly presents the facts as they are seen by competent scholars, because as Pericles reminded the Athenians, "The whole world is a sepulcher of famous men." And a reference work can provide a worthy memorial by furnishing an accurate account of their lives so that later generations may pause and reflect on their deeds.

[10]

Style—
The Magic Ingredient

S TYLE is more than a collection of bright sayings or lively ornaments embellishing a subject. In an encyclopedia, it is a means of organizing a theme so all its significant facets are exhibited and illuminated. This can only be done when a subject is thoroughly understood—for without understanding, a glittering prose style is merely an empty affectation concealing an author's ignorance. Buffon has forcefully emphasized the intellectual and intuitive qualities that are the foundation of a successful style:

> To write well is to think deeply, feel vividly, and express clearly—to have intelligence and taste. Style supposes the united exercise of all intellectual faculties. Ideas and ideas alone are its foundation.

It is natural that encyclopedias should employ experts whose background enables them to provide an authoritative account of particular subjects. However, men who have spent a lifetime investigating a specialized area often seek to impart their knowledge in a concentrated form that stresses facts rather than ideas. They tend to take the fundamental principles underlying their studies for granted, and instead of communicating its general aspects, they supply esoteric details in an academic jargon. Articles on religion frequently suffer from this fault. The entry on Jehovah presents a linguistic analysis of various pronunciations of the word, but does not discuss the Hebrew idea of monotheism. The account of Isaiah examines the dates and origins of successive passages, but does not explore the spiritual meaning or poetic grandeur of the prophet's message. Finally, the article on the Book of Exodus neglects the religious significance of the Ten Commandments and the Exodus from Egypt. Instead, it concentrates on scholarly attempts to identify the original sources of the work—and offers such material as:

> It is a plausible conjecture that the original narrative of J and E also contained directions for the construction of an ark . . . and that these commands were omitted by R^P in favour of the more elaborate instructions given in ch. xxv.–xxix. (P).

This heavy-handed treatment is not an isolated case, since it occurs in major entries. An example is Gilbert Murray's essay on Homer:

> Liberties are taken both with accidence and with syntax in order to obtain forms that are metrically convenient; especially conspicuous is the effort to obtain words or phrases which fill the final dactyl-spondee after the Bucolic diaeresis: ἡνιοχῆα acc. of ἡνίοχος, Αἰθιοπῆας of Αἰθίοπες, Σαρπήδοντος for Σαρπήδονος, εὐρέα πόντον (from εὐρέι πόντῳ); the alternation of singular and plural in such words as ἱπποσίνης ἱπποσυνάων, νηπιέη νηπίῃσι, κονίη κονίῃσι, that of active and middle in εἰσορόωντες εἰσορόωνται, μητιόωντες μητιάασθαι are to be explained thus.

Despite the outstanding qualities of the eleventh edition, it was hampered by a pedantic approach. Many contributors sought to create a monument of learning that could be used by specialists—and they ignored the needs of laymen, preparing weighty treatises containing elaborate footnotes and lengthy appendices.

Information was couched in a forbidding language, and articles were cast in a ponderous "Teutonic" style associated with the thick volumes of German scholarship. This heavy manner still survives. The essay on Mystery examines the cults of ancient Greece and supplies a series of footnotes with additional references. It suggests in discussing a pair of divinities "supposed to descend from an aboriginal period of Eleusinian religion":

> [2] See Dittenberger, *Syll.* 83, 39; 200, 21; C.I.G. ii. Add. 1620c; *Ephem. archaiol.* (1886), πιν. 3; Heberdey in *Festschrift für Benndorf*, p. 3, Taf. 4; Von Prott in *Athen. Mittheil.* (1899), p. 262.

How many people can decipher such a footnote, let alone find it useful? Yet such abstruse material is not unusual. The article on the Church Father Origen reports:

> [2] Porphyry says of Origen, κατὰ τὰς περὶ πραγμάτων καὶ τοῦ θείου δόξας Ἑλληνίζων (Euseb: *H. E.* vi. 19).

The biography of the Greek orator Isaeus, in accounting for his extant speeches, provides the following note:

> [1] For the words of Photius (cod. 263), τούτων δὲ ὅι τὸ γνήσιον μαρτυρηθέντες ν' καταλείπονται μόνον, might be so rendered as to imply that, besides these 50, others also were extant. See *Att. Orat.* ii. 311, note 2.

Greek and Latin quotations often appeared in older editions and many of these quotations still remain. The article on Epicurus discusses his atomic theory in the following way:

> Owing to an inherent "swerve" (παρέγκλισις, *clinamen,* Lucret., ii. 292—this, of course, is a necessary postulate, Lucret., ii. 243 Quare etiam atque etiam paulum inclinare necesse est Corpora. Plut. *Mor.* 964 C οὐδὲ γὰρ αὐτοὶ τῷ Ἐπικούρῳ διδόασιν . . . ἄτομον παρεγκλῖναι μίαν ἐπὶ τοὐλάχιστον) the atoms collide and rebound to a lesser or greater distance, thus forming compound bodies of greater or lesser density.

This approach was fashionable in the eleventh edition because it was addressed to an educated elite who had been exposed to the elements of Greek and Latin in British public schools. But it is difficult to justify in recent decades when knowledge of Greek and Latin is no longer common.

Because of such relics from the past, the *Britannica* often resembles a repository of arcane learning rather than a source of vital ideas and concepts. If editors had wisely abridged old articles, they could have eliminated obscure and archaic passages, as well as the pedantry accumulated from earlier editions. Instead they sometimes limit themselves to making typographical changes in material that should be thoroughly revamped. A long treatise on the Crusades in the 1958 edition is studded with scholarly footnotes. This essay was "revised" a few years earlier; but no effort was made to eliminate superfluous footnotes, or incorporate them into the text. Instead, they were merely numbered consecutively. One note, discussing a saga by Albert of Aix, is a full-blown example of the antiquarian approach:

> [39]Von Sybel's view must be modified by that of Kugler, to which a scholar like Hagenmeyer has to some extent given his adhesion (*cf.* his edition of the *Gesta,* pp. 62–68). Hagenmeyer inclines to believe in an original author, distinct from Albert the copyist; and he thinks that this original author (whether or no he was present during the crusade) used the *Gesta* and also Fulcher, though he had probably also *"eigene Notizen und Aufzeichnungen."*

Of course, the same treatment is not suitable for all subjects— an article on Cotton Manufacture or Coal Mining must satisfy different requirements from a survey of the Crusades or an account of the French Revolution. The great variety of topics in an encyclopedia implies a corresponding diversity in the mode of presentation. Consequently an intelligent discussion of style must be limited to a specific class of entries for which uniform criteria can be applied. A general indictment of the *Britannica*'s style is too vague, while citing particular articles has only a limited value in characterizing the defects of thousands of entries. However, the decline in its literary quality can be documented by examining articles reprinted in successive editions.*

* See Note II, p. 356, for an example from the article on Jonathan Swift.

A primary reason for abridging old entries has been to make more room available for science and technology. This has forced editors to condense or drop old material, and often they have done more than create additional space by judicious cutting—they have changed the character of many articles by wholesale deletions. Critical opinions, philosophical asides, and personal reflections have all been sacrificed to preserve factual information. The current notice on Vincenzo Bellini demonstrates the results of this shortsighted policy. Originally, the eleventh edition quoted one of Wagner's letters describing the effect of Bellini's music:

> I shall never forget the impression made upon me by an opera of Bellini at a period when I was completely exhausted with the everlastingly abstract complication used in our orchestras, when a simple and noble melody was revealed to me.

These grateful words have been removed, although they illuminate the bond uniting creative artists and provide a touch of vividness to an otherwise undistinguished entry. Such quotations imparted a special value to old articles because—although their facts might be corrected by later research—their insights often possessed a lasting interest.

In earlier editions, entries were modeled on the English essay. Authors could employ subjective impressions, esthetic insights and philosophical ideas as a means of enhancing their subject. Since extreme brevity was not required, they could stop and relate a bit of history, paint a lively scene or repeat an amusing story. In the ninth edition, the treatise on Virgil began by tracing the development of Latin literature, and the essay on Rembrandt opened with a sketch of seventeenth-century Dutch life.

Although a number of these "classic" essays are still reprinted, many of their lively passages have been eliminated. An instructive case is the splendid essay on Petrarch by J. Addington Symonds. The original in the ninth edition was a stimulating account that portrayed the Italian poet as an individual, and as a representative of the elevated spirit of Humanism. Its literary distinction is hardly evident in the 1958 edition because almost half of Symonds' prose has disappeared. One deleted paragraph described the poet's humanistic ideals:

> Petrarch's ideal of humanism was essentially a noble one. He regarded the orator and the poet as teachers, bound to complete themselves by education, and to exhibit to the world an image of perfected personality in prose and verse of studied beauty. Self-culture and self-effectuation seemed to him the highest aims of man. Everything which contributed to the formation of a free, impassioned, liberal individuality he regarded as praiseworthy.

After portraying Petrarch's lofty ideals, Symonds explored the diverse facets of the poet's personality and dramatically exhibited the conflict between his ideals and his private life:

> Petrarch was made up of contradictions. Praising solitude, playing the hermit at Vaucluse, he only loved seclusion as a contrast to the society of courts; while he penned dissertations on the burden of celebrity, he was trimming his sails to catch the breeze of popular applause. No one professed a more austere morality, and few medieval writers indulged in cruder satires on the female sex; yet he passed some years in the society of a concubine, and his living masterpiece of art is an apotheosis of chivalrous passion for a woman.

Such leisurely analysis, which has been jettisoned, enhanced the value of old essays by allowing them to express the personality and ideas of their contributors.

During the nineteenth century, each volume of the set was sold individually, beginning with the letter A and proceeding through the rest of the alphabet. This encouraged editors to secure outstanding contributions, because income received from earlier volumes financed the publication of later ones. Since it took a number of years to complete an edition in this way, authors were able to prepare a series of articles for successive volumes which furnished a unity and continuity to the set.

As each volume appeared, its contents would be reviewed in leading periodicals, and owners would examine individual entries in much the same way that a collection of essays might be read today. Literary values were stressed, and piecemeal publication encouraged a search for lucid, authoritative articles that would satisfy critics and enlighten the public. This led to a standard of excellence that made the ninth edition an indispensable addition to serious libraries; and its emphasis on literary quality made the work popular in America, where it helped to slake the thirst for worth-while reading matter at a time when books were a major means of filling leisure hours.

Although many of these old essays still appear, editors have often sacrificed their personal verve and individual style by keeping dreary sections and dropping illuminating passages. The article on Rembrandt, taken from the ninth edition, has been cut to its present length by deleting a lucid account of Dutch life as well as an eloquent tribute to the man and his art.

Such deletions might be justified by the necessity for providing up-to-date information, but the article on Rembrandt was not disturbed for thirty years. The effect of this neglect on a simple factual level is illustrated by the description of his most famous painting, "The Night Watch." This work was cleaned after the last war with striking results. It revealed the bright sunny colors hidden for generations beneath layers of discolored varnish, and disclosed fresh details in the painting, such as the names on the scutcheon. Despite the excitement generated by this discovery, the 1958 edition reported: "The background is dark and heavy and the scutcheon on which the names are painted can hardly be seen."

During the nineteenth century, the *Britannica* influenced educated opinion by means of authoritative essay-articles prepared by leading intellectual figures. These contributions occasionally lacked the balance and impartiality of modern articles. Sometimes they were diffuse and neglected important aspects of their theme; but they seldom degenerated into catalogues of undigested factual material because they sought to convey the emotional as well as the intellectual aspects of their subject. The emotional resources of the essay-article may be suggested by Jebb's tribute to Sophocles in the ninth edition. Having translated his work into English, Jebb was deeply moved by the majestic spectacle of

Greek drama. To convey an impression of the rapid march of Sophoclean tragedy, he evoked the swift, momentous opening of *Oedipus Rex*:

> First there is the silent spectacle of the eager throng of suppliants at the palace gate,—young children, youths and aged priests. To them the king appears, with royal condescension and true public zeal. The priest expresses their heartfelt loyalty, describes the distress of Thebes, and, extolling Oedipus' past services, implores him to exercise his consummate wisdom for the relief of his people. The king's reply unveils yet further his incessant watchfulness and anxious care for his subjects. And he discloses a new object to their expectancy and hope. Creon, a royal person, had been sent to Delphi, and should ere then have returned with the response of Apollo. At this all hearts are trembling in suspense, when a figure is seen approaching. He is wreathed with Apollo's laurel; he looks cheerfully. What has Phoebus said? Another moment of suspense is interposed. Then the oracle is repeated,—so thrilling to the spectator who understands the story, so full of doubt and hope and dread to all the persons of the drama: "It is for the blood of Laius—his murderers are harboured in the land of Thebes. The country must be purged!" . . . All this in 150 lines!

Jebb's stirring paragraph has been removed because it is a literary evocation rather than a factual account. The slow sure way it reaches a climax terminating in the chilling cry of the oracle does not follow the modern approach. Therefore it has been discarded.

The leisurely nineteenth-century essay has frequently been replaced by concise articles that satisfy the demand for instant information. This has led editors to cut old entries like bolts of cloth to fit a given space, converting lively essays into dull notices. The biography of Confucius illustrates how much has been lost in the process. The original version in the ninth edition opened with a long description of the social and political conditions in China during Confucius' time, and discussed his philosophy through a series of anecdotes taken from his life.

During his travels Confucius often met recluses, scholarly men of principle who had given up the struggle against vice and disorder by withdrawing from the world. Once when Confucius was looking for a ford in a river, he sent his disciple, Tze-lu, to ask a man working in a field for directions. When the man, who was a recluse, learned that Tze-lu was a disciple of Confucius, he said:

> "Disorder in a swelling flood spreads over the kingdom, and no one is able to repress it. (Rather) than follow a master who withdraws from one ruler and another who will not take his advice, had you not better follow those who withdraw from the world altogether?" With these words he resumed his hoe, and would give no information about the ford.
>
> Tze-lu went back, and reported what the man had said to his master, who observed: "It is impossible to withdraw from the world, and to associate with birds and beasts that have no affinity with us. With whom should I associate but with suffering men? The disorder that prevails is what requires my efforts. If right principles ruled through the kingdom, there would be no necessity for me to change its state."

This tale offers insight into the Confucian principle of *shu,* "heart" for the suffering of fellow men; but the quotation, and the entire story which had such a firm place in the original essay, have been eliminated because there is no room now for extended sermons.

A generation ago, Aldous Huxley emphasized the literary loss that occurred when the eleventh edition was replaced. He observed in his book *Beyond the Mexique Bay*:

> My experience is that if I want information on any subject unaffected by the scientific discoveries of the last twenty years, I am much more likely to find it in the old than the new edition. The old edition was in twenty-eight volumes; the new is in twenty-four. By some curious dispensation, these four additional volumes seem to have contained everything I ever wanted to find out. Skillful writers could probably have crammed the same amount of information into the reduced space. But in many cases. . . no attempt has been made to do

this. The old articles have not been rewritten in a more compressed style; they have simply been cut down. . . . Instead of being compressed into a narrower space, whole chunks of information have simply been cut out. This disgraceful kind of editing is doubly pernicious: valuable facts contained in the old edition disappear and the old articles, many of which were well-designed and well-written wholes, read in their new form like the "essays" of sixteen-year-old schoolboys.

The necessity for shortening articles to make room for new material has disturbed many people. Librarians, in particular, have criticized this mechanical method of revision. As custodians of the world's literary heritage, their reverence for the printed word has been offended by this free and easy policy. Walter Yust, editor of the *Britannica*, recognized this problem in 1940 when he noted that librarians were "troubled by this high-handed treatment of original copy," but he blandly replied in *College and Research Libraries*:

> I have no such reverence for original copy. I have had twenty-six years of experience in the handling of copy and in the writing of it. I have never seen an article the worse for wise condensation. With the possible exception of the Gettysburg Address, the Lord's Prayer, and maybe one or two others, there are few pieces which cannot be condensed to improve them.

Unfortunately, his editorial talent was not utilized when the *Great Books of the Western World* was being prepared. If Mr. Yust had been employed to remove dull parts from the literary classics, the fifty-four volumes of the set could have been reduced to a mere thirty or forty volumes, and the *Great Books* would have become *Greater Books*.

Today the *Britannica* is sold as a complete set and is seldom used as a source of extensive reading. Therefore its loss of distinction has attracted little attention. One significant factor in this decline has been the great increase in the *Encyclopaedia*'s audience. During the nineteenth century, readers were drawn from a limited but extremely literate public. This group supported such influential periodicals as the *Quarterly, Edinburgh* and *Westminster* reviews which published lengthy essays by Macaulay, Carlyle, Huxley and Matthew Arnold. Subscribers to these periodicals formed a discriminating elite, but their small number was a major disadvantage from a business point of view.

Today approximately 150,000 sets are sold annually. Instead of a small group seeking scholarly excellence, the contemporary market consists of a large heterogeneous public which acquires the *Britannica* for a variety of reasons. For some, it is a useful reference work. For others, it is a prestige symbol or a tangible sign of intellectual sophistication; while for still others, it is a testimonial to the persuasive skill of a salesman. In many cases, parents obtain the work, not for their own personal use, but to assist their children in "getting ahead" in the world. Under these conditions, serious defects may escape notice—and editorial needs may be neglected in favor of intensive sales campaigns.

A broad market is a commercial asset, but the pursuit of large numbers poses grave problems for an adult encyclopedia, since it is difficult to maintain intellectual standards while supplying information and enlightenment to a mass audience. One solution to this problem is to abandon high standards by presenting material in an elementary manner. This course has been adopted by several American encyclopedias, and it can easily be rationalized by the desire for increased profits. The *Britannica* has been protected to some extent from this danger because its contents have not been completely revised. This frugal policy, however, has left a mass of print devoted to barren, insignificant topics. As matters now stand, many articles in the humanities are inadequate, not because they are too light or popular, but because they are glutted with pedantic views or obsolete material. The resulting dullness is almost as serious an evil as excessive popularization because it prevents the *Encyclopaedia* from serving as an effective instrument in the diffusion of knowledge.

An encyclopedia deals with a diversity of subjects covering the entire gamut of human experience, history and culture. Of necessity, it deals primarily with facts and concrete information. But buried in its mass of dates and factual detail are accounts of the classics—those works representing the summits of Western civilization. In dealing with them, editors can hardly escape the question the Lord asked the prophet Ezekiel: "Son of Man, can these bones live?" For in recalling the grandeur of the past, they must seek to resurrect the dry bones of those who were truly great, and recover from the devouring shadow of time masterpieces created in a bygone era. In dealing with these works, enthusiasm has a place as well as information and analysis. If in attempting to portray the grandeur of the classics by bold flights of rhetoric, contributors should fly too close to the sun and fall into a sea of purple prose, their efforts would not be wholly lost. Superlatives and enthusiastic praise may provide an impression of works whose greatness rests on a vision of man and the human condition that transcends their time and place.

The number of ducats received for a commission, the year it was completed and the church for which it was intended are matters of some importance to the scholar, but they are relatively insignificant to laymen who wish to grasp the esthetic meaning of artistic activity. The *Britannica* usually reverses this order of interest by placing information ahead of understanding; and in doing so, it neglects the emotional experience evoked by a work of art. It emphasizes biographical details, even in dealing with artists of the highest rank.

Michelangelo's unfinished Pietàs, Beethoven's last quartets and Rembrandt's luminous self-portraits are monuments marking the limits of art. Each records the lonely voyage of an artist beyond the achievements of middle age until, standing at the gates of death, he gathers up his strength and presses forward to new conquests. These final efforts of the masters, the mixed emotions they arouse with their painful pathos and unexpected depths cannot be fully explained—they must be experienced.

Beethoven stated in the last year of his life that he could never hear in his mind the melody of the slow movement of his B-flat Quartet, Opus 130, without tears coming to his eyes. A note in Beethoven's hand above the contrasting section of this movement reads *Beklemmt*—"oppressed"; or as Ernest Newman has suggested, "with a tightening of the heart." Donald Tovey writing about this quartet in the *Encyclopaedia* describes it as "dark with excessive bright." Such works, he says, "are transparent as far as our vision extends, and their darkness is that of a depth that shines as we penetrate it." Tovey's acute observation reflects his profound understanding of Beethoven's work, but such penetrating remarks are an exception rather than the rule.

Despite the solemnity often attached to masterpieces marking the close of an artist's creative life, the *Britannica* frequently manages to dispose of these works in a few brief sentences. The article on Verdi devotes only a few sentences to his greatest works, *Otello* and *Falstaff*. The first is cited as "subtle and profoundly moving" and the second for its "flawless refinement"; but there is no description of the action of these operas or the unusual circumstances surrounding their creation in the eighth decade of Verdi's life.*

The article on Verdi illustrates the truism that style cannot be separated from substance. It is a dull notice because it fails to follow the dramatic evolution of his art. Such misguided treatment is hardly the work of a sensitive critic anxious to make the most of his subject; rather it recalls the cautious pedant who mechanically transfers the facts he has collected from filing cards to the printed page without bothering to consider their meaning or significance.

The 1958 entry on Titian devotes an entire page to an elaborate catalogue of his paintings. It cites more than fifty of his works and carefully notes their location in museums and churches throughout the world, but does not discuss his artistic achievement. The article makes no attempt to trace the extraordinary development that led to the strange masterpieces of his final years which are painted so loosely that the figures can hardly be distinguished from the background. The Venetian master suffered the same fate as Rembrandt. The world eagerly sought the works of his middle age but neglected the products of his last years when, isolated by the death of his friends, he continued to pursue

---

* See Note III, p. 357, for a discussion of these circumstances.

his art in a manner that was no longer favored by the rich and the powerful. Despite his fame and achievement, Titian was forced to write Philip II of Spain for money the monarch owed him. In an unsuccessful effort to arouse the king's sympathy and secure new commissions, Titian reminded his royal patron that he was ninety-five years old and could not hope to live much longer.

A generation earlier, at the height of his mature style, Titian had posed Venetian courtesans on broad beds and with his brush transformed their luxurious bodies into sumptuous golden images of the Goddess of Love surrounded by gay lute players, handsome young men and other symbols of sensual delight. But in his old age, figures disappeared in semi-darkness as the painter completed his canvases "more with the finger than the brush." The flesh which once had glowed with a splendid animal radiance now dissolved into a spiritual essence as the master meditated on the dreams that culminate in a beautiful body. This metamorphosis of Venus from an earthly goddess to a dim creature enveloped by a mysterious atmosphere was not understood by the young painters who were employed in his workshop. When they saw their master retouching his paintings with his fingers, they thought he had become senile, but Vasari knew better. As the first and most famous biographer of the artists of the Italian Renaissance, Vasari justly praised Titian's final style:

> His first works were finished with great diligence, and might be looked at near or far, but the last were worked with great patches of color, so that they cannot be seen near, but at a distance they look perfect. This is the reason that many think that they were done without any trouble, but this is not true. And this way of working is most judicious, for it makes the pictures seem living.

These words were written by a contemporary of Titian, but the *Encyclopaedia* finds no need to quote them because its article does not examine the evolution of his style or the haunting works of his final period.

Occasionally, the importance of an artist's words are recognized as an authentic expression of his creative intentions. The

Britannica's biography of Gauguin draws upon his journals and letters in discussing his work. It describes the circumstances surrounding the creation of his last major painting, which was completed under the shadow of an attempted suicide. Gauguin called this final masterpiece by the enigmatic title, "Where are we from? What are we? Where are we going?" He described the emotions that led to this work in a letter written from the South Seas shortly before his death:

> Before I died I wished to paint a large canvas that I had in mind, and I worked day and night that whole month in an incredible fever. . . . I put in it all my energy, a passion so dolorous, amid circumstances so terrible, and so clear was my vision that the haste of execution is lost and life surges up. It does not stink of models, of technique, or of pretended rules, of which I have always fought shy, though sometimes with fear. . . . Where does the execution of a painting commence and where does it end? At that moment when the most intense emotions are in fusion in the depths of one's being, when they burst forth like lava from a volcano . . . ? The work is created suddenly, brutally if you like, and is not its appearance great, almost superhuman?

These words recall Gaugin's determination to paint, his ambition and personal suffering. They remind us of his profound commitment to his artistic destiny in a way that could never be captured by a catalogue of facts, a list of paintings, or a chronicle of wanderings. Therefore they justly belong in his biographical article.

Although the modern entry on Eugene O'Neill is less than a page long, it is a good example of effective prose. It notes that his plays are infused with a "melancholy that clung like poison gas"—and emphasizes the dilemma that faces O'Neill's characters by quoting a cry from *The Great God Brown:*

> Why am I afraid to dance, I who love music and rhythm and grace and laughter? Why am I afraid to live, I who love life and beauty of the flesh and the living colors of earth and sky and sea? Why am I afraid of love, I who love love? . . . Why was I born without a skin, O God. . . . Or rather Old Greybeard, why the devil was I born at all?

The article aptly portrays the central role occupied by O'Neill in the development of the American theater and observes: "Actually his plays were cardiograms of the outraged heart, poignantly charting the canceled dream, the twisted love, the thwarted hope." Such vivid writing demonstrates that it is still possible to find contributors who can present their subject in a forceful way, despite the limited space available, so that an arid manner is neither necessary nor inevitable.

All good writing implies selection and organization. Effective exposition occurs when the extraneous elements surrounding a subject have been stripped away to reveal its logical structure and essential ideas. Even the simple process of presenting factual material can produce a powerful effect if it is controlled by a unity of purpose and intention. At its highest level this process is represented by Dante who created a vision of the Almighty in the *Paradiso* by filling canto after canto with medieval astronomical lore; on a lower plane this art is practiced by every skilled historian who marshals his material to provide a coherent picture of an era or an epoch. Unlike a poet who must create a fresh work of art, the author of an encyclopedia article is only required to supply a straightforward account of his subject in a way that can be understood by educated laymen. In accomplishing this task, a contributor may never attain the heights of literary eloquence, or plumb the depths of artistic experience, but he will remain faithful to the cause of learning as long as he presents the central aspects of his subject in a clear, direct manner.

Of course, it is not always true that a fresh article is better than its predecessor. A new entry may be more accurate, but it may emphasize unimportant details, rather than essential matters. A good illustration is the article on Cervantes. The ninth edition contained a vivid survey of his life and a luminous discourse on the spiritual significance of *Don Quixote*. This splendid essay was replaced in 1910 by a feeble article that neglected the meaning of his work by engaging in biographical speculations, even though Cervantes is one of those authors, like Shakespeare, whose life is shrouded in obscurity. This arid article was retained for a half-century, although it fails to discuss *Don Quixote*—one of the great turning points in the transition of European literature from the medieval world of romance to the modern concern with reality.

Cervantes completed his masterpiece in a backward province of Spain, burdened by poverty and plagued by misfortune. He created a unique world in which the Knight of the Mournful Countenance could sally forth to uphold the ideals of chivalry accompanied by his skeptical squire, Sancho Panza. In this world, windmills become giants—and milkmaids, ladies in distress. Here Don Quixote can dream of emulating the heroes of the past and rhapsodize on the Age of Gold.

After the first volume of *Don Quixote* appeared, another writer published a crude, cruel parody containing further adventures of the Don and his squire. Angered by this insult, Cervantes was inspired to create a sequel that was even greater than its original. Deeper in humanity and fashioned with greater artistry, it broke down the barrier between reality and illusion. In it, the Duke and Duchess can attempt to deceive Don Quixote by pretending that his imaginary world is real, and that he is indeed a true knight-errant. But through all his trials, he is inspired by a vision of valorous deeds—and in the end when he lies dying, he can humbly ask Sancho Panza to forgive him for leading him astray, saying, "I was mad and now I am sane: I was Don Quixote de la Mancha, and now I am Alonso Quijano the Good. . . ."

Once in a while, the *Britannica* is illuminated by a burst of enthusiasm, but its object may seem as strange as the raptures of Don Quixote over the beauty of his lady, Dulcinea del Toboso. The entry on Modern Gastronomy lyrically conveys the exquisite delights that tickle the palates of civilized epicures. The author of the article, Paul Reboux, states that gastronomy is an art because it appeals to all the senses. To support his claim, he itemizes these sensations in detail:

> The crispness of fried dishes and pastry is agreeable to the ear. The softness of well thickened sauces and melting *foies gras,* the succulent freshness of fruit, are pleasant to the touch. Is there anything more delightful to the eye than

a dish *au gratin,* with its captive flavours imprisoned under its golden dome? Do not odours like those of seasonings of herbs, or of truffles, afford the highest possible gratification of the sense of smell? Of the palate there is no need to speak.

As a true gourmet, the author harshly rebukes Molière who "talked like a Philistine when he made one of his characters say that 'we eat to live, we do not live to eat.' " Monsieur Reboux is not content to recount the tantalizing sensations produced by a master of French *haute cuisine;* he vigorously proclaims the place of gastronomy in civilized life. He assures us that eating is more than a pleasure, it is a fine art. Indeed:

> It may even be said that gastronomy is a perfect art, for so wide a range of enjoyment could not in the opinion of the present writer be obtained from listening to a symphony, hearing a poem read, or gazing at a beautiful building. Indeed, it would not be unreasonable to maintain, not merely that gastronomy is a perfect art, but that it is the only art which is perfect.

Unlike factual errors which can often be corrected by changing a few lines here and there, serious literary defects cannot be remedied by minor surgery. The mass of arid, archaic articles, the erratic patchwork of old and new material, and the labored accumulation of factual information cannot be corrected by gentle pruning. So many entries are plodding exercises in pedantry that the *Encyclopaedia*'s lifeless style cannot be cured by replacing a small set of articles. In most cases, piecemeal revision is out of the question—entirely new contributions are required to present the insights of modern scholarship in a stimulating manner and to regain the literary standards that were once a proud trademark of the *Britannica*.

[11]

History
and Its Legends

Laymen reading historical works are apt to assume that all
their facts are indubitably true. Scholars, however, realize it may
be difficult to settle even simple questions about the past, since
many episodes rest on flimsy conjectures or doubtful testimony.
They are skeptical about colorful traditions based on hearsay or
dubious documents, and their reluctance to accept such material
may be unsettling to laymen. However, the aim of their study is
to establish *facts* about the past, not comfortable beliefs. This
forces scholars to reject many picturesque incidents that are a
familiar ingredient of historical romances and patriotic appeals.

Even a date may pose difficulties. An example is Columbus'
birthdate, which was unknown for a long time because neither
his son nor his first biographer furnished any information on the
matter. During the 1830's, Washington Irving assumed that he
was born about 1435 and was an aged mariner when he made
his celebrated voyage. Later historians, on the basis of fragmentary evidence, believed he was born at least a decade later, but

were unable to fix the exact year. The mystery was solved in 1904 when an Italian scholar published a legal document establishing that Columbus was born in 1451, between the twenty-fifth of August and the end of October.

The article on Columbus in the 1958 edition does not present the currently accepted birthdate, but claims that it is uncertain and offers two alternatives—1446 and 1451. The article also asserts that the only authentic portrait of Columbus is in the possession of the De Orchi family. But this painting shows the explorer with a round head and brown eyes, whereas contemporary observers have recorded he had a *long* face and *blue* eyes.

Almost everyone has heard that Columbus proved the earth is round. Schoolchildren learn about his struggle against the prejudice of his contemporaries who believed in a flat world. Elementary geography books contain vivid pictures illustrating the idea of a flat world, but they never explain how Columbus overthrew this belief. Their failure is not surprising because this feat is a modern fabrication.

The ancients had observed that the horizon at sea is a spherical arc, and they realized that a spherical earth would explain why, when a ship approached from a distance, its mast would first appear above the horizon, and then its hull. The radius of the earth had been measured in antiquity, and a spherical earth was adopted by Ptolemy in his astronomical work. When Dante assumed a spherical earth in *The Divine Comedy* in 1300, he was merely following an accepted belief. All the educated men of Columbus' time thought the earth was round; the only dispute was about its size, and the location of Asia with respect to Europe.

Since Columbus felt it was possible to reach the Indies by sailing across the Atlantic, he eagerly embraced any information that would diminish the distance. This was necessary because the existence of America was unknown, and an accurate estimate would have made such a voyage a practical impossibility. Columbus underestimated the diameter of the earth by 25 percent, and assumed that China and Japan were located in the middle of the Pacific. As a result of these errors, he calculated that the distance from the Canary Islands to the east coast of China was 3,550 nautical miles, when it is actually about 11,700 miles. Although his geographical estimates were grossly inaccurate, his persistence and enterprise led to the discovery of the New World. Had he calculated correctly he might never have undertaken this epochal voyage, for it would have been unthinkable to attempt a voyage of 11,700 miles in the frail ships of his time.

Washington Irving is responsible for perpetuating the legend that Columbus proved the earth is round. He wrote a popular biography containing a dramatic scene portraying Columbus disputing the question with a formidable group of learned men. This conflict of ideas was effectively conveyed when Irving presented a picture of "a simple mariner standing forth in the midst of an imposing array of professors, friars and dignitaries of the church; maintaining his theory with natural eloquence, and as it were, pleading the cause of the new world." The contrast between the simple mariner and the multitude of prejudiced professors and friars made an effective tableau; for here was a single self-taught sailor who successfully challenged and held his own against a host of scholars, and who was to be triumphantly vindicated by the discovery of America.

Actually, when the commission of scholars heard Columbus, they decided his claim that there was a narrow channel between Spain and the Indies could not possibly be true—and they were correct. But the public likes to believe its heroes are always right, so the Columbus legend continues to flourish. It enjoys wide currency because elementary schoolbooks are often prepared by rewriting earlier texts and employing encyclopedias for background material. As a result, when reference works fail to expose familiar myths and fallacies, these may be repeated until they are accepted as common knowledge. In the case of Columbus, the *Britannica* devotes five pages to his life, but only notes: "He believed the earth to be a sphere; he underestimated its size; he overestimated the size of the Asiatic continent." No further details are supplied, although this estimate was a vital factor in his efforts to obtain financial support.

The failure to comprehend his achievement may be demonstrated in a rather striking manner. The *Encyclopaedia* ran a series of advertisements in a number of British tabloids including the *Sunday Pictorial* (February 26, 1961) stressing the theme, "You ought to learn more about the *Britannica.*" Each advertisement was subdivided into a number of panels illustrating information found in the set, and they each concluded with the slogan, *"It's all in the Britannica."* One of the panels stated:

> Before Columbus proved the world was round, people thought the horizon marked its edge. Today we know better.

Indeed we do.

A colorful legend can be launched even if it is flatly contradicted by existing evidence. All that is required is a facile imagination and a vigorous style that can transform a prosaic incident into a lively episode. A vivid instance is Franklin's experiment of flying a kite in a thunderstorm to test the equivalence of lightning and electricity. In the usual version, Franklin is accompanied by a small boy who, it is often claimed, helped him fly the kite. A picture of this episode is shown in the *Britannica Junior,* but the actual circumstances were somewhat different. Franklin was indeed accompanied by his son when he performed this experiment, but his son was twenty-one years old at the time.

This scientific experiment is omitted from the *Britannica*'s biography of Franklin, although it is a familiar story in elementary textbooks. In other cases, well-known episodes are treated inconsistently.*

Probably the most famous legend in American history is that of Washington and the cherry tree. According to the well-worn tale, when George was six years old, his father gave him a little hatchet, and with this hatchet he barked his father's favorite cherry tree. When his father questioned him about what had happened, he replied in the famous climax of the story, "I can't tell a lie, Pa; you know I can't tell a lie. I did cut it with my hatchet." (In the modern version, George chops the cherry tree down and replies, "Father, I cannot tell a lie.") This episode

---

* See Note IV, p. 359, for accounts of Betsy Ross and the first American flag and of Stephen Foster and "My Old Kentucky Home."

was first recorded by Parson Weems in his life of George Washington. He introduced the anecdote in a string of stories about Washington's childhood, saying: "The following anecdote is too valuable to be lost, and too true to be doubted for it was communicated to me by the same excellent lady to whom I am indebted for the last [story]." According to Weems, this aged lady was a distant relative of the Washington family who had spent some time with them when she was a child.

Historians, however, have dismissed the hatchet and the cherry tree because Weems failed to include the story in the first edition of his biography in 1800. He only introduced the tale in the fifth edition which appeared six years later, although he reported hearing about the episode twenty years earlier. Weems had no scruples about inventing picturesque tales, for he sought to increase the sales of his books by making them entertaining and edifying. This objective is evident in the title of his biography which is called *The Life of George Washington; With Curious Anecdotes, Equally Honourable to Himself and Exemplary to His Young Countrymen*. The first edition boasted it was "faithfully taken from authentic documents," but this claim disappeared from the title page by the time the fifth edition appeared. Instead the author described himself as "Formerly Rector of Mount-Vernon Parish"—a flattering invention which had no factual foundation, since there was no parish in Mount Vernon. The first edition was a modest pamphlet of eighty pages that began with Washington's service in the French and Indian Wars; but by the fifth edition, it had grown to a full length book of 250 pages that commenced with colorful stories of Washington's childhood and youth.

The cherry-tree legend possesses a remarkable vitality; it continues to persist although it has been assailed many times. A singular confirmation is provided by the *Britannica*'s essay on George Washington, written by Allan Nevins. When this essay originally appeared in 1929 it stated:

> Little has been recorded of Washington's childhood in the small four-room farm house on the Rappahannock, a fact which invited Mason L. Weem's *absurd fictions* regarding the

hatchet and the cherry tree, and his repugnance to fighting. (Italics added.)

This blunt and forthright dismissal of a venerated bit of Americana was retained as late as 1956; but the following year Professor Nevins' attack was deleted—not because of new historical evidence—but presumably in response to protests from owners of the set. A new sentence was introduced that avoided this sensitive issue by noting:

> Little has been recorded of Washington's childhood in the small four-room farm house on the Rappahannock, although Mason L. Weems told the story of the hatchet and cherry tree and of young Washington's repugnance to fighting.

Thus the legend was no longer dismissed, but presented as if it had some factual basis.

Nothing is more helpful in launching a new myth in American history than invoking the name of George Washington, since his countrymen seem ready to accept almost any story elevating his stature and reputation. This may be seen in the customary account of Monroe's re-election as President. His biographical entry asserts:

> In 1820 he was re-elected, receiving all the electoral votes but one, which William Plumer (1759–1850) of New Hampshire cast for John Quincy Adams, in order, it is said, that no one might share with Washington the honour of unanimous election.

This is not true. Plumer was one of the few electors in American history who acted in accordance with the wishes of the Founding Fathers by exercising his own judgment in the selection of a new President, without regard to partisan or factional considerations. Plumer, a hard-headed New England individualist, bluntly stated in his autobiography that he had voted against James Monroe because he did not approve of his fiscal policies, and this statement is confirmed by contemporary newspaper reports of the election. This reason, however, was too prosaic for writers who wished to eulogize Monroe's second administration as the "Era of Good Feeling." In the 1880's two historians, Edward Stanwood and James Schouler, invented the story that Plumer's vote was withheld because of his reverence for George Washington; and this tale is repeated by many reference works, even though such reverence for Washington is much less "American" than the independence of a presidential elector who followed the dictates of his conscience.

Sometimes poets have been responsible for the popularity of certain legends. Almost everyone has heard of Paul Revere's exploits, yet his "midnight ride" only became well known after Longfellow's poem appeared in 1863. Longfellow related that Paul waited impatiently for a signal to be given by lanterns in the belfry of the Old North Church—"one if by land, and two if by sea"—so he could warn the Minute Men of approaching Redcoats. Yet it was Revere who ordered lanterns placed in the North Church after learning that the British would travel by sea, because he was afraid it might be difficult to cross the Charles River without being stopped. After the signal had been set, he crossed the river to the Charlestown side, borrowed a horse and began his famous ride. Revere, however, was captured by a British patrol after leaving Lexington, so he never reached Concord. These facts were disregarded by Longfellow who rearranged the actual events to make his poem more effective. He exercised poetic license in describing:

> It was twelve by the village clock
> When he crossed the bridge in Medford town.
> . . . .
> It was one by the village clock
> When he galloped into Lexington.
> . . . .
> It was two by the village clock
> When he came to the bridge in Concord town.

Despite its inaccuracy, Longfellow's poem has been accepted by careless writers as an authentic account of a familiar episode in Revolutionary history. The resulting confusion can be easily

documented in the *Britannica*. Its entry on Paul Revere is historically correct when it states:

> His midnight ride from Charlestown to Lexington on April
> 18–19, 1775, to give warning of the approach of British troops
> from Boston, is Revere's most famous exploit; it is commem-
> orated by Longfellow, who, however, has "paid little attention
> to exactness of fact."

But the article on Boston follows the fictional description given
by Longfellow:

> On the evening of April 18 an expedition was sent out.
> By an agreed plan of signals Paul Revere, *waiting at the
> Charlestown shore, learned the route* by which it had started
> and on a horse borrowed for that purpose, rode through the
> country arousing the inhabitants. (Italics added.)

Artists, as well as poets, have the power to single out individuals and make them part of a national tradition by depicting
scenes filled with patriotic or religious sentiment. The work of
Benjamin West is a notable example. His painting of Penn's
Treaty with the Indians helped fix the event in the minds of
schoolchildren who were told it established peaceful relations
between the Indians and the settlers of the new Pennsylvania
Colony. The article on William Penn observes:

> Realistic and entirely imaginative accounts . . . inspired
> chiefly by Benjamin West's picture, have been given of the
> treaty which there seems no doubt Penn actually made in
> November 1683 with the Indians.

But no contemporary evidence has been found of this treaty,
although scholars have diligently searched through the files of
the Penn family, the archives of the English government and the
state of Pennsylvania, as well as in many historical collections.
Although there is nothing to show that this treaty was ever consummated, the *Encyclopaedia* confidently fixes its date as November, 1683, and this assertion is repeated in the article on Pennsylvania.

The only basis for the treaty is Benjamin West's painting,

which was commissioned by Joseph Penn and completed in 1771, almost a hundred years after the supposed event. West wrote a friend that his ambition in composing the scene was "to express savages brought into harmony and peace by justice and benevolence." His effort was remarkably successful; the public relished the way in which he combined the exotic aspects of Indian life with the Christian sentiments of peace and brotherhood. West employed his relatives and other contemporaries as models, but later writers have treated his painting as if it were a photograph of an actual event. The most astonishing performance was given by that tireless myth-maker, Parson Weems, who wrote a biography of William Penn containing the dialogue between the Indians and the white men at this historic occasion. He recorded that the Sachems said:

> Bad white men to kill their red brothers! But you no bad white man! Oh no; you good white man! You all same as red man! You one brother! You bring red men good things! We give you land, and deer, and turkeys plenty! You live with us, all brothers together, long as the sun and moon give light.

After giving a detailed report of what transpired, Parson Weems recorded that Penn and his followers gave the Indians in return for their land a long list of items including twenty guns, one hundred bars of lead, forty pairs of stockings, twenty tomahawks, five gallons of molasses and one barrel of beer—items whose cash value totaled $515.50.

Although Penn's Treaty with the Indians possesses an ancient pedigree, other stories are modern inventions. An example is the saga of Paul Bunyan, the mythical hero of the lumber camps of the Pacific Northwest. It is only recently that Bunyan and his Blue Ox have been recognized by reference works. In 1929 the *Britannica* was the first encyclopedia to include an entry on Paul Bunyan. It recorded:

> . . . The legend which is said to have begun in the Papineau rebellion in Canada in 1837 . . . had, by 1860, spread throughout the northwest, and perhaps even into the south

where under the name of John Henry he became "the man worth talking about" in the work of the camp gang.

This version has been repeated by many reference works, although Paul Bunyan is not an authentic figure of American folklore. He was created to encourage the sale of lumber by a talented advertising executive from vague stories he had heard as a youth. Bunyan first appeared in 1914 and 1916 in two small booklets containing tales of his adventures and advertising material promoting the Red River Lumber Company. The booklets were written by W. B. Laughead, advertising manager of the company, and the title of the first pamphlet was appropriately called "Introducing Paul Bunyan of Westwood, Cal." It offered a skillful blend of "folk material" and advertising copy by reporting:

> Paul Bunyan's greatest asset was Babe, the Big Blue Ox. Babe was seven axe handles wide between the eyes and weighed more than the combined weight of all the fish that ever got away. . . . Babe used to pull the water tank with which Paul iced his roads from Dakota to Lake Superior. Once this tank burst and that's what started the Mississippi River and has kept it flowing to this day.
>
> Paul will not need Babe in California for The Red River Lumber Company has installed steam and electric appliances there that would make Babe hang his head in shame.

At first, this effort to publicize Bunyan as a folk hero and guardian spirit of the Red River Lumber Company was not very successful, but when a new booklet was prepared in 1922 entitled "The Marvelous Exploits of Paul Bunyan," an edition of ten thousand copies was rapidly exhausted. Soon other writers discovered Bunyan and hastened to capitalize on his popularity by offering fresh adventures. The most successful was James Stevens who wrote a book in 1925 which sold more than 75,000 copies. Stevens catered to prevailing tastes by depicting a hero who attacked prohibition, professors and poetry, and who was an outspoken advocate of free enterprise and the twelve-hour day. Stevens was not content to elaborate the Bunyan mythology,

but proceeded to invent a new genealogy that would add fresh
luster to his figure. He maintained, without offering any evidence,
that tales about Bunyan were originally of French-Canadian
origin and were modeled after a real person who had fought in
the Papineau rebellion of 1837. These changes were introduced
to make Bunyan a super-patriot. According to Stevens, Paul
originally spelled his name as Bunyon and called his calf Bébé,
but Paul had a vision in which he saw his true destiny as an
American:

> Now Paul Bunyon lifted his hands solemnly and spoke in
> the rightful language of Real America.
> "In becoming a Real American, I become Paul *Bunyan*,"
> he declared, "I am Paul *Bunyon* no more. Even so shall my
> blue ox calf be called Babe, and Bébé no longer."

This picture of Bunyan as a rustic patriot is accepted as genuine folk material by many encyclopedias which portray him as an
authentic figure of the logging camps, even though he was actually created by an advertising manager in 1914. Since his mythical status has been affirmed by the *Britannica* for a generation,
it is only natural that he should be welcomed in children's books
and advertising copy as a lively bit of Americana.

Pocahontas is another example. Her rescue of Captain John
Smith, who was about to be executed by her father, Powhatan,
is supposed to have occurred in 1608. But immediately thereafter
when Smith described his experiences in his book, *A True Relation*, he failed to include this astonishing event. It was only
reported sixteen years later in his *Generall Historie*. The entire
episode occupies only ten lines, but subsequent writers have
seized on the incident and transformed it into an exciting adventure.

Smith's story was challenged in 1860 by Charles Deane, who
published a diary by Edward Wingfield, the first president of the
Virginia Colony. The diary traced the history of the Colony and
independently confirmed Smith's early account in *A True Relation*, which had merely identified Pocahontas as a ten-year-old
child and said nothing about her feat of saving his life. Once

Smith's truthfulness was questioned, a lively debate ensued. Edward Arber, who edited Smith's papers, accepted the Pocahontas story and attempted to rehabilitate Smith's reputation. But Henry Adams attacked the legend in a penetrating essay in the *North American Review*. Adams compared parallel passages in Captain Smith's reports of 1608 and 1624. He showed how Smith's later account systematically exaggerated his adventures among the Indians. In 1608, eight guards were sufficient; but in 1624, twenty or thirty were necessary to prevent his escape. In 1608, only four guides escorted him back to Jamestown; but twelve accompanied him in 1624. Adams pointed out that none of the other leaders who wrote about the early history of the Virginia Colony seemed to know anything about this remarkable event which was revealed by Smith, and Smith alone. Therefore he concluded that the dramatic rescue by Pocahontas was a figment of Smith's imagination, but his cogent arguments did not succeed in destroying the legend.

The *Britannica*'s article on John Smith describes this episode in the following way:

> It was on this trip that . . . the best-known incident of his life occurred, namely, his rescue by Pocahontas, who . . . threw herself upon him and by her entreaties prevailed with her father to spare his life. This was the act of a kind-hearted, simple little Indian maiden of twelve or thirteen years of age who had been entertained by Smith with stories and sights of marvels in the time he had been at her father's residence before the execution had been decided upon.

The entry on Pocahontas adopts a more critical attitude. It traces the controversy that has arisen over the story and notes: "Due to the fact, however, that no mention of this experience is made in the minute personal narrative covering this period, written by Capt. Smith at the time of the supposed occurrence and published immediately thereafter . . . doubts have arisen as to the authenticity of the tale."

The *Encyclopedia Americana* supplies an interesting footnote to this divergence of opinion. Its article on John Smith traces the history of the controversy, but contains no reference later than

1914. It advances an unexpected witness for the Virginia Captain by declaring: "Smith has found many defenders, such as Arber in his memoir in the *Encyclopaedia Britannica* (9th edition, 1887)." To find the *Americana,* which claims to be preeminent in American biography, offering an antiquated reference in the *Britannica* as an authority is as surprising as discovering Khrushchev quoting Kennedy.

Sometimes the *Britannica* critically analyzes dubious material. The entry on William Tell carefully examines the tradition surrounding his legendary encounter with the tyrant Gessler which is lost in the obscurity of early Swiss history. It observes that the date of his defiance varies in early accounts from 1260 to 1334, and records that all efforts to demonstrate the existence of a real William Tell who lived in the fourteenth century break down completely. This candid examination of a Swiss national hero differs sharply from the indulgent treatment of well-known figures in American history whose exploits are often accepted at face value.

It is only fair to point out, however, that there are occasional exceptions. The essay on Baseball effectively discredits the idea that the game was invented in 1839 by Abner Doubleday at Cooperstown, New York—a tradition enshrined by the Hall of Fame erected in Cooperstown. This myth was launched in 1908 by a commission set up by A. G. Spalding, a sporting goods manufacturer, who wished to establish the American origin of the game. The commission reported that baseball was based on the children's game "One Old Cat"; but this theory was demolished in 1939 by Robert Henderson of the New York Public Library who demonstrated that it was actually derived from the English game "Rounders." Thus America's "national sport" originated in the British Isles, just as intercollegiate football evolved from the English sport of rugby.

In themselves, the legends of American history seem harmless enough. Pocahontas, Betsy Ross and the exploits of Christopher Columbus have amused and excited countless children. "Why can't we leave these instructive stories alone? Can't we keep them just like Santa Claus? After all, he doesn't exist but look what he does for Christmas." So goes the refrain. It all appears reasonable and sensible—until we realize that once the standard of truth is abandoned we are helpless against those who demand that history further special political, religious and national interests. Not long ago Europe was engulfed by those who believed in the Master Race and wished to rewrite history as the inevitable triumph of Aryan nations possessing "pure blood." Today Marxists attempt to present history as a record of the class struggle and the victory of communism. All these efforts have one feature in common—the wish to arrange and present the past so it will agree with fixed, preconceived ideas.

Once we refashion the past to agree with current ideas, we destroy its educational value. Instead of providing a means of learning about the diversity of human experience, it merely becomes a mirror of contemporary confusions and preconceptions. When we know who will triumph and who will be defeated, it is easy to attribute confidence and assurance to those who will succeed, even if they did not possess such optimism. Such hindsight is offered in the usual version of the vision that occurred to St. Ignatius of Loyola. According to the *Britannica*:

> On the road to Rome a famous vision took place. In a certain church near Rome, whilst in prayer, he was aware of a change in his soul; and so openly did he see God the Father associating him with Christ who said "Ego vobis Romae propitius ero," that he could not dare doubt the reality of his vision.

The words, "I will be propitious to you at Rome," were not included in the saint's autobiography. He merely recorded that "he felt so great a change in his soul and he saw so clearly God the Father placing him with Christ His Son that he could not dare to doubt the experience."

The quotation was first revealed by his follower Laynez twenty-two years later. He added that Ignatius did not understand the meaning of this vision because the saint said: "I know not what will happen to us. Perhaps we will be crucified in Rome." This response by a religious mystic who has just had a vision of God and His Crucified Son is not surprising: it lends psychological weight to Laynez' report, which was made by a single witness long after the event. This troubled and uncertain reaction, however, has been dropped by clerical writers who prefer the simple-minded picture of a self-confident saint who possessed no inner doubts, because they know that after reaching Rome he will be authorized by the Pope to found the Society of Jesus, which will stem the tide of the Reformation. Consequently they merely repeat the optimistic words, "I will be propitious to you at Rome," and ignore the saint's perplexity.

Emotional factors often play a decisive role in perpetuating historical legends. In a few instances, however, they have been stimulated by commercial considerations. An example is the widespread belief that tartans—worsted cloth woven in colored stripes that alternate in a definite sequence—were employed by ancient Scottish clans as a means of identification. This idea permits individual patterns to be associated with specific clans possessing a long and illustrious history, and it encourages consumers to select patterns used by the heroes of an earlier day. The article on the Tartan follows this tradition in describing the distinctive attire of the Scottish Highlanders:

> For this costume, and the tartan of which it is composed, great antiquity is claimed, and it is asserted that the numerous clans into which the Highland population were divided had each from time to time a special tartan by which it was distinguished.

This claim, which has been reprinted for seventy years, has no factual basis. In examining seventeenth- and eighteenth-century portraits, scholars have discovered that leaders of the Scottish clans were not identified by distinctive tartans. The origin of this idea can be traced to a visit of George IV to Edinburgh in 1822, which coincided with an outburst of interest in early Scottish history produced by Walter Scott's novels. In honor of the king, a host of new tartan patterns were designed which were arbitrarily assigned to different clans. This furnished the eminent clans of Scotland—Fraser, Forbes, Macgregor,

Macleod and Campbell of Argyll—with individual tartans and provided each design with a unique trade name. Although tartans did not possess a heraldic significance before they were registered in the nineteenth century, textile firms have perpetuated this profitable fiction.

It is possible to dismiss certain historical legends as relatively harmless inventions, but in other instances, they have been employed to justify national interests or colonial ambitions. One of the best known stories of English history is the massacre of the Black Hole of Calcutta. The article on India reports:

> In 1756 the nawab Suraj ud-Daulah attacked and captured the English settlement at Calcutta. He incarcerated 146 English prisoners in the notorious Black Hole, a small military prison 18 ft. by 14 ft. 10 in. in size; and in the morning only 23 persons emerged alive.

This "massacre" is also mentioned in the articles on Clive and Calcutta, and it appears in many English history books to justify British colonial policies by showing that enlightened English rule was necessary to "civilize" the barbarous native princes of India. The picturesque name of the prison as the "Black Hole" helped impress the event in the minds of schoolchildren, yet this name had been assigned to the prison by the British themselves before the massacre occurred.

The story of the Black Hole was subjected to a critical analysis in *Bengal Past and Present* (1916, 1917) by J. H. Little. He pointed out that the "massacre" rested solely on the word of a British colonial official, J. Z. Holwell; and that it is not mentioned in the chief Indian historical work of the period, the *Seir Mutaqherin,* which records other atrocities inflicted on the English. Furthermore, when this work was translated in 1789, the translator stated that the story of the Black Hole was unknown to the inhabitants of Calcutta. Little demonstrated that Holwell was a liar and a grasping mercenary whose primary interest was his own personal advancement. He noted that Clive and his Council were forced in 1766 to inform the directors of the East India Company that the "horrible massacres" Holwell had attributed to the Nawab Mir Jafar were "cruel aspersions on the character of that prince" and had no foundation in fact.

No official report on the Black Hole was ever forwarded to the directors of the company, and Holwell's personal narrative contained many inconsistencies. He supplied a detailed description of the events of that terrible night, even though the prisoners were crowded into a small room whose only illumination came from two windows looking out on a low verandah. The guards were forced to bring up torches to see what was happening inside (this being long before the invention of the electric light), but Holwell was able to record what was transpiring inside, for he stated, "What must ensue appeared to me in lively and dreadful colours the instant I cast my eyes round and saw the size and situation of the room." He managed to maintain a stoic calm while "observing everyone giving way to the violence of their passions." Thus "men who sat down and could not get up again were instantly trod to death by their fellows."

According to Holwell, the tragedy occurred because 145 men and one woman were thrust into a room, eighteen feet cube. Almost immediately they fell into a profuse sweat that brought on a raging thirst. To obtain more air, every man except Holwell and three gentlemen stripped off their clothes. Within an hour, everyone's thirst became intolerable, and respiration grew difficult. The guards brought water which was passed around in hats, but this only increased the thirst of the prisoners. Although Holwell managed to quench his thirst by wringing out the perspiration from his sleeve, he first attempted to drink his urine, "but it was so intensely bitter there was no enduring a second taste, whereas no Bristol water could be more soft or pleasant than what arose from perspiration." Holwell reported that in the morning only twenty-three prisoners emerged alive from the prison. The bodies of the dead were promiscuously thrown into a nearby ditch, and he added in a piquant aside: "The rest, who survived the fatal night, gained their liberty, except Mrs. Carey, who was too young and handsome."

According to Lord Acton, when an interesting statement is discovered, the critical method "begins by suspecting it" because the main thing for the historian "is not the art of accumulating material, but the sublimer art of investigating it—of discerning truth from falsehood." The lurid details of the Black Hole have been questioned several times in recent years. George W. Hartman in the *Journal of Social Psychology* (February, 1948) analyzed some of the emotional factors that have led to the continued acceptance of the "massacre" in the absence of any solid evidence for its occurrence. He noted that despite the emphasis placed on this outrage in schoolbooks, the subsequent Treaty of Alingar in 1757 did not mention compensation for the relatives of those who perished in the Black Hole, although it stipulated reparations for much less serious crimes. Hartman pointed out, "The latest edition of the *Britannica* in what seems like an unconscious imperial mood adds its ponderous authority to this doubtful tradition." Bergen Evans discussed the Black Hole in his book *The Spoor of Spooks and other Nonsense* (1954) and observed that the tale is mentioned in four different places in the *Encyclopaedia*. Despite these critical comments, this story continues to appear.

Examining popular legends is an instructive exercise. It reveals how often they spring from incomplete knowledge or defective evidence and demonstrates the way in which existing documents may be distorted or disregarded when patriotic sentiments are aroused. Sometimes their hold on the public is so strong that major reference works find it difficult to deal with them in a critical manner. If this is the case in matters where the facts can be readily established, is it any wonder that encyclopedias may be unable to treat complex historical questions where wide differences of opinion exist? Presenting an accurate account of major developments such as the Civil War or the Russian Revolution is an arduous task. A mass of evidence must be examined and evaluated, and the resulting material fused into a coherent chronological narrative. Without a critical spirit, history merely becomes a collection of tales—some true and some false—and not a record by which men may hope to grasp the present and prepare for the future. Fiction belongs to the province of literature; for historians only *true* history has a value. For only the truth can elevate history to that sphere where, in the words of Thucydides, it becomes "not an essay which is to win the applause of the moment, but a possession for all time."

[12]

The Historical Vision

Historians seeking to capture the diversity of the past no longer restrict themselves to political and military events, but endeavor to include the art, literature and culture of individual countries in order to portray the life of the people, as well as the celebrated deeds of kings and generals. Thanks to their vision and research, we now pass from the royal palace into the streets of the city; we enter the stalls of playhouses, watch busy artisans at work, and listen to the latest gossip in coffee houses in an effort to perceive the spirit of earlier times.

In examining what Matthew Arnold has described as "the fretful foam of vehement actions without scope that is called history," we soon discover that it is more than a collection of self-evident facts gathered by a group of omniscient, impersonal scholars. To impose a unity on the disordered and often contradictory events of the past, and to illuminate these events for later generations is an act of the whole man. All history is based on a selection and interpretation of existing evidence because it is impossible to deal with more than a tiny fragment of reality in a historical work. Consequently, matters of genuine importance must be emphasized and presented in a way that reflects past reality rather than contemporary attitudes. In earlier times, it was difficult to treat religious questions objectively, since writers frequently acted as propagandists who employed history as a weapon of theology. Fortunately, this type of bias is relatively rare today: scholars no longer seek to settle disputed theological questions with tainted evidence or spurious documents. As a result, patriotic emotions and inadequate scholarship, rather than religious zeal, are a primary source of historical bias in the *Britannica*.

Religious influences, however, are not entirely absent. A good place to seek such influence is in articles dealing with the Catholic Church, because the Church has maintained since the Middle Ages that it is the ultimate repository of religious truth. This position has forced Catholic advocates to attack ideas that might undermine the Faith. A century ago, Cardinal Newman felt it necessary to surround the pursuit of knowledge with proper safeguards to protect those truths the Church holds sacred. He stated in his lecture "Christianity and Scientific Investigation":

> . . . There must be great care taken to avoid *scandal*, or of shocking the popular mind, or of unsettling the weak; the association between truth and error being so strong in particular minds that it is impossible to weed them of the error, without rooting up the wheat with it.

If Cardinal Newman, a liberal and progressive thinker, asked scientists to avoid giving scandal, others with a more orthodox outlook have gone much further. They insist that history justify the actions of the Church. To satisfy their demands, apologists have sought to depict earlier ages in a way that would cast a favorable light on the Church.

A good example of clerical apologetics is the 1958 entry on the Society of Jesus, which first appeared in 1936. It replaced an earlier account whose frank description of the rise and fall of the Jesuits was offensive to the Society and its members. The new article was written by the editor of the conservative Catholic weekly, *America,* which had repeatedly attacked the *Encyclopaedia*'s treatment of the Jesuits. In discussing the "evil day" when the order was initially suppressed in 1773, the article quotes from the Pope's breve: "For the sake of peace, and because the Society can no longer attain the aims for which it was founded, and on secret grounds which we enclose in our heart, we suppress the said Society." The article then comments on this passage as follows:

> The "secret grounds" have never been disclosed, but it is probable that Clement XIV. meant the threats to which he had been subjected. The Brief became effective only when promulgated by the Bishops. It condemns neither the teaching, nor the morals, nor the discipline of the Jesuits. As Spittler notes, "It is useless either as a justification or as a condemnation" of the Society. It was not preceded by any judicial investigation, and Clement XIV. based it upon motives of policy.

The earlier essay on the Jesuits described the charges contained in Clement's breve, which included their defiance of their own constitution, their acquiescence in heathen practices in the East, and the disturbances they created in Catholic countries by meddling in political affairs. These charges were outlined because, as the author of the essay explained:

> It has been necessary to cite these heads of the breve because apologists of the Society allege no motive influenced the Pope save peace at any price, and that he did not believe in the culpability of the fathers. The categorical charges made in the document rebut this plea.

The modern article is not satisfied with a misleading account of the suppression of the Society; it offers a sharp critique of this action:

> Some verdicts of historians upon the Suppression merit notice. Ranke (Romische Papste III, 205) writes: "The Jesuits were destroyed chiefly because they defended the strongest conception of the supremacy of the Roman See." St.

Alphonsus Ligouri declared that the Suppression was due to "a plot of Jansenists and infidels." Pope Pius XI. called the Suppression "a painful page of history."

St. Alphonsus and Pius XI are hardly impartial judges, but the opinion of Leopold von Ranke must be carefully considered. He was one of the leading historians of the nineteenth century, and his tesimony carries special weight because, as the founder of the modern school of "scientific" historiography, he was noted for his objectivity, which is exemplified by his famous dictum that history should be presented *wie es eigentlich gewesen*—"as it actually was."

An examination of the third volume of Ranke's *History of the Popes* discloses that the sentence quoted in the *Britannica* has been torn out of context. This is a common fault of religious apologists who are willing to prove their case at any cost. Ranke deals explicitly with the suppression of the Society in an earlier paragraph when he states:

> And herein, as I think, lay the principal and most profound reason for the suppression of the order. It was an institution contrived for the purposes of war, and which, in a state of peace, was no longer in its place. Since then it would not yield a hair's breadth of its constitution, and obstinately rejected all reform, greatly as this was needed on other grounds also, it may be said to have pronounced sentence on itself. It is in fact of the highest moment, that the papal see could not succeed in upholding an order which had been founded for the purpose of opposing the Protestants—that a pope deprived it by an act of his unbiased will.

Ranke's words can hardly be reconciled with the *Encyclopaedia*'s apology for the Jesuits, yet he is advanced as a witness for the Society. He observes that the suppression was caused by the failure of the order to adapt to changing conditions, but the *Britannica* fixes the blame on malevolent external agents by declaring:

> It seems clear that the elements that pushed forward the Suppression were the Jansenists, the anti-Christian philoso-

phers, and the advocates of unlimited secular absolutism; that Clement XIV. acted under coercion, and that when free, the Bishops, and the laity in general, bore witness to the learning and priestly zeal of the Society.

To fix the downfall of the Society on the Jansenists, atheists and infidels is hardly plausible unless one believes that these groups carried more weight with the Pope than the Catholic rulers of Spain, France and Portugal who demanded that the order be suppressed because it interfered in their internal affairs.

The earlier article on the Jesuits reflected the outspoken character of the eleventh edition, which did not shirk controversy, but sought to examine disputed subjects in a forthright manner. Its point of view was lucidly set forth in the editorial introduction in the first volume:

> In a work indeed which deals with opinion and controversy at all, it is manifestly impossible for criticism to be colourless; its value as a source of authoritative exposition would be very different from what it is if individual contributors were not able to state their views fully and fearlessly. . . . The easy way to what is sometimes considered impartiality is to leave controversy out altogether; that would be to avoid responsibility at the cost of perpetuating ignorance. . . .

Because of this philosophy, the eleventh edition dealt candidly with religious topics. Its article on Heresy explained that as long as the Christian Church was itself persecuted by the pagan empire, it advocated freedom of conscience and insisted that religion could only be promoted by instruction and persuasion, but as soon as Christianity was officially adopted by the Roman empire, it began to persecute men for other religious opinions.

The eleventh edition recorded that thousands of heretics were slain during the Albigensian Crusade—and it noted that Protestants also persecuted heretics once they gained power. The modern treatment, however, is quite different. It discusses "scientific" heresy and the theological disputes of early Christianity, but glosses over Catholic and Protestant persecutions, so that one must turn to other entries to learn something about the subject.

From a comparison of the eleventh edition and the current set, one might conclude that the *Encyclopaedia* has simply adopted a policy of appeasing different religious groups. Such a hypothesis seems plausible. However, it is contradicted by articles that disagree with orthodox opinion. An example is the essay on the Reformation which describes the abuses of the monastic system, the corruption of the Holy See and the widespread sale of indulgences that led to the Protestant revolt against Rome. This essay does not conceal the nature of the conflict that ensued because it seeks to present an accurate picture of a turbulent era—something that will hardly soothe sensitive spirits. Such an outspoken treatment would not appear if a strong Catholic influence permeated the entire *Britannica*. Although clerical pressure seems to have operated on some material, the primary reason for defective historical articles is not religious bias, but the frugal practice of reprinting entries long after their ideas and concepts have been abandoned by contemporary scholars.

If a Catholic point of view were forcefully expressed, a positive contribution would be a comprehensive essay on the Middle Ages when the Church was supreme and the Christian faith synonymous with European culture. But this is not the case. The medieval period is discussed in a scrappy two-page article that fails to explore its panoramic richness or to describe the role of the Church in regulating the social, political and economic life of Europe. Instead it advances the controversial thesis that "it is no longer possible to draw a sharp distinction between culture or intelligence in medieval and modern times"—and despite the tremendous impact of science and technology, it claims, "There has never been anywhere a complete breach with medieval institutions or modes of thought."

Although the Middle Ages is slighted, the Renaissance is covered in a twelve-page essay by John Addington Symonds, who vigorously portrays the diverse features of this exuberant era. He describes the rise of humanism and the revival of learning, the emergence of science, and the philosophical and educational ideals of the age. He concludes by examining the development of the Renaissance in various European countries, and his essay is supplemented by separate entries on Renaissance art and architecture.

The disparity between the treatment of the Renaissance and of the Middle Ages can be easily explained. The Renaissance has been recognized as a distinct historical period for almost a century, and it has benefited from many full-length studies. The Middle Ages, on the other hand, has been a subject of intensive research only during the last fifty years. Historians, such as Johann Huizinga, Henri Pirenne and Marc Bloch, have explored the diverse manifestations of medieval life and interpreted its social, economic and intellectual aspects. Their comprehensive studies have dispelled some of the misconceptions surrounding the period, and made it possible to provide a survey that could equal in richness and detail the *Encyclopaedia*'s account of the Renaissance.

In the past, an era encompassing a thousand years of European history—from the fall of Rome to the invention of printing—was dismissed by many writers as a bleak epoch filled with ignorance and superstition. For Voltaire and other rationalists, the term "Gothic" was an expression of contempt derived from the barbarian invaders of Rome, the Goths, and they used the term to dismiss medieval art and culture as "barbarous and tasteless."

Modern critics and historians have rehabilitated the Middle Ages by separating its genuine achievements from its baser elements. They have stressed the continuity between the Middle Ages and the Renaissance and demonstrated that the sharp division between the two periods assumed by earlier writers is erroneous. Their research has revealed that many of the customs and characteristics of the Renaissance can be traced back to medieval antecedents—and that an understanding of medieval life is necessary to comprehend the development of the Renaissance.

This continuity is disregarded in Symonds' essay on the Renaissance. He allots a page to the Middle Ages, but equates the entire period with the Dark Ages of Mankind in order to contrast the ignorance of the medieval world with the enlightenment of the Renaissance. He trenchantly explains why the medieval era was sterile and unfruitful:

> Superstition and stupidity hedged them in on every side, so that sorcery and magic seemed the only means of winning power over nature or insight into mysteries surrounding human life. The path from darkness to light was lost; thought was involved in allegory; the study of nature had been perverted into an inept system of grotesque and pious parable-mongering; the pursuit of truth had become a game of wordy dialectics.

Symonds notes that progress was impossible during the Middle Ages because it lacked "the right touch on life, the right feeling for human independence, the right way of approaching the materials of philosophy, religion and scholarship." He portrays the medieval period in such dark hues to provide a bold contrast between the static sterility of medieval thought lost in "wordy dialectics" and the bustling energy of the Renaissance, which was creating a new world. This comparison is quite effective, but it fails to explain how the Middle Ages could have produced the poetic vision of Dante, the intellectual order of St. Thomas Aquinas and the mystical fervor of St. Francis of Assisi. Such a rationalistic view ignores the religious faith expressed in the architectural rhetoric of the Gothic cathedral whose vocabulary was the pointed arch and flying buttress, and whose austere sculpture embodied the spirit of the Gospels in material form. Consequently there is no place for the splendors of Chartres, Amiens and Notre Dame whose majestic forms have come to symbolize the imposing faith of medieval Christianity.

Symonds depreciated the Middle Ages because of his enthusiasm for the values of the Renaissance which exalted individual freedom and the development of the whole man. His zeal was understandable. During the nineteenth century, the inevitable march of progress seemed firmly grounded on scientific principles and it was easy to believe that man would reach new levels of perfection through social evolution. Today, this optimistic belief in progress has been seriously undermined, and the medieval period is no longer dismissed because it lacked the dynamic values of the Renaissance. Rather the reverse has occurred. Clerical advocates now exalt the static, changeless aspects of medieval life to demonstrate the beneficent influence of the Church—and some writers, not content with the real accomplishments of the period, have attempted to endow it with modern characteristics.

This may be seen in the article on the History of Education when it reaches medieval times. It glosses over the widespread ignorance and illiteracy prevalent even in religious orders:

> No doubt, in times of spiritual and intellectual lethargy, the practice fell short of theory; but on the whole it may be concluded that the provision for higher instruction was adequate to the demand, and that, relatively to the culture of the time, the mass of people were by no means sunk in brutish ignorance.

Such a statement is as exaggerated as Symonds' dismissal of the Middle Ages because it neglects the oppressed condition of the great bulk of the population who were struggling to survive as serfs under the feudal system. What is required is not a brusque summary, or a few slogans about medieval life, but an effort to portray and synthesize its diverse aspects with the aid of insights and information supplied by modern scholarship.

Despite its brilliant literary style, Symonds' essay on the Renaissance has been superseded by advances in historical knowledge which have discredited many of its views. In 1929 the editors attempted to correct this outmoded treatment by adding a brief supplement citing some of its major deficiencies. But despite these faults and the growing inadequacy of this seventy-year-old essay, no effort has been made to replace it by a fresh contribution. Instead it has been reprinted year after year, even though it belongs to the History of Ideas, rather than to contemporary scholarship. This fate is inevitable because our view of the past is not fixed, but is the product of successive generations of scholars who interpret earlier ages in the light of new discoveries, interests and ideas.

This process is vividly portrayed in the *Britannica*'s essay on History, which specifically cites the changing conception of the Middle Ages and the Renaissance:

> Hardly an "old master" remains an authoritative book of reference. Old landmarks drop out of sight—e.g. the fall of the Western empire in 476, the coming of the Greeks to Italy in 1453, dates which once enclosed the middle ages. The perspective changes: humanism stretches back into the middle ages and the gap between the Renaissance and the middle ages dwindles. . . . The result has been a complete transformation of history since the middle of the 19th century.

Most people living during the Renaissance did not realize they were passing through a momentous period of change. This only became evident much later. Today the idea of the "Renaissance Man," the forceful individual who pursued many diverse interests is almost a cliché; it has become a romantic ideal in an age dominated by "organization men" and narrow specialists. Journalists are ready to apply the term to anyone who displays a few outside interests, yet the image of *l'uomo universale*—"the all-sided man"—was first created by historians in characterizing the vehement personalities who flourished during the Renaissance. Indeed, the common picture of the period as an epoch of rebirth and renewal is primarily a nineteenth-century idea. It was expressed in 1853 by the French historian Jules Michelet who invoked a vision of its stirring achievements:

> The Renaissance . . . the discovery of the world and the discovery of man. The sixteenth century . . . went from Columbus to Copernicus, from Copernicus to Galileo, from the discovery of the earth to that of the heavens. Man refound himself. While Vesalius and Servetus revealed life to him, his moral mysteries were penetrated by Luther, by Calvin . . . by Rabelais, Montaigne, Shakespeare and Cervantes. He plumbed the profound depths of his nature.

Although the idea of the Renaissance was first sounded by Michelet, its synthesis as a distinct historical period was due to Jacob Burckhardt who in 1860 depicted its essential features in his book, *The Civilization of the Renaissance in Italy*. Burckhardt made no effort to present a chronological account, but sought to capture the spirit of the age by charting the emergence of the modern political state and the exuberant philosophy that liberated the individual by the energetic belief that "men can do all things if they will." For Burckhardt, festivals and fashions, domestic life and the ruins of Rome, all served a means of capturing the varied aspects of the period. Before his work appeared, history was generally regarded as past politics—a chronological account of political events and military campaigns leavened with a bit of biography. But after Burckhardt, historians realized that a mere record of political and military events could not convey the varied life of earlier epochs. As a result, cultural history has assumed a recognized place alongside the political and military chronicles that were once a standard product of historical study.

The *Britannica* fails to reflect this shift in perspective because it has retained material from the eleventh edition that stresses the military aspects of war, rather than its social and political effects. This explains why the current edition contains long, comprehensive treatises on the military campaigns associated with various European wars. Five pages are allotted to the Seven Weeks' War of 1866, and five and one-half pages to the War of the Spanish Succession—and this exhaustive treatment is epitomized by a fifteen-page essay on the Napoleonic Campaigns that traces the marches and counter-marches of Napoleon's armies across Europe. Such entries pay meticulous attention to military strategy and tactics, but neglect the economic and political consequences of the events they describe. An example is the account of the Seven Years' War which observes in its opening paragraph that "this war laid the foundations of the British empire," as well as the foundations of modern Germany. But these momentous results are not discussed in the remainder of the seven-page article.

"History is what one age finds noteworthy in another," Burckhardt has observed. Inevitably we are drawn to recent happenings that are fresh in our minds; and when sufficient time has elapsed, historians are able to offer a coherent picture and interpretation of these events. Thus when the fourteenth edition was being prepared, a great deal of space was set aside for the first World War because it was universally acknowledged at the time to be the greatest conflict in recorded history. This popular absorption in the "war to end war" was expressed in an exhaustive treatment of its major battles and campaigns, and this emphasis can still be found in the current edition because a large amount of material has been reprinted from the fourteenth edition. Thus there are long articles on the battles of Verdun, Ypres, the Somme, Loos, Tannenberg and Neuve Chapelle, as well as on the Dardanelles, Serbian and Salonika campaigns, in addition to a host of entries on leading battles, such as Lys, Rossbach and the Hindenburg Line, describing their action in great detail. Field Marshal Wavell contributed a six-page essay on the Operations in Palestine and a comprehensive series of articles on the Carpathians, Luck, Lemberg, Narew, Narocz and Przemysl. These elaborate entries analyze the tactics of opposing generals and are supplemented by maps clarifying the movements of different army groups.

A high point in this exhaustive coverage is reached in the eight pages devoted to the battles of the Marne. The first battle (Sept. 6–9, 1914) is characterized as "the first great turning point" of the war, and the second (July 15, 1918) as "the turning of the tide in the final year" of the war. Since more than 10,000 words are used to record these four days of battle, the *Britannica* is able to supply an hourly chronicle of the movements of the Allied and German armies. Such minute coverage is not unusual. Ten pages are assigned to the Battle of Jutland, which occurred on May 31, 1916. An elaborate set of tables itemizes the individual ships involved, as well as the various battle squadrons and their commanders. The tenor of this article may be suggested by its observation:

The movements of the fleets and squadrons were necessarily governed to a large extent by highly technical considerations, and the battle is not an easy one for the layman to follow without a painstaking study of its successive phases and the motives that produced them.

The article then furnishes an exhaustive study of the tactics employed by opposing commanders.

One positive result of this emphasis on World War I was T. E. Lawrence's brilliant essay on Guerrilla Warfare, which originally appeared in 1929. He presents a masterly account of the theory, philosophy and strategy of guerrilla war as it was practiced by the Arabs under his command from 1914 to 1916. He points out that the numerically inferior Arab legion could harass a much larger Turkish force by striking at materiel—not men. After noting that "the Arabs might be a vapour, blowing where they listed," he describes their use of the vastness of the desert and their superior mobility to foil their enemies. His account possesses considerable interest and importance because the same strategy has been used in later campaigns. A major portion of his essay is reprinted in the 1958 edition, and it remains a dazzling, and in many ways, a definitive exposition of guerrilla tactics. In view of subsequent events in Indo-China, Algeria, and Laos, Lawrence's observation on the ultimate effect of such methods is quite prophetic:

> Rebellions can be made by 2% active in striking force and 98% passively sympathetic. . . . Granted mobility, security . . . time and doctrine . . . victory will rest with the insurgents, for the algebraic factors are in the end decisive, and against them perfections of means and spirit struggle quite in vain.

The exhaustive treatment of World War I was a significant feature of the fourteenth edition; but when World War II occurred, it was impossible to supply the same comprehensive coverage because of the limited space available. When the war was over, no attempt was made to carry through a complete revision of the *Encyclopaedia*'s contents, so that the military events of World War II are covered only by a few general survey articles. There are no entries on individual campaigns or battles, such as Stalingrad, Guadalcanal and El Alamein, or the great naval actions in the Pacific at Leyte Gulf, Midway and the Solomon Islands—yet ten pages are devoted to Jutland and eight pages to the Marne.

While some scholars endeavor to provide a comprehensive synthesis of the past, others investigate particular facts or special subjects to eliminate the hearsay, errors and bias of an earlier generation. An encyclopedia must keep abreast of these specialized investigations, as well as broader surveys, in order to reflect modern scholarship. Unfortunately, however, this ideal is sometimes honored in principle rather than in practice.

It is a melancholy experience to observe the ease with which reputable writers can excuse the violent deeds committed by church or state. This frailty is disturbing in any work, but it is particularly serious in an encyclopedia because of the popular belief that its facts are truly facts. A painful example is the article on Spain which singles out the Jews as one of the principal factors in the establishment of the Inquisition:

> It was, consequently, a fact of serious political importance that during the anarchy of Henry IV's reign (1454–75) the Jews gained great power and influence. They might compel—sometimes by means of their usury—their debtors to renounce the Christian religion; and Marranos (baptized Jews) often preserved their old religious faith in secret.

During the Middle Ages, the Jews were a small minority living in the midst of a hostile population. As aliens, they were under constant pressure to abandon their religion, and their resistance angered clerical fanatics. The charge that they employed "usury" to gain converts was one of those inflammatory accusations, like ritual murder, that was used to incite their enemies. The article on the Inquisition, which is more accurate historically, reminds us that in Spain "massacres *en masse* and forced baptisms were carried out, instigated by the clergy." Zealous Christians employed force and terror to encourage conversion; and once baptized, Jews would be condemned as heretics if they dared to return to the faith of their fathers. These efforts created a host of *Conversos* (New Christians) who occupied all ranks of Spanish society. When the *Britannica* asserts that Jews were busy converting Christians and adds they might compel their debtors to renounce their religion by means of usury, it supplies an ominous note to a piece of twisted history that will not be lost on modern readers.

The article on Spain is not content to fix the cause of the Inquisition on the Jews—it seeks to exonerate this institution by declaring:

> The familiars of the Inquisition, exercising ceaseless vigilance in the remotest corners of Spain, may be fittingly compared with the justices of the peace who did so much to uphold the throne of Tudor England. . . . It cannot be denied that the Inquisition was guilty of abuses and cruelties in the course of its long history, but it was no more unjust or inhumane than most other courts of the Europe of its day.

This attempt to justify an evil institution is refuted by the article on the Inquisition which reports, "Commerce and industry were rapidly paralyzed by this odious regime of suspicion." It records that the accused were all assumed to be guilty, and that they were secretly tried by individuals who acted both as prosecutor and judge. Whenever the usual methods failed, torture was applied to extract confessions.

In the entire history of the Spanish Inquisition, not a single case of a complete acquittal has been discovered. Those who fell into its hands were doomed. If they were fortunate, their property was confiscated, but if they refused to admit their guilt, they were imprisoned, and even executed. These are a few of the reasons why the Inquisition has become a hateful name to all those who value individual liberty and the rights of man.

As an instrument of coercion and oppression, the Inquisition casts a dark shadow over the history of the Catholic Church. Yet it was founded initially in the belief that the soul of the individual was a precious possession that must be saved from the danger of eternal damnation. If torture was applied, it was used in the hope of eliciting a response from the accused. Pain was not its purpose and death was not its goal. It was only in the twentieth century that human extermination and mass murder became instruments of national policy. This ominous development is largely neglected by the *Britannica*. The entry on Concentration Camps in the 1958 edition occupies only eight lines and simply notes, "The Nazi regime used them in peace and war." For further information, readers are directed—"*see* SOUTH AFRICAN WAR, 1899–1902."

The article on National Socialism ignores the violence and bloodshed that marked the final years of Nazi rule in Europe. Instead it concentrates on the early history of National Socialism before Hitler assumed power. It speaks in vague terms about the Party's "Anti-Judaism," but says nothing about the liquidation of European Jewry during the war. There is nothing about the dark reign of terror which comprised the closing chapter of the Third Reich when all Europe suffered under German occupation, and the Gestapo became a synonym for wickedness and brutality. The article glosses over the grim consequences of a political movement that began by exalting the Aryan race and the philosophy of *Deutschland über Alles*. It is not difficult to explain why these matters are neglected. The article on National Socialism was written during the war before the Nazi harvest of misery and suffering was complete. When it first appeared, the latest reference in its bibliography was 1941; and after the war, despite the lurid evidence given at the Nuremberg trials and the mass of captured German documents revealing the depths of Nazi depravity, no attempt was made to recast this inadequate entry. Instead it was revised by inserting a few references in the bibliography—and a few sentences in the text that ironically neglect German atrocities by stating: "National Socialism under Hitler's leadership ended thus in complete failure; the national socialist Reich ended in total catastrophe after 12 years' existence."

Lord Acton once insisted in his lectures that a strong man with the dagger should not be followed by a weak man with a sponge who wipes out the crime. He felt "the great achievement of history is to develop, perfect and arm conscience," and he asked his fellow historians "to suffer no man and no cause to escape the undying penalty which history has the power to inflict on wrong." His request was made before the deeds of the twentieth century were to provide examples of terror spread across a continent, when evil was to become an instrument of national policy, and crime was to be executed on a scale so vast it can neither be explained nor understood by men who believe in the inexorable progress of law and order. For the historian who believes that history is *Quidquid aguni homines*—"Whatsoever things men do"—these events can hardly escape scrutiny and reflection because they raise profound questions about man's guilt and responsibility. Yet here, as in so many other important topics, the *Encyclopaedia* fails to meet the moral challenge posed by contemporary events.

Although the article on Anti-Semitism is eight pages long, it allots only a single page to the systematic destruction of European Jewry. Separate sections trace the history of anti-Semitism in individual countries, such as Hungary and Poland, but they ignore the period of mass extermination by skipping the years 1941–45. This momentous era is discussed in a brief factual résumé that recounts some of the statistics relating to Nazi genocide, without examining the subject in any depth. It concludes by describing Christian efforts to save Jewish lives, and these acts of heroism are emphasized, considering the limited space available, but no effort is made to present the other side of the picture. If some individuals attempted to aid the Jews, others were eager to assist in their destruction. An honest account should record how Hungarians and Ukrainians joined in pogroms in German-occupied territory, and report how Poles frequently blackmailed Jews hiding from the Gestapo. Such facts are mentioned in the essay on the Jews, but they are neglected in the article on Anti-Semitism which declares:

Not all opposition to Nazi anti-Jewish excesses was crushed, however. Even in Germany, many Jews owed their lives to the help of their Christian neighbours who sheltered them or their children. There were Protestants and Roman Catholics who consistently opposed Nazism. . . .

Nothing is said about the action of the German chemical industry which supplied the cyanide and Zyklon B gas used in the extermination camps; nothing is said about the complicity of industrialists who built factories near concentration camps where forced labor was readily available; and nothing is said about the army of slave laborers employed during the war under subhuman conditions in the Krupp factories whose industrial empire is still in the possession of the Krupp family.

Any effort to explore the relation of the Christian world to the fate of the Jews must consider the action of the Allied Powers. In 1939 the British government sealed the gates of Palestine by issuing a White Paper barring further immigration into the Holy Land. As late as 1943, when the Nazi policy of liquidating the Jews was well known in Allied capitals, Cordell Hull, the American Secretary of State, was attempting to convince other countries such as Madagascar, Ecuador and the Dominican Republic to accept Jewish refugees. To talk only of those who aided the Jews, while neglecting the others, is to look out into the darkness of recent history and report only flashes of heroism while ignoring the mass of suffering, cruelty and indifference.

Conventional ideas about the goodness of man and the triumph of reason are inadequate in describing the fate of the Jews. This is ignored by the article on Anti-Semitism which offers reassuring sentiments of Christian brotherhood and compassion that will comfort those who wish to find something positive in these melancholy events. But the true facts are of another order. To take only a single example: captured German documents and testimony at the Nuremberg trials indicate that the Nazi plan of exterminating the Jewish population was developed only gradually. The decision to introduce "the final solution" of the Jewish question was made during the summer of 1941, when it became obvious that no country would accept large-scale immigration from German-occupied Europe. The problems of guilt and responsibility cannot be easily unraveled in dealing with the monumental crimes of the Nazi regime, because the very magnitude of their deeds involved statesmen in other countries who observed their action and did nothing. A small illustration may suffice.

In December, 1941, a group of 760 Jewish refugees managed to escape from Rumania aboard a converted yacht. The British Colonial Office, however, refused to allow the refugees to enter Palestine, and the Turkish government would not permit them to remain in Turkey. Their overloaded ship, the *Struma*, was towed from the harbor of Istanbul, and the following day it struck a mine and sank with its passengers in the Black Sea. This ill-fated episode stirred public opinion. In reply to Parliamentary critics, Harold Macmillan, who was then Colonial Under-Secretary, issued an official statement in the House of Commons:

> His Majesty's Government greatly deplores the tragic loss of life which occurred in the disaster. . . . His Majesty's Government earnestly hopes that such a tragedy will not occur again. It does not lie in their power, however, amid the dangers and uncertainties of war to give any guarantee, nor can they be party to any measures which would undermine the existing policy regarding illegal immigration to Palestine, in view of the wider issues involved.

The *Britannica* fails to note or even hint that the Allied Powers were unwilling to take any action in behalf of the Jews. Thus, by emphasizing some facts and neglecting others, it provides a misleading account of the extermination of the Jews.

Hegel once remarked that history is the slaughtering bench of humanity, and his aphorism has become a grim truth in our time. Nazism demonstrated the pernicious effect of the totalitarian state based on propaganda and coercion, and its legacy has not disappeared. The questions raised by its reign of terror still persist: How was it possible for a tiny band of political adventurers to gain the overwhelming allegiance of the German people, and why were men at all levels ready to follow Hitler's mad dreams even into the abyss of national destruction? To what extent was the German worship of obedience and authority responsible for the excesses of its leaders? What protection is there for the private citizen when the machinery of government is seized by a small group of men and employed as an instrument of force and terror? How secure, indeed, is freedom in modern society? Such questions are still relevant and disturbing. Surely any treatment of recent German history must depict not only the crimes of Nazism, but also the historical conditions that made this movement possible. These requirements are not met by the *Encyclopaedia*'s survey article on Germany. More than ten thousand words are devoted to the events of 1933–45, but there is little attempt to explore the evils of Nazism or to comprehend the nightmare that seized Germany for twelve years. The Nazi regime is described as a "totalitarian police state," but its monumental crimes are neither examined nor discussed. One paragraph is allotted to the treatment of the Jews. It states:

> . . . Jews were restricted to a ghetto-like existence until the war when they were systematically put to death in different extermination camps. Altogether in German-occupied Europe, out of a total of 8,300,000 Jews, 6,000,000 were so killed or died of starvation and disease.

There is no endeavor to explain how these events came to pass, or indeed, how they were possible. After all, they did not occur in the barren steppes of Central Asia or the jungles of South America; they took place in the heart of Europe amid a people who boasted of their culture and learning, under the auspices of a government that was enthusiastically supported by its citizens and whose malevolent acts were inflicted on so many people that they cannot be dismissed merely as the work of a small group of criminals and psychopaths.

The article on Germany devotes seven pages to the history

of the Nazi era, but its wartime atrocities are limited to a single paragraph. It notes that German economic exploitation of occupied Europe was ruthless, and it reports:

> At Mauthausen, one of the extermination camps in Austria, close to 2,000,000 people, mostly Jews, were exterminated between 1941 and 1945, at Oswiecim (Auschwitz) in Poland, 2,500,000 were executed in gas chambers, while another 500,000 died from starvation and disease.

There is no comment on these acts, and there is no effort to relate them to the nature of the Nazi regime. Indeed the article on Germany says nothing about the International Military Tribunal which was convened in Nuremberg after the war to try major Nazi leaders for crimes against humanity.

Robert H. Jackson in his opening statement at the Nuremberg trials said, "History does not record a crime ever perpetrated against so many victims or ever carried out with such calculated cruelty." Yet there is no account of the Nuremberg trials in the *Encyclopaedia* and no description of Nazi atrocities. There is no map to show how Nazi terror spread across Europe from the early political concentration camps at Dachau and Buchenwald, deep in the heart of Germany, to the giant death factories at Auschwitz, Maidanek and Tremblinka in Poland. There are no photographs of the twisted emaciated bodies, the mass graves and the piles of shoes left behind by those who perished. There is no effort to translate bare numbers into realities—for those who died, died as individuals and not as ciphers in a ledger book of genocide. It may be natural that Germans should wish to shield their eyes from the crimes which were committed in the name of a greater and more glorious Germany, but why should such reticence be practiced by the *Encyclopaedia Britannica*?

An effective examination of contemporary history must deal with grave moral issues—for if the twentieth century has witnessed the triumph of science and technology, it has as a corollary seen the growth of awesome means of mass destruction that threaten the very basis of civilization. Such developments are usually avoided, or treated in a very superficial manner in the *Britannica*.

One of the most ominous events of World War II was the dropping of atomic bombs on Hiroshima and Nagasaki. Two brief paragraphs in the article on Atomic Energy dispose of this fateful topic. They merely note that 66,000 people were killed at Hiroshima and 39,000 died at Nagasaki—and this information is repeated in the seventy-five-page survey of World War II which allots only two short paragraphs to the subject. There is no discussion of the decision to use the atomic bomb against a civilian population, and there are no photographs of the ruins of Hiroshima and Nagasaki.

A brief résumé is given of the subsequent development of the hydrogen bomb, but the wider significance of these new weapons is not evaluated. Yet the subject of nuclear warfare has been of deep international concern for more than a decade. Surely some attempt should be made to communicate the far-reaching effects of atomic weapons on international diplomacy and the balance of power. Ironically, Norman Cousins and Adlai Stevenson, who are on the *Britannica*'s Board of Editors, have repeatedly warned the public of the imminent dangers of nuclear destruction, but their persuasive arguments have had little influence on the *Encyclopaedia*'s coverage.

Even the casualty figures presented may be questionable since they exclude military personnel. In particular, the presence of 70,000 Japanese soldiers in Hiroshima is ignored. Although the number of deaths caused by the atomic bomb at Hiroshima will probably never be known exactly, Japanese sources estimate that about 200,000 were killed, rather than the 66,000 reported by the *Britannica*. In the case of Nagasaki, where more accurate figures are available, Japanese sources set the total number of deaths at 74,000 (not 39,000). It is interesting in this connection that the 1947 edition carried an article on the Atomic Bomb which reported only ten thousand people killed at Nagasaki. Such inaccurate figures may be due to carelessness, but the failure to discuss the bombing of Hiroshima and Nagasaki seems motivated by a desire to avoid an unpleasant subject—one that might be painful to Americans who would be reminded that the destruction of these cities was the result of a decision made by a small group of men in Washington.

The *Encyclopaedia*'s blindness to moral issues is demonstrated by the article on Bacteriological Warfare which opens with the chilling observation:

> Biological warfare—often referred to as germ warfare, bacteriological warfare or BW—represents another attempt to examine and control the forces of nature for the use of civilization. . . .

The article then examines the possibility of employing germs as an instrument of war, and its enthusiastic tenor is illustrated by the remark that "biological warfare, in a certain sense, can be considered to be aiding nature in the spread of disease and germs. . . ."

Although war has long been considered a scourge of mankind, this is not obvious in the *Britannica*. It presents comprehensive surveys of World War I and II that treat military developments in great detail, but disregard the devastation and suffering that followed in their wake. There are no photographs showing the destructive consequences of war; instead there are exhaustive military reports of individual campaigns and battles. This gray factual approach, so neutral and lifeless, is hardly adequate in rendering the varied scenes of human history. It may enable entries to speak in a low and muted voice, in which the facts are discreetly organized so that the lurid but true colors of history are obliterated. It may insure that no sensibility will be shocked, and no eye horrified by the outrages of the past—but it reduces history to a dry chronicle of events from which human feelings and emotions have been eliminated.

This shallow approach to modern history is demonstrated in the 1958 edition by the article on the city of Dresden. It contains an elaborate description of the city, as well as a series of photographs of leading landmarks, but these sites no longer exist. The article declares, "There was a good deal of fighting in the streets during 1919," but neglects to mention the wholesale destruction of the city during World War II. Ironically, however, the entry on Fire reports: "In the closing days of World War II, Dresden was subjected to air attack which probably dwarfed all previous attacks on German cities. No detailed evaluation of damage was published but estimated deaths of 300,000 . . . suggest it was the greatest fire of World War II."

The *Encyclopaedia*'s inability to deal with the consequences of war or the events at Hiroshima and Nagasaki raises a disturbing question about its reliability and authority. If the *Britannica* slights momentous issues such as the dangers of nuclear warfare or the crimes of National Socialism, if it does not provide an adequate account of major historical periods such as the Renaissance and the Middle Ages, if it offers an elaborate exercise in clerical apologetics in treating the Jesuits, or attempts to defend the evil practices of the Inquisition, can one trust its judgment and opinion on other subjects?

[13]

Knowledge
and Public Policy

POLITICAL programs are conditioned by intellectual doctrines. This point was forcefully expressed by John Maynard Keynes when he wrote: "Practical men, who believe themselves to be quite exempt from any intellectual influences, are usually the slaves of some defunct economist. Madmen in authority, who hear voices in the air, distill their frenzy from some academic scribbler of a few years back."

An encyclopedia, in surveying politics and the social sciences, can illuminate the interaction between abstract ideas and concrete events, and show how political actions have been influenced by philosophical beliefs and recent historical experience. Thus Herbert Hoover was unable to cope with the Depression because he believed in the nineteenth-century ideals of individual enterprise and laissez faire. He could not take the bold steps required to check the breakdown of the American economic system because he was trapped by a set of ideas no longer relevant to modern conditions. The *Britannica* does not discuss this failure in its biography of Hoover because it devotes only a few paragraphs to his presidential career and ignores the extensive literature dealing with his administration. This negligence is not an accident. The article on Franklin D. Roosevelt was written twenty-five years ago by Allan Nevins—and it has been reprinted ever since. The only change has been to add two short paragraphs on the presidential elections of 1936, 1940 and 1944. No bibliography accompanies this article—and for information on Roosevelt's second and third terms, readers are directed to the entry on the United States. One might suspect this obsolete notice is retained because FDR is still a controversial figure in certain circles, but this seems rather farfetched since William Benton and Adlai Stevenson are members of the *Britannica*'s Board of Editors. A much simpler explanation is that if the one-and-three-quarter page article on Franklin Roosevelt were expanded to include the events of his second and third terms, it would be necessary to disturb the "classic" five-page essay on Theodore Roosevelt which has been reprinted for thirty years.

If an American is dismayed by the brusque treatment of FDR, what is a Frenchman to think when he discovers there is no entry in 1958 on Charles de Gaulle—but individual notices are assigned to a number of French leaders including Edouard Daladier, Léon Blum, Pierre Laval and Marshal Pétain? If this were an isolated instance, one might excuse it as an oversight. But it is not a unique case.

One of the grave problems of the postwar era has been the emergence of the Cold War and the struggle against communism. Under these conditions, Marxist theory has assumed a special importance because of its influence on the foreign and domestic policies of the Soviet Union. Despite this development, the *Encyclopaedia*'s only treatment of Marxism is in the biography of Karl Marx prepared by the British Socialist, G. D. H. Cole. After outlining some of the basic tenets of the theory he concludes:

> No attempt has been made in this article to criticise or evaluate the Marxist doctrine as a whole. It has been confined to an attempt to state clearly the main outlines of the Marxian

system. . . . In the note below, mention has been made of books both favorable and unfavorable to the Marxian standpoint.

But the most recent book listed (with the title given incorrectly) is *Marx, Lenin and the Science of Revolution* by Max Eastman, published in 1926!

Such negligence is not unusual. The entry on Public International Law goes only as far as the Hague Convention of 1907 —and until 1954 the *Britannica* offered a startling prediction in an article on Pacific Questions:

> One of the most interesting of Pacific Questions is how far Bolshevik Russia will succeed in the Orient. In China its propaganda is probably doomed to failure because of the almost universal peasant-proprietorship.

The 1958 edition contains a long essay on the Far Eastern Problem that reports, "As long as there has been a far eastern problem China has been its center." But this essay stops at the events of World War II and completely ignores the existence of Communist China.

Sometimes old material contains views that are offensive to foreigners. In 1958 a Singapore newspaper editor complained about the article on the Malays which asserted:

> The Malays are indolent, pleasure loving, improvident, fond of bright clothing, of comfort, of ease, and dislike toil exceedingly. They have no idea of money, and little notion of honesty where money is concerned. . . . They are addicted to gambling, and formerly were much given to fighting, but their courage is not high judged by European standards. The sexual morality of the Malays is very lax. . . .

This passage was written by a British colonial official for the eleventh edition, and was retained for almost fifty years. When *Time* magazine (January 19, 1959) asked John V. Dodge, Managing Editor of the *Britannica*, about this passage, his abashed reply was: "I wish to say we are embarrassed by the paragraph you quote. . . . It obviously should have been replaced long ago—and I cannot say why it was not."

On July 28, 1962, the *New Yorker* exclaimed, "Boy, is the

Encyclopaedia Britannica in need of revision!" It announced that its 1960 copy of this compendium records that the Masai, one of the chief tribes of Tanganyika, "are a tall, well-built, slender people with good features," and that it observes:

> The two lower incisors are removed. . . . The warriors wear their hair plaited into queues hanging down the back and over the forehead. . . . Women and old men eat flour and vegetables in addition to the milk, blood and meat which form the staple diet of the tribe. . . . Their weapons are spears . . . clubs and a peculiar sword.

The *New Yorker* then described an interview with a young Masai studying in America whose incisors were intact, whose hair was not long, and who did not drink blood. The student reported that his people are not allowed to carry spears or clubs today except for occasional ceremonial gatherings. "They don't even *make* spears any more," he said. "Our spears now come from Germany."

This is not the only entry in the 1958 edition that might disturb foreigners. The article on the Caribbean Sea states: "The possession and fortification of the Panama Canal has, as the much-quoted phrase expresses it, extended the southern border of the United States to the Canal." The article presents an elaborate defense of American foreign policy in the area by observing:

> Landings of American marines have invariably been in small numbers, and on the ground of protection of American lives and property. . . . The system has been declared paternalistic, but the standing of United States officials is always maintained in the most rigorous etiquette, and the position of decision and immense power wielded by these representatives of Washington are entirely the gift of the countries themselves. . . .

Thirty years ago, when this article first appeared, it was taken for granted that Latin American countries should serve as an outlet for American commercial interests, but today such outspoken "Yankee imperialism" no longer reflects the policy of the United States.

Editors are often reluctant to discard material by prominent figures. An instructive case is George Bernard Shaw's essay on Socialism: Theory and Prospects. It carries an editorial footnote explaining: "This article . . . is presented for its historical interest as the expression of a leading figure in the Socialist movement, although his analysis does not tally at all points with equally widespread notions and practices of Socialist theory." Shaw begins his critique by stating:

> Socialism, reduced to its simplest legal and practical expression, means the complete discarding of the institution of private property by transforming it into public property and the division of the resultant public income equally and indiscriminately among the entire population. . . . In Socialism, private property is anathema and equal distribution of income the first consideration.

The idea that income would be equalized under socialism is not shared by other Socialist thinkers. Marx offered the ideal "From each according to his abilities, to each according to his needs"; and Socialists have generally recognized that it would be neither feasible nor desirable to divide all income equally. This, however, does not deter GBS from presenting some of his own eccentric ideas on socialism. His essay, written in the 1920's, contains some of the anti-democratic sentiments which were to become a prominent feature of his closing years. He announces: "Democracy, or votes for everybody, does not produce constructive solutions of social problems; nor does compulsory schooling help much." He then declares:

> It is an historic fact, recurrent enough to be called an economic law, that Capitalism, which builds up great civilizations, also wrecks them if persisted in beyond a certain point. It is easy to demonstrate on paper that civilization can be saved and immensely developed by, at the right moment, discarding Capitalism and changing the private property profiteering state into the common property distributive state.

And Shaw concludes that a stable Socialist state will be impossible until "the two main tenets of Socialism—abolition of private property . . . and equality of income have taken hold of the people as religious dogmas."

Such views originally possessed a wide interest because they emanated from a famous playwright and intellectual gadfly, but they are hardly an adequate description of the theory and prospects of socialism today.

The desire of editors to "puff up" their product with famous names has encouraged them to retain "classic" articles for many years. Some of these essays may be valuable contributions, but they prevent scholars from furnishing a fresh account of important subjects. Whenever an article possesses appeal for more than a generation, it should be regarded as a "classic" belonging to the history of the subject, rather than as current scholarship. Fundamentally an encyclopedia should be a vehicle of contemporary learning, since there are few subjects that cannot be illuminated by fresh information.

The *Britannica*'s negligence in dealing with significant social problems may be seen in the article on Birth Control which reflects a point of view fashionable during the 1930's. It stresses that "the poorest and least successful families, commonly handicapped in health and education as well as economic resources, produce and rear more than their proportion of children." Then, after citing a number of studies, it notes: "The story is almost invariably the same; it is the successful members of the more industrialized and supposedly advanced populations who seem headed for extinction for lack of fruitful breeding." This view of birth control antedates the "population explosion" and the sharp rise in population after World War II. The antiquated character of the article is obvious when it predicts:

> In the United States all statistical studies of birth rates and population trends indicate that this country is likely to reach a population of approximately 160,000,000 between 1960 and 1980, followed by a decline in numbers.

Despite this pessimistic prophecy, the 1960 census reported that the population of the United States had reached 180 million and is increasing at the rate of three million a year.

The essay on Slavery maintains: "Liberia is controlled by American Negroes who have little in common with the indigenous population." The latest information in the essay is that "in Aug. 1937 the Government informed the Slavery Committee (of the League of Nations) that slavery does not exist in Liberia." Clearly this section was written some time ago—and a closer examination reveals that the bulk of this thirteen-page essay has been taken from the eleventh edition. This may explain why it examines in great detail efforts to suppress the slave trade, but devotes only a single page to the institution of slavery in the United States which has left such a deep impression on American racial attitudes. In 1911, when the *Britannica* was a British work, it may have been natural to slight the effects of slavery in the United States, but it hardly seems justified in a contemporary American reference work.

Racial problems in the United States have attracted wide attention because of the emergence of independent nations in Asia and Africa. This change, however, is not reflected in the article on Lynching in the 1958 edition which maintains:

> After reconstruction, with the increase of Negro crimes, came an increase of lynchings, because of prejudice, the fact that for some time after reconstruction the governments were weak (especially in the districts where Negroes outnumbered the whites), the fact that Negroes nearly always shielded criminals of their own race against whites, and because of the occurrence of the crime of rape by Negro men upon white women.

This passage does not rest on facts, but is merely an attempt to justify Southern mob violence. It was written in 1910 by a dean of Vanderbilt University, a Southern white school. Although the article was revised within the last decade to include recent statistics on lynching, the only change made in this biased passage was to alter its punctuation and capitalize the word "Negro."

Three-fourths of the 3,693 people lynched in the United States between 1889 and 1929 were Negroes. Of this number, 17 percent were accused of rape and an additional 7 percent of attempted rape. Needless to say, in many cases these charges were unfounded; consequently, there is no basis for citing rape as a major cause of lynching. Gunnar Myrdal in *An American Di-*

lemma explains the prevalence of a sexual element in lynching by observing:

> . . . A mob which makes the accusation of rape is secure against any further investigation, by the broad Southern definition of rape to include all sexual relations between Negro men and white women; and by the psychopathic fears of white women in their contacts with Negro men. The causes of lynching must, therefore, be sought outside the Southern rationalization of "protecting white womanhood."

Occasionally the *Britannica* deals vigorously with social issues. Its essay on Civil Liberties boldly portrays the struggle to maintain free speech in the United States, and its article on Propaganda explains that in totalitarian countries a world of ritual and ceremony is exchanged for discussion, so that current happenings are used as fables about the infallibility of the ruling class.

Such essays may be the exception rather than the rule, but they suggest that a reference work can effectively examine contemporary issues. This goal is explicitly stated in James Harvey Robinson's article on Civilization and Culture, which was originally prepared for the fourteenth edition:

> This encyclopedia itself is a description of civilization for it contains the story of human achievement in all its bewildering developments. It shows what men during hundreds of thousands of years have been learning about themselves, their world and the creatures which share it with them.

Our language, laws and cultural patterns are products of individuals living together in society. This is a significant aspect of human history. Anthropologists have endeavored to discover and understand the operation of these patterns in primitive societies. One of the early motivations of their studies is emphasized in the article on Primitive Economics which states: "An adequate knowledge of the economic organization of a native people is essential before we can govern them, trade with them, utilize their labour, secure their co-operation in political affairs, or preserve them from the worst effects of contact with white civilization." These practical motives have stimulated investigation of primitive life and encouraged anthropologists to seek out different cultures before they are submerged by outside influences. Unfortunately the resulting expansion of knowledge is neglected because many articles in this area—such as Matriarchy, Polygyny, Primitive Trade, Primitive Labor, Primitive Religion and Primitive Land Tenure—have been reprinted since 1929.

The survey article on Anthropology emphasizes physical anthropology—the study of the physical characteristics of various races and groups. Although it contains separate sections on culture and society, and culture and personality, the article does not mention the work of Margaret Mead or Ruth Benedict whose analysis of the patterns and style of life of primitive groups have exerted a deep influence on anthropological research. Paradoxically, however, a separate entry on Social Anthropology notes their important contributions.

The *Encyclopaedia*'s reverence for outmoded material is illustrated by Malinowski's long essay on Marriage, which first appeared in 1929. Although he concludes with the remark, "Marriage like most problems of anthropology is ceasing to be a subject of speculation and becoming one of empirical research," his article has not been revised to include the wealth of anthropological data accumulated during the last generation. Inevitably, despite Malinowski's pioneering studies in the South Seas, his essay has been superseded by later research. An example is the distinction between the conjugal and consanguine family introduced by Ralph Linton in 1936. In the conjugal family the marriage tie is primary, and the family normally consists of a father and mother raising children; while in the consanguine family, organized about a group of blood relatives, marital ties are secondary to blood relationships. This distinction between the extended, joint or multiple family and the nuclear, primary or simple family is now widely employed—but it is not discussed in Malinowski's article because this classification was introduced after his article was written.

Many significant areas in sociology are neglected in the 1958 edition. There are no articles on Bureaucracy, Ideology, Social

Structure, Mass Communications or the Sociology of Knowledge —and the index fails to reveal further information on these subjects. Yet each of these topics is an active area of social research. The article on the City does not depict its sociological characteristics, but simply cites legal definitions used in England and America. The brief notice on Demography defines the subject as "that branch of statistics that deals with the life-conditions of people"; but it neglects to explain the significance of these statistics in clarifying shifts in population, industrial development and economic activity.

Examples of neglect can be found in other areas as well. Advances in psychology and psychoanalysis have thrown fresh light on the motivation of historical figures and political leaders. The ideas of Freud and other investigators have provided a deeper understanding of the emotional factors affecting political behavior, and have illuminated the role of irrational impulses in molding social change. The *Britannica*, however, does not effectively exploit these insights.

Its essay on Character attempts to explain the psychological basis of human behavior without employing the ideas of psychoanalysis or other schools of psychology. It begins by noting: "Instincts, habits, impulses, desires, emotions, sentiments all belong to it"; and then asks:

> But what relation do they bear to one another? What part is the part of character that has to be controlled and what is its controlling part? Whence come those things that are called "principles" of conduct, and "ideals," and the multitude of "qualities of character"—courage, steadfastness, sincerity, tolerance, generosity, patience and honesty and their opposites?

The article answers these questions with a simple reply—"We do not know." It then vainly attempts to examine different aspects of human character without referring to the name or work of a single psychologist.

A similar failure occurs in the essay on Personality which treats the views of different investigators in a verbose fashion.

Instead of critically discussing rival theories, it endeavors to accept the contributions of all schools without evaluating their claims in the light of existing evidence and informed professional opinion.

Certain individuals have left a deep mark on the social sciences and exerted a profound influence on the outlook of social critics and men of power. We recognize this fact when we identify a body of ideas with Marxism, Freudian psychology or Keynesian economics. An encyclopedia should describe the work of such major figures, whose names and concepts have become an essential part of the intellectual atmosphere of our time. Sometimes their achievements are recognized in survey articles, but are slighted in biographical entries. The article on Sociology states, "Of the pioneer sociologists, perhaps the most influential in terms of the impact of their work on other sociologists were Durkheim, Weber and Cooley." Despite this judgment, there is no article on Cooley, and the entry on Durkheim is a superficial notice that fails to describe his fundamental studies of suicide and social disorganization. The biography of Max Weber merely lists the titles of his works, without discussing his analysis of Western and Far Eastern religions, or his searching examination of the bureaucratic mind. It neglects his analysis of charismatic leadership and his celebrated thesis that the Protestant ethic was a powerful force in the evolution of capitalism. Therefore anyone who runs across the name of Weber or Durkheim in his reading and turns to the *Britannica* for enlightenment will hardly be satisfied.

Perhaps the most flagrant case is the biographical notice on Sigmund Freud. The main section of the article traces his career to 1913; everything after that date is summed up in exactly seven lines, which record his election to the Royal Society in 1936, the publication of *Moses and Monotheism* and his death in London in 1939. The entire bibliography consists of four references: Freud's *Collected Works* in German, and three articles that appeared in British medical journals a few months after his death. The article on Freud was prepared by Ernest

Jones a generation ago. It was revised in 1940 by condensing the article and adding a few new lines. But the added material is quite defective, since Freud's speculation that Moses was an Egyptian is described in the following fashion: "In 1939 he published *Moses and Monotheism* in which he set out to psychoanalyze anti-Semitism."

In a similar fashion, John Maynard Keynes receives a brief, superficial notice, although his economic ideas have revolutionized the fiscal and tax policies of governments seeking to control the violent oscillations of the business cycle. His biography reports: "In his hands economics became less a descriptive science defending the *status quo*, more an instrument of social control to achieve such broad objectives as maximum national income, full employment and international monetary stabilization." But the exact nature of these contributions is not explained in this article or elsewhere in the *Encyclopaedia*. Yet their impact is noted in other entries. The essay on Unemployment states:

> Lord Keynes made an attempt to synthesize from all these ideas a comprehensive theory which would satisfactorily explain the economic factors contributing to the business cycle. His *General Theory of Employment, Interest and Money* (1936) is a landmark in economic theory, and economic thinking since the publication of his great book has been influenced by his ideas.

Although Keynes' economic remedies have provided an effective means of shoring up the capitalist system, he was not fond of its conventional wisdom. He sharply questioned the notion that "free competition built man" and he scorned the belief that state interference in economic matters would "retard the onward movement . . . by which we ourselves have risen like Aphrodite out of the primeval slime of Ocean." Despite his energetic program for stimulating consumer demand by means of deficit spending during economic recessions, he had a rather low opinion of business morality. In 1932 he wrote: "The Capitalist is a fair-weather friend. As soon as the storm passes, he abandons the duties of a navigator and even sinks the boats that might carry him to safety, by his haste to push his neighbor off and himself in." The following year he recorded:

> The decadent international but individualistic capitalism in whose hands we find ourselves is not a success. It is not intelligent, it is not beautiful, it is not just, it is not virtuous—and it doesn't deliver the goods. In short, we dislike it and are beginning to despise it. But when we consider what to put in its place, we are extremely perplexed.

Keynes shifted the emphasis of economics from the problems of production to those of demand by emphasizing the importance of consumption, overproduction and unemployment. Before his time, classical economists believed that supply created its own demand—and they did not anticipate the possibility that production could outstrip the purchasing power of consumers. This difficulty was clearly recognized by Keynes, who insisted that the economy must be stimulated by government spending. When his *General Theory* first appeared, reviewers did not grasp its significance; but within a few years it became the most influential work in economics since Marx's *Das Kapital*. It provided a rational justification for deficit spending and furnished a concrete program for governments faced with mass unemployment and economic stagnation. Although his book is written in a technical style inaccessible to laymen, his ideas have exerted a profound influence on professional colleagues. Keynes realized the importance of his work. He told George Bernard Shaw, "When my theory has been duly assimilated and mixed with politics and feelings and passions, I can't predict what the final upshot will be in its effects on action and affairs. But there will be a great change."

In an earlier era, a distinguished Englishman like Lord Keynes would have received a long biography. But such coverage rarely occurs today because of the shortage of space, so that major intellectual figures are often assigned brief entries. The total space devoted to the biographies of Freud, Durkheim, Weber and Keynes in the 1958 edition is little more than one page, but six pages are allotted to the biography of Auguste Comte, one of the early founders of sociology. This disparity has a simple explanation. The article on Comte was reprinted from an even longer essay by John Morley which appeared in the ninth edition. Morley supplied an interesting sketch of Comte's early life as well as a detailed critique of his philosophical ideas. He described Comte's idolization of Benjamin Franklin and his attempt to imitate his behavior by quoting an enthusiastic letter written to a friend:

> I seek to imitate the modern Socrates not in talents, but in way of living. You know that at five-and-twenty he formed the design of becoming perfectly wise, and that he fulfilled his design. I have dared to undertake the same thing, though I am not yet twenty.

This revealing passage has been deleted from Morley's essay, as well as his description of Comte's early career. Nevertheless, the article records that John Stuart Mill and his friends raised a subscription to finance Comte's studies—and relates Comte's refusal to read any newspapers, reviews or scientific transactions once he had gathered his basic stock of material because he did not wish to be influenced by contemporary events or ideas. Morley's essay, despite its condensed form, presents a comprehensive account of Comte's theories and their influence on later critics. Yet he confesses at the end of his essay:

> Seriously to examine an encyclopaedic system, that touches life, society and knowledge at every point, is evidently beyond the compass of an article such as this. There is in every chapter a whole group of speculative suggestions, each of which would need a long chapter to itself to elaborate or to discuss.

The limited horizons of personal experience and the simplified images of the mass media fail to provide an adequate description of the political and social developments affecting our lives. Information obtained from newspapers and television must be supplemented by deeper sources of knowledge. Encyclopedias can be useful for this purpose if they present the principles and insights of the social sciences and show how they provide a better understanding of contemporary problems. In doing so, they can bolster democratic processes that should depend on the existence of an enlightened public opinion, rather than on the arbitrary dictates of a small ruling class—and therefore encyclopedias can contribute to the ideals of a free society.

[14]

Fanciful Zoology

THERE has always been a widespread interest in animal life, and many authors have sought to capitalize on this by preparing popular surveys of natural history. Two hundred years ago, Oliver Goldsmith wrote a book on the subject that enjoyed a great vogue. He stated that the purpose of his work was "to drag up the obscure and gloomy learning of the cell to open inspection; to strip it from its garb of austerity, and to shew the beauties of that form, which only the industrious and the inquisitive have been hitherto permitted to approach."

When Dr. Johnson heard of the project, he remarked: "Goldsmith, Sir, will give us a very fine book upon the subject; but if he can distinguish a cow from a horse, that, I believe, may be the extent of his knowledge of natural history."

In the past, it was difficult to supply an accurate account of animal life because of the confusion between fact and fable. Pliny's *Natural History* included many legendary creatures and fabulous tales, and medieval bestiaries continued this tradition.

They catalogued the inhabitants of the animal kingdom and described their habits, but their material was usually based on older books, rather than fresh observations. They sought to inculcate moral lessons from the Scriptures, and usually repeated the colorful stories of earlier travelers and naturalists.

A more critical attitude arose during the Renaissance, when men began to question traditions inherited from antiquity. The new spirit was expressed by Thomas Browne in 1646 when he published his *Pseudodoxia Epidemica,* or *Enquires into Very Many received Tenets and Commonly presumed Truths,* which, he said, when examined prove but vulgar and common errors. His book attempted to meet the "Goliath and Giant of Authority" by an appeal to experience, and it was inspired by Bacon's vision of a positive science that would dispel ancient errors by experiment and logical analysis.

Browne attacked many myths and legends and endeavored to explain their widespread popularity. One reason, he observed, "is the Credulity of men . . . whereby men often swallow falsities for truths, dubieties for certainties, feasibilities for possibilities, and things impossible for possibilities themselves." Another cause is the "neglect of Enquiry . . . rather believing, than going to see; or doubting with ease and *gratis,* than believing with difficulty and purchase."

Browne devoted a great deal of space to erroneous beliefs in natural history. Among the ideas he criticized were that goat's milk will soften a diamond; that the chameleon feeds on air; that the urine of toads is poisonous; and that the bear licks her newborn cubs into proper shape.

Today it may seem easy to dismiss such tales because observation, rather than authority, has become the final judge in dealing with the natural world. Yet strange things do occur in nature. The blood of tunicates contains concentrated sulphuric acid, as well as oxides of the rare element vanadium. The horned toad squirts blood from its eye when it is excited; and the male hornbill walls up its mate in a hollow log and feeds her through an opening while she is incubating her eggs. Therefore one cannot always recognize fanciful stories. The *Britannica* records:

There is a family (Pygidiidae) of tiny, slender degenerate catfishes, which are parasitic, and attach themselves to other fish or animals like leeches. One of these, the candiru (*Vandellia*), which commonly lives inside the gill cavity of other fishes . . . has the evil reputation of at times entering the urethra of unwary bathers.

Although these attacks sound unbelievable, they actually occur. This indicates why it is necessary to secure definite evidence before discounting unusual reports.

Open-mindedness, however, should not be confused with a blind acceptance of old beliefs without critical examination. Pliny stated that camels can go for long periods without water because they store water in special pockets in their stomach. This idea was accepted by Buffon and Cuvier, and it is repeated by many encyclopedias without any further proof. It reappears in the *Britannica*'s essay on the Alimentary Canal, which refers to the "well known water cells" in the camel's stomach. These water cells, however, hold only about four and one-half gallons, whereas a camel may drink in ten minutes as much as twenty gallons, which is rapidly dispersed through the body.

An even less accurate explanation is offered in the entry on the Camel: "Water is stored in the body tissues, chiefly in the hump; little is stored in the stomach." The hump, however, is composed of fatty tissue used as a source of food, and not for storage of water.

The recent researches of Schmidt-Nielsen and his collaborators have explained why the camel can go so long without water. They have shown that the cells of its complex stomach are associated with the digestion of food rather than the storage of water, because these pouches are lined with thousands of glands. They have established that the camel can survive in a desert climate because its fur provides an effective thermal insulation that minimizes the amount of water lost by sweating. In addition, it can survive a water loss equal to 30 percent of its body weight without any ill effects. (In other animals, including man, a water loss of 20 percent is usually fatal because the blood becomes viscous and circulation is impaired.) These physiological findings are not mentioned by the *Britannica* since its article on the Camel was prepared fifty years ago.

Because an encyclopedia is usually prepared by a large number of contributors, it may provide contradictory information on disputed matters. An example is the way in which newborn opossums reach their mother's pouch. Since they are born after a gestation period of only thirteen days and weigh only one two-hundredth of an ounce at the time of birth, it was once difficult for naturalists to understand how such tiny, immature creatures could travel from their mother's cloaca to her pouch. The article Opossum repeats a traditional belief when it records: "At birth the immature and helpless young . . . are placed by the mother in her pouch, where they cling to the nipples by their mouth." The entry on Marsupialia, however, correctly notes:

> In the case of the Virginia opossum, immediately after birth the young animal uses these large fore-limbs and claws in climbing along the under-side of the mother's body from the cloaca to the mammary field, where it attaches itself to one of the teats.

Direct observation has shown that while she is giving birth, the mother licks the hair of her body in a line between the cloaca and her pouch, and the infants make their way along this dampened track of hair without any help from the mother. Since this journey takes only about sixteen seconds, it was not noticed by early investigators who assumed that the mother lifted her minute offspring into the pouch.

The tendency to generalize from limited observation is often a source of error. An illustration is the death march of the lemmings. According to the *Encyclopaedia*:

> The circumstance which has given popular interest to the lemming is that certain districts . . . of Norway and Sweden, where under ordinary conditions they are unknown, are at certain intervals overrun by an army of lemmings. These emigrations, which usually last three or four years . . . are always down toward the sea. . . . The lemmings advance steadily and slowly, regardless of all obstacles, swimming streams

and even lakes of several miles in breadth. . . . None returns and the onward march of survivors never ceases until they reach the sea, into which they plunge and are drowned. . . .

Those that finally perish in the sea, committing what appears to be voluntary suicide, are only acting under the same blind impulse which led them previously to cross shallower pieces of water with safety.

This graphic account has been taken from the 1910 edition, but the bibliography cites a book by Charles Elton published in 1942 which discredits this lurid tale. He points out that a great increase in the number of lemmings every three or four years forces them to leave their mountain habitat in search of food. As a result, they move toward the plains, and therefore toward the sea; but this migration to the lowlands is due to their overpopulation, rather than a blind suicidal impulse. Oddly enough, the *Britannica*'s erroneous account still appears, although it was criticized for its inaccuracy in 1946 by Bergen Evans in his *Natural History of Nonsense*.

Another popular notion is that wolves travel in packs. The *EB* states:

> Except during the summer when the young families of cubs are being separately provided for by their parents, they assemble in troops or packs, and by their combined efforts are able to overpower and kill deer, antelopes and wounded animals of all sizes.

This information is contradicted by the naturalist Ernest Seton who declares that "the ordinary wolf pack seen in the summer and autumn is merely the family under the guidance of the parents, though on rare occasions, two families may unite for a time." Major Seton adds, "The most I ever saw in a band was five." This testimony is confirmed by Vilhjalmur Stefansson who recorded, after studying wolves in their natural habitat, that he had never seen a wolf group larger than a single family, including the parents and cubs. For a number of years, he checked many accounts of wolf packs, but was unable to substantiate a single report. Thus the notion that wolves hunt in large packs belongs to the realm of folklore, just as does the literary idea that wolves may attack and kill human beings.

Such beliefs spring from the desire to impose human characteristics on animal life. The familiar figures of fable and mythology, such as the wily fox, the regal lion and the deadly wolf, reflect an anthropomorphic outlook, which is often accompanied by a willingness to accept fanciful tales of animal behavior. The essay on Fishes says about the stickleback:

> It is now seen that his formidable armature of spines is more for attack than defense. Though not ordinarily a rapid swimmer, when on the war path he shows great speed and dexterity in the water. Battles between males are frequent and sometimes to the death.

This vivid vignette is contradicted by the naturalist Konrad Lorenz who notes that any "fighting" between sticklebacks is only a symbolic demonstration of territorial rights which occurs when an intruder approaches a nest at mating time. In such an encounter, the winner, regardless of the size of the opponents, is almost always the fish that is closest to his nest. Lorenz observes that the report that sticklebacks fight to the death, which occasionally appeared in older acquarium literature, is incorrect because:

> . . . Even a dead stickleback will slip [from] under the sharpest scalpel before one is able to penetrate the tough skin, even in places where it is not reinforced with bony armour. . . . Owing to the extreme toughness of the sticklebacks' skin, no serious wounds can be inflicted in their natural battles which, as compared with those of fighting fish, are absurdly harmless. Of course, in the confined space of a small tank, a stronger stickleback may harry a weaker one to death, but rabbits and turtledoves, in analogous conditions, will do the same thing to each other.

A credulous spirit may explain why certain unusual powers are accepted with a minimum of proof. The *Britannica* asserts:

> The Alaska blackfish (*Dallia pectoris*) is a large-mouthed hungry little fish. . . . It is said to freeze solid in winter, but be as lively as ever when spring thaws it out.

This remarkable ability is reiterated in the 1961 edition of the Merriam-Webster Unabridged Dictionary. It was first described by an explorer in 1886 who stated that blackfish in Alaska "will remain frozen in grass baskets for weeks, and when brought into the house and thawed out will be as lively as ever." He claimed that "the pieces which are thrown to ravenous dogs are eagerly swallowed; the animal heat of the dog's stomach thaws the fish out, whereupon its movements soon cause the dog to vomit it up."

This ability to withstand complete freezing was sharply questioned on physiological grounds as early as 1890, but it was only subjected to a direct test in 1938 by N. A. Borodin of Harvard University. He discoverd that Alaska blackfish could survive a forty-minute exposure at $-20°$, but died after an hour's exposure. Furthermore, his specimens all died after being frozen in water. These observations were repeated in 1953 by Scholander and his collaborators who found that when blackfish are partially frozen, they can survive for a few days, but circulation in the frozen parts is never re-established. If they are completely frozen, rigor mortis ensues. After an extensive series of experiments, they concluded that freezing causes irreversible damage to the tissues and that it is out of the question that the fish as a whole can withstand freezing.

The *Britannica*'s erroneous information is usually the result of its neglect of current knowledge. As a result, it sometimes questions true stories, as well as accepting legendary ones. The current article on the Swift was prepared in 1910. It cautiously states that more observations will be needed to verify whether swifts actually pair in mid-air and spend the night on the wing at great heights. However, recent findings have confirmed both phenomena.

Sometimes ideas that have been discredited as superstitions are shown to have a factual basis, so that wholly denying an ancient belief may be as incorrect as accepting it. The essay on Ornithology declares:

> Another superstition centering around migration has been the supposed hibernation on the part of some birds, a belief that dates back to early times. . . . Aristotle attributed hibernation to the swallow and various other birds, saying that

some individuals became torpid and so passed the winter in the shelter of caves or hollow trees in a state of suspended animation. In later years hibernation was used mainly to explain the disappearance of swifts, swallows and sora rail. . . . In short, though hibernation, or its correlate aestivation, is common among mammals, reptiles, amphibians and even fishes, it has never been proved among birds.

This assertion is no longer true. Edmund Jaeger in 1949 described the hibernation of a poor-will discovered in the Chuckawalla Mountains of the Colorado Desert. He noted that the Hopi Indians call the poor-will, *Hölchko,* "the sleeping one"—and reported that the specimen he examined remained in a torpid state for several months. Subsequent investigators have recorded that hibernation occurs in several species of swifts and hummingbirds, and other birds as well. They have induced hibernation experimentally and found by direct measurement that the body temperature drops by more than 10° C. in this state. Unlike other animals, however, a bird may enter and awake from a torpid state within a few minutes. Thus hummingbirds become dormant every night as a means of conserving their metabolic energy; but in this case, hibernation lasts only a few hours, instead of months.

Encyclopedias are continually faced with the problem of keeping up with current scientific knowledge. Because of the rapid tempo of research, authors can no longer rely on information presented in books, but must search the periodical literature for relevant facts. The growth of knowledge in zoology can be graphically demonstrated. In the middle of the eighteenth century, when Linnaeus published his classification of plants and animals, only 4,400 different species were known. Today by conservative estimate, more than a million animal species are known, and they include more than 750,000 different kinds of insects.

Since many entries on zoology are taken from old editions, they do not take advantage of modern research which has resolved many questions. The article on the Onychophora, a small wormlike arthropod, states:

> The eggs are fertilized internally and it has been stated that the male of the Cape species deposits its spermatozoa on

the surface of the female. Since the uterus is said never to contain spermatozoa, the mode of entrance into the body would be a complete mystery.

This mystery was solved in 1938 when S. M. Manton described how the sperm packets deposited by the male reach the female ovaries. The skin of the female develops an ulcer, and white cells from her blood open a passage through the skin, so that sperm can pass into the body cavity where they can migrate directly to the ovaries.

It may be unreasonable to expect the *Britannica* to be up to date in all areas of zoology, but it should record major advances that have become familiar to laymen. An example is the remarkable "language" used by bees to indicate the location of food, which was first described by Karl von Frisch in 1923. He discovered that, after returning to their hive, foraging bees perform a dance to indicate the location of nectar. If the source is less than a hundred yards away, the bee does a "round dance" in a circular track. But if it is at a greater distance, the bee performs a "tail-wagging" dance by flying in a figure-eight path and waving its tail during the straight portion where the two loops join. The more distant the food, the slower the dance and the more often the tail is wagged. The direction of the food with respect to the sun is indicated by the orientation of the dance. When the sun is obscured by clouds, bees are able to infer the position of the sun from a patch of sky, because they are sensitive to the polarization of light scattered from the sky.

Although Frisch's findings were doubted at first, experimental studies after World War II confirmed the existence of this unusual means of communication. The *Encyclopaedia*'s article on the Bee devotes six pages to beekeeping, but it fails to mention this remarkable discovery. Such lapses are symptomatic of an editorial neglect that makes it hard to accept the set as a reliable authority in the biological sciences.

[15]

The World of Science

A<small>N</small> enormous expansion has occurred in the rate of scientific research during the last two centuries. This increase is reflected in the mounting volume of scientific publication. In 1790, a generation after the *Britannica* was launched, only five periodicals in the world were devoted to biological research. By 1880, when the ninth edition was being issued, the number had reached 235. In 1910, it was 690—and by 1955, there were about 3,500 journals in biology. This number has been doubling about every eighteen years during the last two centuries, and if the present rate of growth is maintained, by 1975 there will be about 7,500 biological research journals publishing half a million articles a year. New journals have appeared even more rapidly in engineering, medicine and agriculture; while in the physical sciences there has been a marked expansion in the size, as well as the number of many existing journals.

The volume of technical publication has become so great that many scientists find it difficult to keep up with progress in their own fields. Each year about 50,000 journals in science and technology are published containing over a million articles. In addition, some 60,000 new scientific books and 100,000 technical reports appear annually, and this number continues to mount. Special journals are devoted to the publication of abstracts—brief résumés of original papers in particular fields. But even abstract journals are becoming unwieldy. *Chemical Abstracts,* issued twice a month, attempts to survey chemistry and its allied fields, which accounts for 20 percent of the scientific literature. It selects articles from eight thousand journals in fifty-two languages; and to cover a single year of research in 1960, its abstracts contained as many words as the entire *Britannica.*

The *Encyclopaedia* has attempted to keep up with this printed avalanche by periodically revising its scientific entries and allocating more space to technical topics. Despite these efforts, however, a good deal of antiquated material appears in the 1958 edition. The article on Mars, prepared in 1929, says nothing about the composition of the Martian atmosphere, or the intriguing question of whether life exists on Mars. The entry on Helium does not describe Helium II, whose remarkable properties were discovered by Kapitza and Allen in 1938; and the entry on Vaporization contains a graph with an experimental point marked "Latest—1928."

Similar lapses take place in dealing with medical subjects. The discussion of Aphasia carries a footnote citing views advanced in 1906—and many articles on comparative anatomy have been taken from the eleventh edition, including the Coelum, Liver, Mouth, Pharynx, Skull and Teeth. As a result, the essay on the Nervous System presents a table which claims to give "a fair idea of the present state of our knowledge of nerve components in the Mammalia"; but this table has been reprinted without change since 1911.

Similar gaps occur in engineering and technology. The article on Power Transmission states, "Cotton ropes are used extensively in transmitting power in factories"; and this outmoded observation is repeated in the entry on Rope and Rope Making. The essay on Hosiery describes the manufacture of stockings, but ignores nylon because it only goes as far as 1940. The latest information on the Airscrew (the propeller) is:

> During 1933 the Hamilton standard came into universal use on the air transport lines of the United States, and the propeller was awarded the Collier trophy for the greatest advancement in aviation during the year.

In a similar fashion, the article on the Strength of Materials reports:

> . . . The literature bearing on the subject of fatigue is now very extensive. Only the merest outline can be given here: the reader is referred to a very clear and complete account by H. J. Gough, *The Fatigue of Metals* (1924).

A separate discussion of the Fatigue of Metals notes, "The importance of an understanding of fatigue phenomena in its relation to industry cannot be over-estimated"; but this entry and the one on the Strength of Materials were not revised for thirty years.

The tempo of technical change makes it difficult to justify such obsolete material. Yet in the 1958 edition, articles appear that are fifty years old including those on Carpentry, Masonry, Glazing and Shaft-Sinking. The entry on Roofs refers to the London Building Act of 1895; and the essay on the Chair concludes with an account of the *art nouveau* school, which flourished between 1895 and 1910, and maintains, "there have been practically no novelties since that time."

Such old material is not confined to minor topics; the treatise on Heat occupies thirty pages, but nine-tenths of its text is taken from the eleventh edition. It contains a graph of the diurnal variations of heat for May, 1895, and cites research on the specific heat of combustion gases dating from 1910. The article hopefully concludes in one of its more recent sections:

> Thus since 1928, a science has developed which might be called properly "molecular engineering. . . ." This promises of yielding a new order of detailed knowledge in the study of the effects of heat in matter.

No further information is provided on this "new order of detailed knowledge"; and if a reader turns to the entry on Band Spectrum, he is erroneously told, "The spectra of even common chemical molecules consisting of more than two atoms are practically unknown."

Robert Hutchins has attempted to defend the *Encyclopaedia* by declaring in the *Columbia Forum*: "One thing can be said with certainty, that is that the *Britannica* reflects modern scholarship." To bolster this claim, Dr. Hutchins refers to the forty Nobel Prize winners who have contributed to the set. This large number, however, proves just the opposite. Forty Nobel Prize winners appear because many of their articles have been reprinted for decades. This is a serious defect because they deal primarily with scientific subjects that rapidly go out of date. In the 1958 set, they include Rayleigh's explanation of why the sky is blue, from the 1911 edition—plus entries by Einstein, Hopkins, Bohr, Rutherford and Michelson from the 1929 edition. In some instances, contributions by Nobel laureates have been retained without change for thirty years. Examples include Adrian on Chronaxie, and Siegbahn on X-ray Spectroscopy. A glaring case of editorial neglect is Sherrington's essay on the Brain, which fails to mention "brain waves" because it was written before this discovery was made public.

The danger of relying on old scientific material is demonstrated by the analysis of the Compton Effect prepared by A. H. Compton who received the Nobel Prize for his discovery of this effect. In discussing the properties of the photon, he asserts:

> It also has a mass, the essential characteristic of matter, its mass being $2.19 \times 10^{-38}\lambda$ grams, where λ is the wave-length of the radiation expressed in centimeters.

Thirty years ago when Compton wrote this article, it was generally believed the photon had a mass; but the relation quoted has been printed incorrectly because it shows a mass dependence proportional to λ, and not $1/\lambda$. In any case, it is now known that the photon possesses a momentum, and not a mass. In discussing the absorption and re-emission of photons, Compton cites a suggestion "made by G. N. Lewis (1926) that the photon is really retained by the atom and does not lose its identity"; but this suggestion does not agree with modern quantum theory. As a result, although the article on the Compton Effect was prepared by its discoverer, it contains serious defects.

Another example is the history of non-Euclidean geometry written by A. N. Whitehead and Bertrand Russell for the eleventh edition. An article in *Science* pointed out that their discussion was defective. Undue prominence was given to Gauss, who never published anything on the subject, and the possibility was mentioned that Gauss may have influenced Lobachevski and Bolyai, despite conclusive evidence that they worked independently. It is rather disconcerting to find these deficiencies in the current edition which reprints Whitehead's and Russell's essay. The only difference is that their treatment of non-Euclidean geometry has been sharply condensed and the initials identifying them as the authors have disappeared. Therefore neither Russell nor Whitehead is listed as a contributor—an omission that seems rather odd considering the editors' penchant for boasting about their Nobel Prize winners.

In 1912 the *Encyclopaedia*'s treatment of psychology was subjected to a detailed analysis by E. B. Titchener in the *American Journal of Psychology*. He observed that many articles in the eleventh edition were taken from earlier editions, and after examining many entries, he concluded, "My general impression, after this survey, is that the new *Britannica* does not reproduce the psychological atmosphere of its day and generation." One example he cited was the account of Weber's Law, which was essentially a reprint from the ninth edition of 1889. This essay appears in the 1958 edition, although it was criticized for its obsolescence and inaccuracy in 1912. It asserts: "In the 'chemical' senses of taste and smell experiments are almost impossible." Yet this statement is contradicted by the article on Smell and Taste which states that experiments have been made on the threshold and differential sensitivity for olfactory materials, as well as for saline and sweet solutions.

Titchener noted in his critique that a great deal of favorable material is presented on spiritualism and psychic phenomena— and this influence persists in the 1958 edition. The entry on Spiritualism by Oliver Lodge reports that a body of careful investigators who founded the Society for Psychical Research in London "have accumulated a great mass of evidence" in favor of spiritualism. He describes the powerful force of "exteriorised protoplasm now generally known as ectoplasm" in the following terms:

> The force exerted by ectoplasm can be quite considerable. For instance a table can be raised completely off the ground; and the weight of a man clambering on the table need not be sufficient to bring it down. The forces have sometimes been measured by spring balances. . . .
>
> In quoting such assertions it is not supposed that they are as yet fully accepted; but they indicate the lines on which the investigation should proceed.

Lodge's rambling, superstitious essay was written a generation ago. Fortunately, there is a separate entry on Psychical Research which is far more critical in character.

Recently C. P. Snow, in a provocative essay, *The Two Cultures,* illustrated the wide gulf separating scientists and humanists by asking how many classicists and men of letters were familiar with entropy and the second law of thermodynamics. Yet a humanist would be frustrated if he attempted to fill this gap in his knowledge by means of the *Britannica.* It presents an elaborate treatment of thermodynamics containing more than a hundred equations, but entropy is mentioned only in passing. At the end of a long discussion of the Carnot cycle, it declares:

> The quantity Q/T which remains constant in a Carnot cycle of any range bounded by two adiabatics, is called the entropy of the heat Q supplied at a temperature T.

Later the article notes, "If a small quantity of heat dQ per unit mass is supplied to any substance at a temperature T, the corresponding increase of entropy $d\Phi$ is dQ/T." Finally a separate section on Thermodynamics and Physical Chemistry briefly comments on the second law, which "is derived from the fact that heat can only flow down a gradient of temperature."

This cursory information, however, is lost in a mass of details, so the average reader would never realize that the second law is one of the unifying principles of thermodynamics. Such an approach ignores the function of an encyclopedia, which is to explain general principles, rather than specialized details. This requirement has only been recognized in recent times. Fifty years ago, the eleventh edition was filled with advanced treatises. Lord Rayleigh provided a lengthy memoir on the Diffraction of Light, the article on Tides employed harmonic functions, and the essay on the Calendar contained an elaborate set of equations for fixing the dates of the Julian and Hebrew calendars. Such comprehensive articles made the eleventh edition a mine of information for scholars and scientists, but most of its technical material was incomprehensible to the general public.

Yet there were protests when this austere style was abandoned. A reviewer in the *British Medical Journal* (April 15, 1911) complained: "The article on the blood is somewhat diffuse in style, and in our opinion, considerably disfigured at the outset by a discussion on the conversational vulgarities of the lower strata of the population; this is rather out of place in an anatomico-medical journal." The article in question opened with a discussion of the etymology of the word "blood" and observed:

> The common English expletive "bloody," used as an adjective or an adverb, has been given many fanciful origins. . . . The *New English Dictionary* suggests that it refers to the use of "blood" for a young rowdy of aristocratic birth, which was common at the end of the 17th century, and later became synonymous with "dandy," "buck," &c.; "bloody drunk" meant therefore "drunk as a blood," "drunk as a lord."

The esoteric style generally employs abstract words and long sentences, or a heavy dose of technical jargon and mathematical symbols. Its popularity may be explained by the desire of certain scholars to awe the public with the mysterious terms of their profession, and enhance their status by emphasizing the knowledge that separates them from outsiders. This learned manner may be seen in the biographical article on Johann Herbart which notes that after a time *t,* when a portion of ρ represented by ω has actually been brought into consciousness, the help afforded in the next instant is given by the equation

$$\frac{r\rho}{\pi} \frac{\rho - \omega}{\rho} \ dt = d\omega,$$

and therefore

$$\omega = \rho \left(1 - \epsilon^{-\frac{rt}{\pi}}\right).$$

Fortunately this mathematical mode is rare outside of the sciences, but it suggests how the *Encyclopaedia* can lose sight of the average reader.

This is a danger in dealing with subjects possessing a specialized language and symbolism. An illustration is musical notation which uses staffs, time signatures and various notes as directions for musicians. To what extent should articles on music rely on musical notation? Apparently this question has not been seriously examined, since the *Britannica* contains a wide variation in the amount of music quoted. The essay on Contrapuntal Forms cites brief musical excerpts to clarify points made in the text—but the entry on the Fugue contains two pages from Bach's *Wohltemperierte Klavier.* An outline of the scherzo of Beethoven's Seventh Symphony comprises the bulk of the article on the Scherzo, and a précis of the first movement of the *Eroica Symphony* occupies three pages of the essay on Sonata Forms. In such cases, printed music has largely replaced the text and become an end in itself. Although the amount of music to be quoted in an encyclopedia is a matter of opinion, it seems rather clear that such a specialized language, which many readers cannot follow, should be used with moderation.

This precaution has been disregarded in many scientific articles which rely heavily on mathematics. The treatise on the Genetics of Populations is an extended exercise in the theory of probability. Its character may be suggested by the following figure:

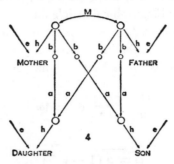

FIGURE 4. RELATIONS AMONG GENOTYPES AND CHARACTERS OF
PARENTS AND OFFSPRING, AS DETERMINED BY AUTOSOMAL GENES

An explanation of the mathematical implications of this diagram occupies half a column. A typical sentence reports: "It may be readily seen by tracing the connecting paths that the correlation and offspring is $h^2ab(1+M)$ relative to a locus and that between brothers is $2h^2a^2b^2(1+M)$ where M $(=F/b^2)$ is a correlation coefficient that sums up all possible connections between the parental genotypes." Such a technical account reads like an advanced text in population genetics, but despite this sophisticated approach, the article does not explain the significance of these studies for fundamental questions in evolution and biology, or describe their practical implications for animal and plant breeding or human genetics.

Articles on scientific subjects should emphasize basic principles rather than technical details because they are intended for laymen rather than trained specialists. An encyclopedia can provide only an introductory survey of many subjects requiring long and diligent study for their mastery. Nevertheless, the growing importance and complexity of scientific research makes such broad surveys valuable for people who wish to keep up with contemporary progress. This goal, however, is sometimes ignored. The article on the Theory of Games presents a detailed exposition of

Von Neumann's minimax theorem, as well as a number of tables of different strategies for various two-person games, but it fails to explain the general implications of this work, which have assumed considerable importance in recent years.

Scientists seeking advanced material turn to textbooks or monographs for enlightenment rather than to encyclopedias, so it seems pointless to include mathematical methods or scientific procedures that can be employed or understood only by professional research workers. The article on Differential Equations devotes five pages to various techniques for solving these equations, and even integrates particular cases. Thus

$$\frac{d^2y}{dx^2} + 3\frac{dy}{dx} + 2y = 4x + 11 \cos x$$

is solved by the method of undetermined coefficients, and

$$(1 - x)\,\frac{d^2y}{dx^2} - 4\frac{dy}{dx} - 4\frac{dy}{dx} + \frac{2}{1 - x}\,y = 0$$

by power series. Yet few scientists are likely to consult the *Britannica* when they wish to solve a differential equation. Despite the space allotted to integrating these equations, the article does not present a history of the subject, or survey in a general way the role of differential equations in analyzing physical phenomena; instead it heaps up a mass of mathematical material that is meaningless to the average reader.

It is difficult to justify such articles because the editors firmly remind contributors that they are writing for "a person of average education who is in search of clear and simple information." Despite this admonition, many entries resemble excerpts from an advanced treatise or textbook. An example is the article on Lattice Theory which deals with "the relation of different parts of the same whole to each other." It develops a series of laws of which a simple illustration is the *modular* law:

$$\text{if } x \geqq z, \text{ then } x \cap (y \cup z) = (x \cap y) \cup z.$$

Such an equation can be interpreted once its symbolism has been mastered, but this is not true of the essay on Logic which is filled with very abstruse material. It enunciates Lukasiewicz's axioms of propositional calculus:

1. $p \supset q \supset \blacksquare q \supset r \supset \blacksquare p \supset r$
2. $\sim p \supset p \supset p$
3. $p \supset \blacksquare \sim p \supset q$

and then derives a large number of theorems with the aid of the symbolism and operations of the propositional calculus. Such an article is beyond the capacities of anyone but a specialist in the subject, yet this entry is not a brief notice, but a ten-page essay.

Certain subjects are difficult to explain without a considerable display of symbols, and technical complexity cannot be avoided in dealing with some advanced topics. An appreciation of the higher functions of mathematics requires considerable technical background, so that few laymen can grasp the *Encyclopaedia*'s sophisticated treatment of Spherical Harmonics. The article on Elliptic Functions summarizes the properties of these doubly periodic functions, as well as theta functions and Weierstrass' theory. It observes:

> The theory is however more simply developed if we define **p** (u) not by inversion, but as a double series which converges everywhere except at the poles, has two periods chosen arbitrarily subject to the condition that their ratio is not real, and has a double pole in each parallelogram.

Sometimes the *Britannica* is needlessly obscure in dealing with topics that could be presented in an interesting manner. The forbidding character of the article on Topology may be suggested by the following definition:

> The 1-dimensional "Betti number modulo 2 of K," denoted by $p^1(K,2)$ (or simply p^1 when the modulo 2 algebraic operations are understood to be used without explicit mention) is the greatest number of 1-cycles $Z_1^1, Z_2^1, \ldots, Z_{p_1}^1$, of K that satisfy no homology of the form $a_1^1 Z_1^1 + \ldots + a_i^1 Z_i^1 + \ldots + a_{p_1}^1 Z_{p_1}^1 \sim 0$ modulo 2, where the coefficients a_i^1 are all 0 or 1 but not all 0 (we make the convention that $0 \sim 0$).

This level of discussion is maintained in the rest of the article. Yet many of the ideas and problems of topology can be presented in a simple manner, since it deals with certain general properties of geometrical figures and treats a number of unusual objects—such as the Möbius strip which possesses only a single surface, and the Klein bottle which has neither an inside nor an outside surface. Some of its results can easily be grasped by laymen. An illustration is Euler's theorem connecting the number of edges, faces and corners in a simple polyhedron. Another is the unproved four-color theorem which states that it is possible to color any plane map with four colors so that countries with a common boundary will not possess the same color.

Other entries show that it is possible to present mathematical material in a lucid manner. The article on Algebra explains the aim and content of college algebra and presents a brief history of the subject. The entry on Diophantine Equations offers a compact résumé of what has been accomplished in this field; and on a more advanced level, the article on the Theory of Numbers describes the basic elements of the theory and reports on recent progress in solving some of its famous problems, such as Waring's Conjecture and the Riemann Zeta Hypothesis.

Every science has its own special language and vocabulary. The symbols of organic chemistry express in a compact fashion the spacial configuration of carbon atoms in different organic compounds. Therefore they are fruitfully employed in the article on Isomerism in explaining why compounds with the same composition, but different orientation of atoms, such as graphite and diamond, possess different physical and chemical properties. Sometimes, however, chemical formulas are used so extensively that they take precedence over the printed text. This is true of the entries on Camphor, Naphthalene, and Quinones; Pyrene, Pyridine, Pyrones, Thiazines and Thiazoles. They resemble the style of a chemical handbook and provide such esoteric information as:

> The reduction of a phenazothionium salt yields a true phenothiazine. The phenothiazines corresponding to the simpler thiazine dyes are colorless and are therefore called leuco bases.

Chemical equations are a convenient means of representing the molecular changes occurring in chemical reactions, and they are a valuable aid in dealing with chemical subjects—but they become a problem when used as a primary means of communication. The three-and-one-half-page article on Grignard Reagents outlines the application of these reagents in preparing various organic compounds. Dozens of equations are listed showing how they react with organic halides, aldehydes, ketones, carboxylic esters and other compounds; but despite this mass of complex material, the importance of these reagents is not explained in a simple manner. This defect disfigures the discussion of organic reactions in the survey article on Chemistry. A host of equations are listed, including eleven separate Grignard reactions. A typical one is:

$$\alpha - C_{10}H_7MgBr + \alpha - C_{10}H_7CN \rightarrow (\alpha - C_{10}H_7)_2C{=}NMgBr$$
$$\xrightarrow{(H_2O)} (\alpha - C_{10}H_7)_2C{=}NH + MgBrOH$$

A set of Friedel-Crafts reactions are also presented, as well as an elaborate classification of different types of organic reactions. The section concludes with a discussion of the synthesis of panthothenic acid, one of the vitamins of the B complex—but such specialized material is hardly suitable for a person "who is in search of clear and simple information."

This advanced treatment reaches a climax in the fourteen-page treatise on Synthetic Dyes, which outlines the reactions involved in the production of a variety of dyes including indigo, malachite green and rhodamine 6G. A sample reaction may be quoted to suggest the nature of this article:

Anthraquinone sodium β-sulphonate — Fused with NaOH and NaNO₃ at 160-200° C. → Alizarine (turkey red when applied with an Al-Ca mordant)

Weak oleum at 120-140° C.

Purpurine (bluer shade of red)

Strong oleum at 180-200° C.

Alizarine bordeaux (purple)

Such reactions are used throughout the article. Although structural formulas are essential in explaining why certain organic compounds are colored and others are not, the article is not content with general principles, but supplies such exotic information as the synthesis of violantrone and the chemical reactions involved in the manufacture of vat khaki 2G and vat olive AR.

Such presentations are extreme cases, but they illustrate the problem of communicating scientific material. Although most entries are not written on such an advanced level, excessive mathematics or chemical symbolism is responsible for many defective entries. The appropriate treatment is a matter of editorial judgment, since some background in physics, chemistry and mathematics is essential to assimilate the results of modern research. A reasonable standard might be that a good deal, if not all, the material in scientific articles should be understandable to students who have taken a year of the subject in college, and the remainder should be accessible to those who have majored in it in college. Such a standard would avoid the danger of excessive popularization, and also insure that material is directed toward intelligent laymen rather than professional specialists.

The heavy, labored jargon of some articles is emphasized when they are compared with outstanding entries that lucidly delineate the basic principles and results of modern science. The essay on Cosmogony contains a stimulating discussion of the origin of stars and planets, as well as the origin of chemical elements. It is supplemented by a separate entry on Cosmology describing various relativistic models of the universe. A comprehensive fifty-page treatise examines the morphology and structure of crystals, and a long essay on Particle Accelerators analyzes different "atom smashers." In addition, there are excellent treatments of the Nucleus and Cosmic Rays.

This list of outstanding articles could easily be supplemented with entries in engineering and technology that demonstrate the *Encyclopaedia*'s ability to deal with technical subjects. There is no reason today for inadequate scientific material, the great increase in the number of scientists and engineers during the last generation has supplied a host of individuals who could provide good articles on their professional specialties. Unlike the social sciences, where imaginative editorial pioneering is often required, sound coverage of the physical sciences could be insured if the *Britannica* would diligently keep abreast of major areas of research. If this were done, the set would no longer be marred by antiquated articles or incomprehensible material, but would serve as a useful source of information on scientific subjects.

[16]

Men of Science

One of the striking developments of the twentieth century has been the emergence of scientific research as a major intellectual activity. It has created new industries and products, transformed our environment and profoundly affected our outlook. The advances of modern research have been felt in almost every area of contemporary life so that an understanding of its aims and achievements has become a necessity for enlightened citizens.

Science is not a fixed body of learning, but a means of extending our knowledge of the natural world, so its methods must be grasped as well as its results. The accomplishments of a Newton, a Darwin or an Einstein illuminate the way scientists can explain the mysteries of nature by bold theories and patient observation. Biographical articles in an encyclopedia can illustrate how scientists isolate fundamental problems and correlate a mass of data by discovering the principles governing natural phenomena. The *Britannica*'s efforts in this direction, however, are often limited because it relies on entries taken from the ninth and eleventh editions. Such material in the 1958 set includes the biographies of Boyle, Bunsen, Dalton and Liebig; Archimedes, Kepler, Helmholtz and Laplace; plus Cuvier, Buffon, Jenner and Koch.

Such old entries may be adequate in some cases; but in others, they may neglect important biographical material, or modern developments that place their subject in a fresh light. The long essay on John Hunter, one of the founders of experimental surgery, does not mention his pioneer investigations of venereal disease. Although he infected himself with the disease in order to study its course and symptoms, this aspect of his research is ignored, because the essay on Hunter was prepared eighty years ago during the Victorian era when such subjects were taboo. The biography of Darwin devotes a paragraph to the publication of *On the Origin of Species,* but does not explain the leading ideas of the book. With the aid of the index one can find some scattered information in the *Encyclopaedia* about Darwin's ideas of evolution and natural selection, but there is no systematic account of his theories. One reference cites the survey article on Biology, which observes that his book "created a revolution in England" and "deeply influenced Karl Marx." But instead of analyzing its contents, the article merely states:

> The *Origin of Species* by Charles Darwin appeared in 1859. For the detailed nature of the views there expressed *see* DARWIN, CHARLES ROBERT.

But the article on Darwin does not describe these views.

The biographies of major scientists should synthesize information that may be dispersed over a large number of separate entries. They should provide a unified summary of their principal achievements which, when supplemented by suitable cross references, can enable readers to gain a just appreciation of their work. This requires that biographical material be correlated with scientific entries, so that a portrait emerges that will reflect their current stature. Such a goal is difficult to achieve when old articles are retained, because the scope and significance of a scientist's research may be affected by subsequent developments. An example is offered by the *Britannica*'s biography of James Clerk Maxwell, reprinted from the eleventh edition. It declares that his great treatise on electricity and magnetism is "one of the most splendid monuments ever raised by the genius of a single individual," and justly notes that "for more than half of his brief life he held a prominent position in the very foremost rank of natural philosophers." But the article is unable to discuss the impact of his ideas because it was prepared long before the invention of radar and microwaves, which are based on Maxwell's equations. Maxwell's importance is clearly indicated by a host of references to other articles in the index. Because so many references are given, his biography should summarize his major contributions, since the average reader can hardly be expected to look up and combine the information contained in a dozen different entries.

According to the *Encyclopaedia*, "the name of Willard Gibbs, who was the most distinguished American mathematical physicist of his day, is especially associated with the 'Phase Rule' "— and "his famous paper, 'On the Equilibrium of Heterogeneous Substances' . . . founded a new department of chemical science." The article on Gibbs, however, does not clarify the Phase Rule, or indicate the branch of chemical science he founded, because it was written before the significance of his research was fully understood. In this instance, by consulting the index one can gain some idea of the Phase Rule because it is discussed in other entries, but one can hardly appreciate the totality of Gibbs' achievement, or his historical importance, from the *Britannica*'s fragmentary information.

Other gaps can be cited in the 1958 edition. The notice on Robert Brown does not mention his observations of the Brownian movement that have immortalized his name—and more space is allotted to Moritz Cantor, a nineteenth-century historian of mathematics, than to Georg Cantor whose theory of sets and transfinite numbers has deeply influenced twentieth-century mathematics. There is no biography of Ludwig Boltzmann, one of the founders of statistical mechanics and the kinetic theory of gases, yet there are entries on such obscure Victorian physicists as Joseph Swan and Thomas Preston. Although Henri Becquerel's interest in natural radioactivity inspired the Curies to undertake the separation and identification of radium, his notice is no longer than that given to his father and grandfather who made no significant contributions. Finally, the article on Oliver Heaviside reports that he "had some difficulty in getting his papers accepted for publication," but neglects his development of operational calculus which is widely used by engineers.

Sometimes biographies unwittingly supply misleading information. One of the leading scientific problems in the nineteenth century was the age of the earth. After geologists had discredited the Biblical account of Creation, they sought a chronology that would agree with existing geological evidence. The theory of evolution intensified the search for a time scale that would fix the rate at which different species emerged from the fossil record. Physicists led by Lord Kelvin attempted to determine how long the earth's present climate has remained unchanged by applying the laws of heat conduction to the cooling of the earth. Their calculations are reported in the *Encyclopaedia*'s essay on Kelvin (William Thomson):

> One of his earliest papers dealt with the age of the earth. Thomson's calculations on the conduction of heat showed that at some time between 20 millions and 400 millions, probably about 100 millions, of years ago, the physical conditions of the earth must have been entirely different from those that now obtain. This led to a long controversy with geologists in which the physical principles held their ground.

Geologists could not accept Kelvin's findings because their studies indicated that hundreds of millions of years were required to account for organic evolution and changes in the earth's surface. Contrary to the *Britannica*, Kelvin's conclusions were subsequently discredited because he failed to include the heat liberated by radioactive elements in the earth's interior, but this omission was not realized when his biography was prepared fifty years ago.

Gaps inevitably occur when articles are reprinted from earlier editions. The essay on Leonardo da Vinci, taken from the ninth edition, reports that his scientific studies "seemed to his trivial followers and biographers merely his whims and fancies, *ghiribizzi*, things to be spoken of slightingly and with apology. The mss., with the exception of those relating to painting, lay unheeded and undivulged until the present generation." Since "the present generation" refers to the 1870's, the essay does not supply a rounded picture of Leonardo's scientific work. It fails to describe his anatomical drawings which were based on the dissection of animal and human cadavers, and attempts to compensate for the neglect of his followers by declaring:

> In science he was the first among modern men to set himself most of those problems which unnumbered searchers of later generations have laboured severally or in concert to solve. . . . Galileo, Bacon, Newton, Harvey—he knew what each of them would one day discover.

This excessive claim is not supported by existing manuscripts of Leonardo's work. Despite his brilliant observations of human anatomy, he was not aware of the circulation of the blood, or the mechanical discoveries of Galileo and Newton. His intense interest in the mysteries of nature made him impatient with his brush, and his experimental bent was expressed in an insatiable appetite for facts. He once wrote, "To me it seems that those sciences are vain and full of error which are not born of experience, the mother of all certainty. . . ." This restless curiosity makes Leonardo a fascinating subject for biographical study, but his personality cannot be successfully delineated unless his notebooks, engineering projects and experimental observations are considered, as well as his artistic work.

Goethe is another artist who became obsessed with scientific investigation. He considered his book *Zur Farbenlehre* to be a major addition to world knowledge. This massive treatise savagely attacked Newton's theory of color and dismissed it as "sheer nonsense." In a letter to Eckermann, Goethe wrote, "In what I have done as a poet, I take no pride, but I am proud of the fact that I am the only person in the century who is acquainted with the difficult science of colors." The *Britannica's* biography of the poet discounts his ideas on color which were based on inadequate mathematical knowledge, but it declares:

> Of real importance was . . . his foreshadowing of the Darwinian theory in his works on the metamorphosis of plants and on biological morphology. Indeed, the deduction to be drawn from Goethe's contributions to botany and anatomy is that he, as few of his contemporaries, possessed that type of scientific mind which, in the nineteenth century, has made for progress; he was Darwin's predecessor by virtue of his enunciation of what has become one of the commonplaces of natural science—organic evolution.

This evaluation of Goethe's place in the history of science first appeared in 1910, but later scholars have reached different conclusions. They observe that Goethe's scientific work is important because of the light it sheds on the poet, rather than for its intrinsic merit. They note that Goethe lagged behind his contemporaries in advocating the principle of evolution, that he did not grasp the idea and never championed it, but merely made some casual, scattered remarks on the subject. Finally they maintain that it was not the poet, but his contemporaries, Lamarck and Erasmus Darwin, whose work anticipated the theory of organic evolution.

In other cases, the *Encyclopaedia* repeats discredited legends. Its nineteenth-century biography of Galileo asserts that "from the Leaning Tower of Pisa he afforded to all the professors and students ocular demonstration that bodies of different weights fall with the same velocity." Yet a friend of Galileo performed this experiment and discovered that bodies of different weights fall to the ground in different times because of air resistance. The article on Galileo presents another familiar story when it states:

> In 1581, while watching a lamp set swinging in the cathedral of Pisa, he observed that, whatever the range of its oscillations, they were invariably executed in equal times. The experimental verification of this fact led him to the important

discovery of the isochronism of the pendulum. He applied the new principle to the timing of the human pulse.

This tale was first recorded by Clemente de'Nelli, more than a century after it was supposed to have occurred. He claimed his account was based on old manuscripts in the possession of Galileo's heirs. He explained that he noticed an ancient manuscript wrapped about a piece of meat delivered from a butcher, and subsequently discovered that the butcher had purchased a quantity of similar papers from the heirs of Galileo's son.

According to de'Nelli, Galileo was about twenty years old when he observed the swinging chandelier. He timed its swing against the beating of his pulse and the tempo of music being played in the cathedral, and soon thereafter performed additional experiments with the aid of a friend to confirm his observations. Galileo, however, did not mention this episode in any of his writings, and he did not discuss the behavior of the pendulum until many years later, near the close of his life. Its properties assumed a practical importance only when Huygens invented the pendulum clock in 1656; and this application probably led Galileo's followers to claim that he had anticipated Huygen's invention.

Prominent figures are sometimes associated with a few colorful or dramatic incidents that seem to epitomize their careers. An example is the traditional version of Francis Bacon's death. According to the *Britannica*:

> In March 1626, when driving one day near Highgate, he was taken with a desire to discover whether snow would delay the process of putrefaction. He stopped his carriage, purchased a fowl, and assisted to stuff it with snow. He was seized with a sudden chill, and was conveyed to Lord Arundel's house, near at hand. The chill and the cold are considered to have brought on bronchitis, and he died on April 9, 1626.

This attempted experiment is often cited to demonstrate the inquisitive outlook and empirical temper that marks Bacon as a man of the Renaissance. But it is not recorded by any of Bacon's contemporaries, or in William Rawley's biography which appeared in 1657. It was first reported by John Aubrey, who was born the year that Bacon died. Aubrey presented an account in 1681 which he said originated with his aged friend, Thomas Hobbes. According to Aubrey, Bacon on arriving at Lord Arundel's house was put into a damp bed that had not been slept in for a year. Although the bed was warmed by a pan, it "gave him such a cold that in two or three days . . . he dyed of suffocation."

This would imply that Bacon stuffed a chicken with snow early in April, but the presence of snow at this time of the year seems rather unlikely. Since this episode is based on second-hand testimony long after the event, it must be classed with such apocryphal tales as Washington and the cherry tree, and Galileo and the Leaning Tower of Pisa.

Emotional factors, as well as a love of the picturesque, may transform a theory into a "fact." The article on Veneral Disease maintains:

> The origin of syphilis is obscure. There is no indisputable reference to this disease in European literature prior to the return of Christopher Columbus from the new world, but evidence of syphilis has been found in the skeletal bones of pre-Columbian American Indians. These facts, coupled with its appearance in epidemic form in Europe shortly after Columbus returned, lend support to the theory of the American origin of syphilis.

This idea possesses a wide appeal because syphilis as a sexual disease has frequently been attributed to foreigners. Frenchmen called it the Italian disease, and the Italians, the French disease. However, there is no evidence that Columbus' men became infected after they reached the West Indies. Although Indians were taken aboard Columbus' ship on October 11, 1492, he noted in his Journal six weeks later: "I thank our Lord that, up to this time, there has not been a person of my company who has so much as a toothache or been in bed from illness except an old man who has suffered from stone all his life . . ." Yet the sores and lesions associated with syphilis usually appear about three weeks after exposure to the disease.

The theory of the American origin of syphilis was introduced to explain the outbreak of epidemics in 1493 and 1495, yet none of the pre-Columbian syphilitic bones discovered in the New World comes from the West Indies, the supposed source of the malady. The first author to connect Columbus with these epidemics was John Montanus of Verona who stated in 1550 that Columbus landed in Naples, and explained:

> In the year of Christ's birth 1492, a certain Columbus, a soldier, with many Spaniards, went to the Indies, then new, which is called Calicut, where there is a certain disease which is widespread in the same manner as scabies is with us. And it happened that while they remained there many Spaniards contracted the disease which then prevailed in these regions, and returning to us many people were infected.

Columbus, however, did not land in Naples—and Vasco da Gama did not come back from the Indies until 1499. Furthermore, on March 25, 1493—a month before Columbus reached Barcelona—an edict was issued in Paris against persons with the *grosse vérole*, a medieval name for a disease whose symptoms resembled those of syphilis. This disease was also known as the *bulbus* and *le grand pox*, and it was frequently identified with leprosy, although its symptoms were quite different from the malady caused by Hansen's bacillus. The medieval form could be readily acquired by sexual contact and contained a hereditary component, but modern leprosy is the least easily transmitted of all chronic diseases. It is not inherited or acquired by sexual contact, and its incubation time is three to ten years. The rapid decline of leprosy in the sixteenth century and the simultaneous emergence of syphilis as a major disease suggests that what once had been called leprosy was now diagnosed as syphilis. This inference is strengthened by references in medieval literature to a sickness associated with sexual intercourse that produced lesions.

Because of the primitive state of medicine in the Middle Ages, syphilis was not identified as a separate disease, but its symptoms were described by medieval writers. Thus Gérard de Berri (*ca.* 1300) stated:

> The *membrum virile* suffers from copulation with women who are impure, from corrupt seminal fluid, or from a poison-

ous humor retained at the neck of the uterus: succeeding this infection, sooner or later the whole body is affected.

Thus it is unnecessary to assume that syphilis originated in America when it was known in Europe long before the discovery of the New World.

Providing accurate biographical information is only part of the larger problem of presenting the lives of major scientists. The tremendous increase in the number of research workers during the last generation has altered the nature of their achievements. It has been estimated that 90 percent of all the scientists who have ever lived are alive today, so that the towering figures who dominated earlier periods have been replaced by a multitude of specialists. In the past, progress depended on a limited number of individuals, and major fields were often associated with the pioneering efforts of a single individual. Today as soon as an important discovery is announced, it is exploited by a host of investigators—and the time between successive findings is measured in days and weeks, instead of years. As a result, the individual has been submerged by the advances of his specialty— and the solitary theorist and experimenter has been replaced by an army of essentially anonymous investigators. The *Encyclopaedia* has attempted to deal with this change in scientific activity by including many brief articles on recent Nobel Prize winners. These short accounts, however, are unable to convey the personality of leading scientists because they resemble the factual listings in *Who's Who* rather than the literary memoirs of earlier editions. Therefore they do not portray the quest for knowledge that is at the heart of scientific activity.

The lives of outstanding nineteenth-century figures such as Darwin, Maxwell and Pasteur exhibit a unity and coherence that is not shared by later investigators. Their careers possess a lasting interest as examples of personal accomplishment, even though science is fundamentally anti-historical. Its practitioners are concerned with problems that remain to be solved, rather than the story of its past triumphs. Laymen, however, who stand outside the stream of scientific research are interested in the growth and development of science, as well as its current state, because they wish to understand the factors that have led to its success. This is one of the reasons why the *Britannica* offers long essays on the history of individual sciences as well as biographies of its principal figures.

When scientists are singled out in historical surveys because of their importance, one expects that additional information on their work will be found in biographical entries. This expectation is not always fulfilled. The *Britannica*'s survey article on Medicine cites the major influence exerted by Rudolf Virchow and Claude Bernard on the development of nineteenth-century medical research, and allots a paragraph to each man, but their achievements are treated in a very superficial manner in the biographical entries.

The article on Virchow, one of the founders of medical pathology, does not describe his central position in European medicine for more than half a century. It merely notes:

> In his book on *Cellular-pathologie* published at Berlin in 1858, he established what Lord Lister described as the "true and fertile doctrine that every morbid structure consists of cells which have been derived from pre-existing cells as progeny."

After announcing that "Virchow made many important contributions to histology and morbid anatomy and to the study of particular diseases," the article assigns only a single sentence to these discoveries.

The essay on Claude Bernard, who is frequently called the father of physiology, fails to trace his impact on subsequent research. His ideas on the physiological function of different organs and the role of the blood in providing an interior milieu for the body have stimulated twentieth-century research. They have been fruitfully employed by Walter Cannon on homeostasis, Hans Selye on stress, and Sherrington on the autonomic nervous system. However, these long-range influences could not be examined in an essay prepared in 1910. Furthermore, Bernard's classic *Introduction to the Study of Experimental Medi-*

cine is neglected, although its publication led to his election to the French Academy and inspired Zola's theory of the experimental novel. His *Introduction* was animated by a desire to liberate medicine from the superstitions of the past by transforming it into a positive science—and it observed:

> When an obscure or inexplicable phenomenon presents itself, instead of saying "I do not know," as every scientific man should do, physicians are in the habit of saying, "This is life"; apparently without the least idea that they are explaining darkness by still greater darkness.

Bernard believed that the future of medicine lay in an experimental method which would test medical hypotheses by means of accurate and unbiased observations. He insisted that "science should always explain obscurity and complexity by clearer and simpler ideas"—and he declared: "Facts are neither great nor small in themselves. A great discovery is a fact whose appearance in science gives rise to shining ideas, whose light dispels many obscurities and shows us new paths."

Both Bernard and Virchow wished to base medical practice on the findings of experimental science. Their aim was explicitly stated when Virchow founded his own medical journal in 1847, at the beginning of his career. He announced:

> The standpoint we propose to adopt and which is already manifested in this first issue is simply that of natural science. Practical medicine as applied to theoretical medicine, and theoretical medicine as an embodiment of pathological physiology, are the ideals toward which we shall strive so far as it lies within the scope of our powers.

Virchow and Bernard helped transform medicine from an art to a science, and they profoundly influenced the outlook of subsequent investigators. The result of their work was aptly summarized by Virchow in 1877 when he recorded:

> It is no longer necessary today to write that scientific medicine is also the best foundation for medical practice. It is sufficient to point out how completely even the external character of medical practice has changed in the last thirty years. Scientific methods have been everywhere introduced into prac-

tice. The diagnosis and prognosis of the physician are based on the experience of the pathological anatomist and the physiologist. Therapeutic doctrine has become biological and thereby experimental science.

This change is an important aspect of medical history because a profession is more than a set of empirical rules and procedures; it organizes a body of knowledge in accordance with a special point of view, and provides a framework for future research. Since this outlook has been fashioned by its intellectual leaders, accounts of their lives should examine their subsequent influence, as well as their specific contributions.

Science is an organized body of knowledge, which seeks to give a coherent explanation of experimental observations and a systematic interpretation of natural phenomena. Its ability to predict natural events is not derived from isolated discoveries, but is based on general theories and principles that correlate a mass of data. Scientific observations are like the meanings of individual words, while scientific theories are like the syntax and grammar of a language which enable words to be combined into sentences expressing complete thoughts. Just as knowing the meaning of a small number of words does not provide a mastery of a language, so a few random bits of scientific information do not supply a comprehension of science and its methods.

An understanding of science, like the mastery of a foreign language, is a long and arduous task. Scientific advances frequently baffle laymen, because they may contradict commonsense notions or depend on mathematical reasoning. An encyclopedia must attempt to explain these advances so readers can grasp their historical and intellectual significance. It must illuminate the goals of scientific activity and its philosophical consequences because of the growing importance of research as an end in itself—and as an essential prerequisite for modern technology. Science, as one of the remarkable achievements of Western civilization, must play an increasing role in any contemporary synthesis of learning, and its creators must be acknowledged as major factors in shaping the modern mind. Therefore the treatment of science and its history is one of the great challenges facing encyclopedia editors.

[17]

Editorial Policies

THE *Britannica* is guided by an elaborate organization. Broad business questions are handled by a Board of Directors headed by William Benton, while editorial policies are formulated by a separate Board of Editors led by Robert Hutchins. These boards meet four times a year for intensive two-day sessions devoted to immediate and long-range problems. The Board of Editors is assisted in its deliberations by a committee of faculty members from the University of Chicago representing the University's interest in the scholarly and financial success of the work. The *Encyclopaedia* also employs an international array of 170 advisors or departmental editors, each of whom is an expert in some branch of knowledge. Each advisor is responsible for about 250,000 words, which he is supposed to keep under continuous surveillance so he can periodically advise the editors when major changes are required. He suggests authorities who might be suitable as contributors—and assists editors and authors in preparing fresh material. Thus the scholarly advisors, whose names are listed in the first volume, presumably insure that the work is accurate and reliable—and in some measure they must be held responsible for its defects since they have lent their names and prestige to the set.

A large staff of full-time employees is responsible for the complex editorial labor associated with continuous revision. Their activity is directed by the editor-in-chief. From 1938 to 1960 this position was occupied by Walter Yust, a former journalist and literary critic, who came to the attention of the Company when he wrote a series of favorable columns on the fourteenth edition in the *Philadelphia Public Ledger*. Although Yust was hired in 1930 as an assistant editor, his early years with the Company were spent in writing and preparing advertising copy. He was made editor-in-chief in 1938, and his tenure in this post exceeded that of any other editor in the *Encyclopaedia*'s history.

Under his regime, the system of continuous revision was greatly expanded, and the staff was freed from the restraint imposed by special publication dates. When the 1956 edition was reviewed in *The Booklist* (February 1, 1957) by a committee of the American Library Association, the editors informed the committee:

> All articles in the *Encyclopaedia Britannica* are divided into 30 major classifications . . . and while any article in any classification is subject to revision at any time, all 30 major classifications and *every article in them* are carefully scrutinized, revised or completely rewritten in accordance with a definite timetable. . . . While no claim is made that every article is completely and beyond all question up to date at any particular date on the calendar, it *is* claimed and it *is* true that every article in the entire 24 volumes is being brought up to date according to a definite schedule.

The editors have attempted to demonstrate the effectiveness of this program by citing the number of words altered in the set. Robert Hutchins announced in the *Columbia Forum* (Spring, 1960) that in the decade from 1950 to 1960, 34 million words were revised in 49,000 articles. Since there are about 38 million words and 42,000 entries in the set, this assertion would imply that some articles were revised more than once during this ten-year period. When the 1960 edition was sent to newspapers for review, the press release boasted that the entire work "at any given date is, in the words of John V. Dodge, executive editor, 'as up to date as human ingenuity can make it.' "

Such extreme claims frequently appear in the Company's advertising. An ad in *Look* magazine (March 14, 1960) reports: "*It is truth. It is unquestionable fact. And the beginning, the support, and the constant touchstone of education.*" Even if we allow for the natural hyperbole of advertising copy, this is quite an ambitious statement—yet such claims are not unusual. An advertisement in *Life* magazine (June 6, 1960) maintains that the set is able "to answer almost *any* question fully and authoritatively," since it "contains the accumulated knowledge of the world since creation." Such assertions have been repeated many times, and despite their inflated rhetoric, they furnish a useful definition of the *Encyclopaedia*'s nature and scope because they have been advanced by the Company itself, and not by a captious critic with impossible standards.

While considerable effort has been made in recent years to bring the set up to date, other practices have been retained with persistent tenacity. One of these is the meager scale of payment for editorial contributors. Experts who examine the *Britannica*'s text to determine whether articles should be revised receive five dollars a page. Contributors who prepare original articles are paid two cents a word—a rate that has remained unchanged, despite war and inflation, since 1929. Thus a scholar who completes a thousand-word article earns the grand sum of $20. The Company is not ashamed of these low rates, but likes to boast that Bernard Shaw received only $68.50 for his essay on Socialism, and Albert Einstein $86.50 for his article on Space-Time. According to the editors, they have never had any difficulty in recruiting contributors even at these low rates. *The Great EB* claims, "Many experts and scholars realize the prestige attached to being asked to contribute to the *Encyclopaedia Britannica* and less than 2 percent of those invited have ever declined."

These niggardly rates can hardly be justified on the grounds of economic necessity because the Company is a flourishing commercial enterprise. William Benton stated in an interview in the *New York Times* on May 25, 1958 that many of the Company's salesmen earn up to $20,000 a year, while district sales managers receive about $70,000 a year.

Ironically, Mr. Benton has shown a deep concern for the plight of underpaid American scholars and educators. He discovered after a visit to the Soviet Union in 1955 that scientists and specialists responsible for Russia's striking military and technical feats were being lavishly rewarded. He publicly urged that action be taken to improve the status of hard-pressed American scholars and educators by offering greater financial incentives for intellectual achievement. But while Mr. Benton has vigorously advocated greater monetary rewards for U.S. scientists and educators, he has privately continued to pay the *Encyclopaedia*'s contributors two cents a word.

It would be a mistake to regard Mr. Benton as an absentee owner, since he is actively engaged in all aspects of the enterprise. After his visit to Russia, he prepared a long report for the 1956 *Book of the Year* describing Communist techniques of propaganda and education. During his visit, Mr. Benton conferred for three hours with the editor of the *Great Soviet Encyclopedia* and his associates. After his return to the United States, Mr. Benton graphically portrayed the results of this interview in an article in the *New York Times*. He recorded:

> For the first time, encyclopedists of the free world and the Soviet met and talked shop. We talked paper, printing and binding. We talked sales, collections and profits. Coffee and brandy were served and we exchanged toasts. We agreed to exchange the latest editions of our encyclopedias. More important, we agreed to exchange statistics on population, production, income and other key subjects for possible inclusion in our publications. But it was not so easy to exchange ideas.

Perhaps it is fitting that Mr. Benton, who achieved his first triumph as an advertising executive, should regard himself as an "encyclopedist of the free world"—since he is a self-made million-aire who typifies the American ideal of success, and whose financial control effectively dictates the *Britannica*'s policies.

In February, 1960, Walter Yust retired after twenty-two years as editor-in-chief. The following October, Harry S. Ashmore was appointed to fill this position. The new editor was graduated from Clemson Agricultural College and was formerly editor of the *Arkansas Gazette*. In 1955 he served as Adlai Stevenson's personal assistant in preparing for the 1956 presidential campaign. Mr. Ashmore gained national prominence during the controversy over school integration in Little Rock. His editorials defending the authority of the federal courts were awarded a Pulitzer Prize; and subsequently he was invited by Dr. Hutchins to the Center for Democratic Institutions to direct a study of the mass media financed by the William Benton Foundation. Like his predecessor, the new editor-in-chief was trained in the field of journalism before obtaining this $50,000-a-year position. After his appointment, Mr. Ashmore announced he would commute between the Chicago headquarters, the London editorial offices and Santa Barbara, California, where he would confer with Dr. Hutchins on new methods of editorial revision.

The editors of the ninth edition were scholars, and the eleventh edition was directed by a journalist with scholarly ambitions. Subsequent editors have been journalists; and their ability to edit a monumental work of contemporary learning has been questioned by critics who have been disturbed by the *Britannica*'s superficial tendencies. In 1934 Aldous Huxley asked if eminence in journalism qualified a man for preparing a survey of universal knowledge—and he replied:

> In newspaper work, accuracy is the last consideration. Carrera . . . Cabrera? What earthly difference does it make which name you print in a publication that leaves the presses in the small hours of the morning and by sunset of the same day is already in the fire, the dust-bin, or the cesspool? Obviously, it doesn't matter two pins what you say in a newspaper. But in a work which is to serve for at least ten years as the standard reference book of the English-speaking people all over

the world, this sort of carelessness does matter—matters, indeed, quite a lot.

On December 24, 1960, the *New Yorker* published an interview with Mr. Ashmore, who described the *Encyclopaedia*'s elaborate system of revision which requires a "literary army" of specialist contributors, permanent advisors and an editorial staff of two hundred employees. He noted:

> We pay only two cents a word—we hope to raise the rate—but I have just approved a plan to offer writers of over twenty-five hundred words two alternative rewards: a set of the *Britannica,* which sells for about four hundred dollars, or a set of the *Great Books of the Western World,* which we publish and which costs the same amount. But a lot of our contributors already have both sets and I don't think this is the final answer.

Mr. Ashmore was able to introduce this barter plan because it entails no financial sacrifice for the Company. If authors who qualify for this offer provide an average of three thousand words, they would be entitled to $60—and this is approximately equal to the manufacturing cost of the *Britannica* or the *Great Books.*

The relative weight accorded to scholarship and salesmanship may be suggested by the following consideration. If the *Encyclopaedia*'s 38 million words were replaced, the total payment to contributors would be only $800,000. This sum is far less than its U.S. advertising budget, which was approximately four million dollars in 1960. Although the *Britannica*'s meager rates have been attacked a number of times, the Company has not raised them. One reason may be that the owners are flattered because they can secure the services of famous scientists and scholars for only two cents a word. Under these circumstances, Mr. Benton and the University of Chicago may enjoy the illusion that they are maintaining intellectual standards when they are actually pursuing their own commercial interests. They may rationalize their behavior by observing that the Company is operating in a market economy where rates are fixed by the laws of supply and demand, rather than intrinsic merit. But they conveniently forget that in a free labor market one tends to get what one pays for —and sometimes it must be confessed the articles supplied by contributors are indeed worth no more than two cents a word.

Many scholars who might be interested in writing for the *Britannica* cannot afford to provide their services at these rates. This is particularly true of individuals in the humanities who have so it has sometimes been difficult to replace long essay-articles not enjoyed the financial prosperity of their scientific colleagues; taken from earlier editions. To circumvent this problem, editors seek authors who are willing to write for two cents a word. This may be one reason for the rapid increase in the number of contributors. Eleven hundred names were added to the *EB*'s roster in 1960, and another 1,300 in 1961. This contrasts with 1,500 authorities who were responsible for the entire eleventh edition. The editors have searched rather widely, since many scholars seem reluctant to prepare more than a single article. In 1960 it was reported that the London office translated articles from fifteen different languages, and the resulting diversity and number of contributors has dissipated a good deal of the literary and intellectual coherence which once characterized the set.

One persistent pressure in revising the *Britannica* has been the necessity to squeeze a growing mass of information within a limited space. Since the text has been increased by only three million words since 1929, many old entries have been abridged or deleted. This action has created some concern which was pungently expressed by the Cambridge don, F. L. Lucas, in a letter in *Speaking of Holiday* (February, 1961), a house organ of the Curtis Publishing Company. Professor Lucas announced:

> My next job, alas, is to re-do "Oliver Goldsmith" for the *Encyclopaedia Britannica*. They sent me the old article. I gasped—"That style!—it must be—it is the great Lord Macaulay." I shrieked with horror at the sacrilegious idea of putting my toes in his boots. But no use. Poor Goldsmith is to be cut from 4000 words to 1800. One can't cut Macaulay by half—as well saw ten feet out of the neck of a giraffe. But so goes the world. One's encyclopedias grow less useful, because what one wants to know is crowded out by things one

doesn't want to know, and couldn't even understand. By A.D. 3000, no doubt, dear Oliver will be reduced to a couple of lines!

This process is illustrated by the treatment of Pope Alexander VI. In 1910 he received two and a half pages. In 1958 he was allotted a single page; but today he is covered in two paragraphs occupying only a quarter of a page. Clearly in such a short entry, it is impossible to describe his controversial career, so it can only report: "Alexander's neglect of the spiritual interests of the church worsened the prestige of the papacy."

Space limitations may explain why some figures receive brief biographies in the 1963 edition. General de Gaulle and Harold Macmillan are given only half a page each. Yet room has been found for a number of individuals connected with the *Encyclopaedia* including William Benton, Robert Hutchins and Walter Yust. The article on Mr. Benton states that "in the Senate he became a champion of freedom throughout the world"—and his biography is longer than the entry on either Adlai Stevenson or Richard Nixon.

In the past, it was customary for editors to explain the methods and principles that guided their work. In 1797 the third edition announced:

> To accomplish a task so arduous and so important, neither labour nor expence has been spared. Literary journals; the memoirs and transactions of philosophic societies; and all the most valuable dictionaries of arts and sciences, both in our own and in other languages have been constantly consulted.

Fifty years ago, the eleventh edition opened with an editorial introduction that discussed its point of view and specific editorial problems. The value of such an account was admirably explained in the first volume of the fourteenth edition which stated: "The preface must devote itself to a statement of the spirit animating the newest design; of the scope of its contents and what is notable in their character; and of the methods by which the whole has been framed."

Such a course has not been followed in the 1963 edition.

Its preface consists of a single page which vaguely describes the *EB*'s program of continuous revision. Indeed, it is interesting that in recent times the only coherent exposition of the philosophical nature of an encyclopedia and the practical problems associated with its construction have come from academic figures, rather than individuals employed in the reference book field.

The literary critic Hugh Kenner opens his book, *Flaubert, Joyce and Beckett,* with a penetrating critique of the encyclopedia as a legacy of the Enlightenment. He observes:

> The Encyclopaedia, like its cousin the Dictionary, takes all that we know apart into little pieces, and then arranges those pieces so that they can be found one at a time. It is produced by a feat of organizing, not a feat of understanding. No Bacon, no Aquinas, is tracing the hierarchies of a human knowledge which he has assumed the responsibility of grasping. If the Encyclopaedia means anything as a whole, no one connected with the enterprise can be assumed to know what that meaning is. A hundred contributors, or a thousand, each responsible for squinting at creation through a single knothole, can work in utter isolation, very likely in a hundred different cities, each on his self-contained packet of knowledge; and these packets an editor with a flow-chart may coordinate, if at all, by appending cross-references, and organize only by filing each in its alphabetic place. . . .
>
> The mark of the Encyclopaedia, then, is its fragmentation of all that we know into little pieces so arranged that they can be found one at a time. Nothing, except when a cross-reference is provided, connects with or entails anything else; nothing corrects anything else, or affords perspective on anything else. And nobody, consequently, is talking to anyone else.

A more positive approach has been offered by Jacques Barzun of Columbia University, who considers the problems connected with the creation of a new world encyclopedia. He declares in the *American Behavioral Scientist* (September, 1962) that such a work should not be a practical handbook, a "how to do it" manual, or a guide to the practice of various professions. Rather it should provide a comprehensive survey of all the arts and sciences by concentrating on their fundamentals and not on specialized details. In such a work, articles should resemble an hourglass by opening with general considerations, gripping their subject closely about the waist, and widening out again to consider related subjects and unsettled possibilities. Its architecture should reflect in miniature the organization of a library, since it endeavors to encompass the entire range of men's knowledge. Finally, Professor Barzun observes that a record of its space allotments and hierarchy of entries would constitute a small book which, if published, would serve innumerable readers as a manual for home study and a chart of the circle of learning that would be worth contemplating for its own sake.

Allocating space to various subjects is a primary responsibility of encyclopedia editors. This requires a philosophy of knowledge that can organize and evaluate different areas in the light of current scholarship and the needs of contemporary readers. It is difficult to believe that the *Britannica* has worked out such a scheme, since its entries often vary in an irrational manner. A striking example is the treatment of the French Revolution— a political upheaval that exerted a profound influence on European history and culture. The *Encyclopaedia*'s article on the subject is only one and a half pages long; yet it devotes twenty-four pages to the French Revolutionary Wars.

Similar disparities can be found in almost every branch of knowledge in the 1963 edition. In linguistics, it presents long technical accounts of Balochi and Burushaski, but there is no article on Korean, which is spoken by 35 million people. In music, three-fourths of a page is assigned to the Suite and two and a half pages to the Rondo, but the account of the Mazurka consists of only two sentences:

> MAZURKA, a lively dance, originating in Poland, somewhat resembling the polka. It is danced in couples, the music being in ⅜ or ¾ time.

Such inconsistencies suggest that the distribution of material is not the result of systematic or rational planning, but may be governed by historical accident. This is illustrated in the area of religion where two pages are allotted to Athanasius "the Great," Bishop of Alexandria, and one and a half pages to Polycarp, Bishop of Smyrna—but Moses receives only half a page. His biography observes, after citing some episodes in his life, "the other events need not be detailed." Yet it concludes, "Moses stands out as one of the greatest figures in history."

Despite the current shortage of space, a host of entries are allotted to minor geographical sites. There is a notice on Rajmahal, village in India, one on Hormuz, an island in the Strait of Ormuz, and one on Jamrud, a fort and cantonment in West Pakistan. Articles are assigned to many minor cities and sites in the United States, such as Camden, South Carolina and Dover, Delaware with populations of 6,842 and 7,250—as well as to Stony Point, New York and Sturgeon Bay, Wisconsin. Many small towns and villages in the British Isles also receive notices. Examples include Dunblane in Scotland, Dromore in Ireland, and Midhurst in England—with populations of 2,992, 2,125 and 1,895, respectively. Such entries indicate that the editors have not devised an intelligent way of handling geographical information.

Despite such shortcomings, the Company announces: "Revision is discriminating. The irrelevant, the trivial and the purely transitory are eliminated." And its editorial methods are presented as an ideal to be emulated, rather than censured. This was demonstrated when it launched a new division for the publication of educational and trade books. This venture was described in a three-page advertisement in the *Saturday Review* (September 15, 1962), which declared:

> . . . Britannica has become more than a set of books. It is a concept, a set of standards for all informational publishing that is without parallel in the contemporary world. . . .
>
> The editors of the Encyclopaedia Britannica have always sought out as contributors persons who are both authors and authorities. The editors of The Press will follow in this tradition. They will continue to perform the meticulously careful job of editing that both Britannica authors and readers have come to expect. Only in this fashion can The Press maintain the standards which it has been bequeathed.

[18]

Five Years Later

SINCE a new edition of the *Britannica* is issued every year, the *EB*'s contents are continually changing. During the last five years, many alterations have been made—and these changes shed considerable light on current editorial procedures. The articles in the 1958 edition that have already been discussed are of particular interest because revision of them reveals the quality of recent editorial activity.

More money is available for editorial work than ever before in the *Encyclopaedia*'s history. This has allowed editors to increase their staff, expand continuous revision, and introduce many changes in the set. A large number of color plates have been added, and fresh terrain maps appear in the atlas. Black and white illustrations now break up the printed text, and the index has been rearranged to increase its readability and ease of use. Articles on individual countries are based on up-to-date statistics, and notices on American towns and cities contain the latest census figures. These alterations are part of an active program that has revised a host of old entries and commissioned many new ones.

As a result, the 1963 edition contains essays on Darwinism, Marxism and the Dead Sea Scrolls. In addition, a number of literary omissions have been corrected. The articles on Milton and Cervantes explore the literary qualities of *Paradise Lost* and *Don Quixote*; the essay on Donne cites modern critics who value him for "his power to catch in verse the ring of passion and to render the accent of a 'naked thinking heart.'" Such excellent contributions demonstrate the value of fresh appraisals of major figures.

It would be a mistake, however, to conclude from these examples that alterations automatically correct faults. New articles have been commissioned on Herbart and Kierkegaard, but Herbart is given twice as much space as Kierkegaard. The essay on Pascal analyzes at length an untitled *recueil* of fragments which it calls *Apologie de la religion chrétienne*. But the average reader would have no way of knowing that this is the same work traditionally identified as Pascal's *Pensées*.

A fresh article on Dostoevski begins by acknowledging that he is "one of the profoundest creative artists of the 19th century," but it concentrates on his biography, rather than his literary achievements. It sums up the *Brothers Karamazov* in two vague sentences:

> Quite different was the reception of the *Brothers Karamazov*, undoubtedly his greatest novel, in which he achieves a profundity of thought that surpasses anything written in his or, indeed, any time since. Published at a time when Dostoevski's fame had reached its zenith in Russia, it was recognized at once as the greatest achievement of his genius.

A new entry on Baudelaire does not describe the contents of *Les Fleurs du mal*, but merely observes:

> The consummate art of the collection was understood and appreciated by a few readers . . . but, for the general public, for several generations, the book remained a byword for depravity, morbidity and obscenity.

It notes that when Baudelaire died, his works were all out of print, but subsequently he was recognized as one of the greatest poets of the nineteenth century. However, the article does not explore the specific nature of his poetic art or the reasons for his posthumous fame.

The erratic nature of editorial revision is illustrated by the treatment of Shakespeare. The *Britannica*'s account has been revised for the first time since 1911, but instead of commissioning a completly new article, fresh sections have been inserted in an old essay. The poaching legend is still repeated, and there is no section on Shakespeare as a dramatist; yet the history of Shakespearean criticism is examined at great length. The new treatment, unlike its predecessor, makes no attempt to deal with Shakespeare's genius, so one would never be able to guess from its contents why he looms so large in the English tradition.

The only other substantial review of his work appears in three columns of the survey article on English Literature. It presents a sketchy chronology and summary of his plays; its superficial character is illustrated when it devotes only a single sentence to *Romeo and Juliet:*

> Shakespeare's second tragedy, *Romeo and Juliet* (1594–95), written at about the same time as *A Midsummer Night's Dream,* shares that play's tone of youth and hope.

In the entire *Encyclopaedia,* there is no examination of any of Shakespeare's individual plays. As a result, the article on Hamlet discusses the Scandinavian sources of *Hamlet* and pre-Elizabethan treatments, but says nothing about Shakespeare's play.

Because of the flood of new contributions, many contradictions appear in the 1963 edition. A new account of the Minoan Linear Scripts describes the successful translation of the Linear B form as "one of the great achievements of decipherment in modern times." This conclusion is confirmed in the biographical entry on Michael Ventris which refers to his linguistic solution as the "authoritative work" which was "at once acclaimed as correct." But the article on Greece states that "the decipherment was still imperfect in the middle of the 20th century A.D." This idea is echoed in a fresh essay on Aegean Civilization which debates whether or not the Linear B script is Greek; yet its bibliography cites works by Ventris and Chadwick which prove conclusively that the script is a form of primitive Greek.

Such inconsistencies are the bane of encyclopedia editors; and despite the *Britannica*'s massive revision, contradictions in earlier editions have not been resolved in the 1963 set. An example is the chronology of Abraham. The current article on Abraham states that "it is not possible to be specific either about when he lived or about the details of his life"; and it observes that Biblical narratives authentically reflect the first half of the second millennium B.C., or perhaps the middle of the millennium. On the other hand, the essay on Judaism reports that "the tradition of his birth at Ur may be fearlessly accepted"—and it asserts:

> According to biblical chronology Abraham's migration to the west took place in the late 20th century B.C., a date which . . . fits well into the framework of general contemporaneous history.

But the entry on the Jews records: "The migration of Abraham from Ur Kasdim may be associated with the unsettled conditions in that area during the 18th century B.C." Thus the information presented about Abraham is even more confusing in 1963 than it was in 1958.

The *Britannica* employs an elaborate system to verify the validity of new material. More than five hundred editorial steps occur from the time an article is solicited until it finally appears in print. To insure high standards of accuracy, entries are examined by contributors, editorial advisors and outside experts. Therefore, while fresh articles may occasionally lack the literary distinction of older essays, they are presumably more accurate. But this is not always the case.

Tovey's biography of Beethoven has been superseded by a new account written by a musicologist from Cologne. He opens a brief discussion of Beethoven's last quartets with the observation:

The third group, op. 127, op. 130 to 135 and op. 137 (1824–26), explores further problems. These quartets are remarkable for their wonderful transparent texture. . . .

But two of these works are not quartets. The opus 134 is a brief fugue for string quintet composed in 1817, and the opus 137 is a two-piano arrangement of the *Grosse Fuge*. Oddly enough, the opus 137 is correctly identified on the preceding page in the *Encyclopaedia*.

Such blunders raise serious questions about the *EB*'s current editorial methods. A disturbing example is Chesterton's famous article on Dickens, which has been revised by deleting a good deal of his vivid prose and adding some new information. This has led to a confusing treatment of Dickens' separation from his wife. Some of Chesterton's erroneous speculations have been retained, and the article now claims:

> For many years the marriage was a happy one, and when the separation came it seems largely to have been due to Dickens' overpowering restlessness, to his demand to put himself and his writing first. . . .

Later this hypothesis is discarded, and the essay candidly reports:

> . . . Even before the separation, there is no doubt that he was deeply attracted by a young actress, Ellen Ternan. It seems clear that sometime during the 1860's she became his mistress. He provided her with somewhere to live; he left her £1,000 when he died; and meanwhile, he divided his time between her, his public career and what remained of his family at Gad's Hill.

The Company has released impressive figures on its continuous revision program, which has been in force for three decades. It claims that 32 million words, or the equivalent of 85 percent of the *Encyclopaedia*'s text have been changed in the last five years. In the 1963 edition, 10,300,000 words were "revised"; and 17,900 articles—almost half of the *EB*'s entries—were reviewed and corrected. From these figures, one might assume that all the *Britannica*'s obsolete material has been eliminated. This optimistic conjecture is contradicted by the presence of many old articles in the latest edition. Apparently, whenever a change is made in an entry, its entire text is counted as revised. Thus the article on Tchaikovsky has been "revised" by altering the spelling of his name and making a few minor changes in its text. Perhaps this explains why the editors can assert that tens of millions of words have been altered, when so much of the *EB*'s contents have been left undisturbed.

These dubious statistics perpetuate the illusion that the set is an authoritative source of modern knowledge, since these figures, taken at their face value, imply that outmoded information no longer appears. This is far from true.

The appendix contains a selected list of 666 articles in the 1963 *EB* that have been reprinted from the ninth, tenth or eleventh edition.* Each of these articles occupies more than half a page in the *Encyclopaedia,* and except for cuts or minor additions, they have been retained for more than fifty years. The first eight volumes of the 1963 edition supply only eleven of the articles in the list, and the remaining 655 appear in the last fifteen volumes. The alphabetical separation between old and new articles is quite sharp, since fifty-six old articles appear in volume nine. It is difficult to understand why this particular set of entries has been reprinted while others have been revised; and this array of antiquated articles effectively refutes the claim that the latest edition of the *Britannica* is a mirror of contemporary knowledge.

Revision is often a haphazard affair. A new article has been prepared on Béla Bartók, but Paul Hindemith is represented by a meager notice which cites *Mathis der Mahler,* composed in 1934, as his most recent composition. Despite the millions of words that have been replaced, two dozen of Tovey's old essays on music have been reprinted.

Archaic material can be found even in areas that have been extensively revised. Many fresh biographies have been prepared on the fine arts, so that major artists such as Leonardo, Titian, Tintoretto, Velazquez and Rembrandt are treated in accurate, informative articles based on modern scholarship. Yet the essay on Greek Art employs old-fashioned engravings and a text published in 1910. Since this account occupies seventeen pages in the *Encyclopaedia,* it can hardly be dismissed as a minor oversight.

* See Appendix, p. 363-73.

The *Britannica* sometimes fails to utilize visual aids in an effective manner. Although the 1963 edition includes a new description of chairs and sofas, it is not supplemented by any pictures that would identify the distinctive styles of different historical periods. The article on Furniture contains no illustrations of twentieth-century furniture; the only examples in the entire set are a few perfunctory photographs in the survey essay on Design.

The Company has widely publicized the *EB*'s editorial innovations. An example is the appearance of color plates in the body of the printed text. This feature was introduced in a tentative fashion in the 1963 edition, but the objects portrayed have been chosen in a very arbitrary manner. There are color plates of pears and peaches, but the unfamiliar passionflower is represented by a black and white illustration. The 1963 article on the Punic War contains colored diagrams of the battle of Cannae. Yet the text of this article has been taken from the eleventh edition and carries the following footnote:

> The chronology here given is the traditional one, but recent researches tend to show that many events have been antedated by one year.

These "recent researches" were published in 1901 and 1902!

As a result of continuous revision, the *Encyclopaedia* is in a state of flux. It is like a city; some landmarks are being demolished, and others renovated. At first sight, this editorial activity is impressive. However, a closer inspection reveals that some alterations are defective. The essay on Sophocles supplies a graphic account of his dramatic art, but it still recommends Jebb's archaic translations. The article on Goya rejects legends about his life, but fails to mention the Duchess of Alba or the famous maja paintings. The entry on Verdi ignores Boito, although it discusses Verdi's association with Merelli, the director of La Scala. Consequently a reader must turn to the entry on Boito to learn about his collaboration with Verdi.

The treatments of Grant and Lincoln reflect modern historical views, but the biography of Edward VII is a reverential eulogy:

> Few men had a surer knowledge of human nature and a shrewder grasp of what was happening. The prince hardly

ever read a book; his letters were perfunctory trifles, but it was Sir Charles Wentworth Dilke, with advanced opinions on home and imperial affairs, who noticed that "it is worth talking seriously to the prince."

Despite this erratic record, a number of outstanding articles should be cited, because they demonstrate the importance of fresh material in the humanities. The essay on Nietzsche is a brilliant survey of his philosophy that forcefully exposes the attempt of his sister and later critics to distort his message. The article on Boswell draws upon his journals for a lively portrait of his personal life. The entry on Coleridge relates his opium-taking, procrastination and domestic difficulties to psychological factors, rather than to innate hereditary causes. The essay on Burns now frankly examines his promiscuous love life and the sexual elements in his poetry. And the biography of De Quincey reveals his fascination with London prostitutes and the softening of references to them in later editions of the *Confessions* to suit Victorian tastes. These splendid articles show that the *Encyclopaedia* can occasionally secure distinguished contributions from contemporary scholars.

Some myths and legends have disappeared in the 1963 edition. The pictures of the Betsy Ross House in Philadelphia and the Rowan Manor in Kentucky have been removed—and the biography of George Washington now identifies the hatchet and the cherry tree as an apocryphal tale. In other cases, traditional stories are treated in an inconsistent manner. The article on William Penn states that Benjamin West's painting of his treaty with the Indians "must be regarded as an exercise of the historical imagination," but the reality of this treaty is affirmed in the entry on Pennsylvania. The biography of Galileo speaks of his supposed observation of the swinging lamp, as if it had some historical reality, yet its discussion appears in a section entitled, "Legend of the Lamp."

Since the *Britannica* rarely examines or analyzes familiar myths, readers are unable to gain an insight into their origin and continued popularity. Thus the biography of Galileo dismisses his experiment from the Leaning Tower of Pisa as fictitious, but it fails to describe the source of the colorful tale. An exception is a new article on Paul Bunyan which carefully traces the genesis and growth of the Bunyan saga. This article is an outstanding contribution because it lucidly explains how an occupational folk tradition has been transformed into a national legend. However, the disappearance of well-known fictions seems to be a haphazard affair, since they have been retained in many instances. Although new information has been added to the entries on Calcutta and India, the story of the Black Hole massacre has not been disturbed. A revised essay on Venereal Disease continues to present the Columbian origin of syphilis, yet it cites some of the arguments of E. Herndon Hudson who has decisively refuted this theory. Hudson observes in his monograph:

> Sheer post hoc reasoning is the only basis for attributing to Columbus the introduction of syphilis into Europe. . . . The return of Columbus with his 44 sailors and 10 Indians affected the history of treponematosis not a whit. Blot out the return of these 55 men; the march of events as regards syphilis remains as it was, a consistent historical whole.

Although some legends have been eliminated, others have entered the set. This is illustrated by a new article on Columbus. It contains a long discussion of his estimates of the size of the earth, but offers eccentric views about his genealogy. It claims that Columbus was not a Genoese "patriot," that he never declared himself a Genoese, and never went back to the city. Furthermore, he never wrote in any form of Italian, but used Spanish even in his private notes. "One explanation of all these facts," the article asserts, "as well as certain features of his character, is that Columbus came from a Spanish-Jewish family settled in Genoa."

This hypothesis has gained considerable popularity in recent years, thanks to a biography by Salvador de Madariaga, who is also the author of the *Britannica*'s article on Columbus. However, no positive proof can be advanced to support this theory, and it is flatly contradicted by existing evidence. The Castilian employed by Columbus in written documents contains many examples of Portuguese usage, which suggest that he learned the language at the Court of Lisbon, where both Castilian and Portuguese were used concurrently. Columbus stated in his first will that Genoa was his birthplace, and in a letter dated April 2, 1502, he made the city of Genoa the beneficiary of one-tenth of his revenues from the Indies. Therefore there is no need to invoke a "Jewish hypothesis" in explaining his background.

There is no easy way to correct errors and defects. A great deal depends on the diligence of editors and contributors. A lavish set of color plates has been added to the essay on Fishes, but it still asserts that sticklebacks fight to the death and blackfish can survive freezing. A fresh article on Hibernation discusses the temporary dormancy of certain birds, yet it categorically maintains: "No birds are able to enter a state of prolonged hibernation"—despite experimental evidence to the contrary. Finally, the entry on the Wolf now records:

> Wolves usually hunt in small groups, rarely in large packs, catching larger prey—deer, caribou, bighorn, moose—by a chase during which they display both speed and endurance.

But in 1956, Crisler reported in the *Journal of Mammalogy* that wolves are unable to capture caribou in a chase, because caribou are swifter animals—and are in danger only when they are sick or injured.

A new essay on Spiritualism describes the occult powers possessed by certain mediums, but it does not present the scientific objections against spiritualism, or critically examine experimental studies of such supernatural phenomena. The naïve tenor of the article is evident when it concludes: "At least it may be safely said that there is a strong prima facie case for some communication from human spirits that have survived death." The author of this essay also provides an account of Levitation that considers the ability of mediums, saints and holy men to lift themselves into the air by supernatural means. He neither accepts nor rejects these claims, but cautiously declares:

> There are obvious difficulties in the way of experimental study of levitation since it is a rare phenomenon that cannot be produced at will. However, the motion-picture camera and the use of infra-red photography provide means of objective recording that might settle the question of the reality of levitation.

Such "open-mindedness" indicates that the *Britannica* has not adopted a skeptical attitude in dealing with certain popular beliefs.

The *Encyclopaedia*'s analysis of various subjects gradually shifts from year to year because of continuous revision; and these alterations are frequently a revealing index of contemporary ideas and attitudes. Such changes have been particularly marked in sexual areas, since many Victorian entries have been removed and new articles inserted that reflect current freedoms rather than ancient taboos. The 1963 edition discusses Homosexuality, Enuresis, Lesbianism and Nudism; and the shifting attitude toward sexual matters is quite obvious in an analysis of Sexual Deviations that candidly examines such topics as sodomy, bestiality and sadism.

This progress toward greater frankness, however, has definite limits. The *Britannica* does not consider the cultural or social aspects of human sexuality. Instead its essay on Sexual Behaviour presents an elaborate explanation of why these aspects are neglected. In the first place, it claims that to explore the subject from every possible point of view would require more space than is available; yet the essay is more than four pages long. It notes that the sociological approach would presumably deal on a descriptive level with the sexual mores and practices of various human cultures; "but valuable as such data undoubtedly are, they are limited in the sense that they apply only to one of thousands of species that inhabit the earth." The article declares that the treatment of the ethical features of the subject would be "of questionable value, for moral standards change from generation to generation and vary widely from one society or culture to another." Finally, it concludes that the biology of sexual behavior "is a basic part of natural science which can be considered objectively, without reference to moral values; and the zoological approach permits description of the behaviour of any animal, including man, in strictly factual terms."

This zoological approach ignores the findings of modern psychiatry, anthropology and psychoanalysis which demonstrate the pervasive influence of sexual impulses on human culture, behavior and thought. Such a narrow view reduces the sexual responses of *homo sapiens* to a form of mammalian activity, without relating it to its social or historical context. This shallow treatment is not limited to sexual behavior.

The *Britannica*'s index contains fifteen references to "love." They deal with such themes as love in Chinese philosophy, courtly love, Platonic love, and the Christian idea of *agape*; but there is no coherent historical or sociological account of love in the entire *Encyclopaedia*. Instead the subject is discussed parenthetically in more than a dozen different entries. Thus the article on Emotion presents a brief psychological résumé couched in a scientific jargon that may be as illuminating in its own way as the *EB*'s description in 1797:

> Love is the term used to describe such diverse manifestations of behaviour and experience as the parent-child relationship, attachment between the sexes, attachment to places, to things, to occurrences or to food. Most experimental studies on love reactions have been based upon mating and maternal behaviour of animals. Such studies have shown that this behaviour has a substantial innate component and becomes evident later in life through biological maturation rather than through experience and learning.

Providing fresh information is only one aspect of the editors' responsibility. They must insure that changes are made in accordance with a well-coordinated plan, since hundreds of individuals are working on the set. It is difficult to discern such a plan in the 1963 edition, since alterations frequently occur in a random manner. Thus, although some articles on World War I have been condensed or deleted, a host of others have been reprinted without change. Furthermore, the relative neglect of World War II has not been rectified. An exception is a new entry on the Battle of Midway, which is described as "the most decisive battle of World War II in the Pacific." But this entry is only one-fourth as long as one on the Battle of Heligoland Bight, a sweep by British light naval forces on Aug. 28, 1914.

A similar pattern emerges in the social sciences. Many defective essays have been replaced, such as Lynching, Personality and the Caribbean Sea—and new material has been added on such topics as Bureaucracy, Interracial Relations and Abnormal Psychology. Comprehensive treatises have been prepared on Africa and Latin America, but despite these changes, gaps still remain. There is no entry on the Middle East or the Near East, and there is no reference in the index to these important geographical regions. The article on the Far Eastern Area stops with 1928, and a long description of the Russian province of Kamchatka contains no information after 1926. A new essay on Guerrilla Warfare ignores its recent development as a revolutionary instrument by Communist and nationalist movements; and despite the triumph of Castro's guerrilla campaign in Cuba, the essay declares:

> Because guerrilla bands are loosely knit, poorly disciplined, and must remain so, they can never overthrow an enemy or win a war.

The 1963 edition presents critical accounts of Christian Science and Mary Baker Eddy, but it usually assigns Catholic subjects to Catholic scholars who repeat orthodox views. The treatment of the Society of Jesus has been revised by a Jesuit who attributes the suppression of the Order to external agents, rather than internal causes. He states that "the decades preceding the suppression were not a time of either spiritual or intellectual decadence in the society," and he asserts that "the suppression of the society is probably best seen as a prelude to the French Revolution." This deference to clerical ideas may explain why a fresh article on Birth Control which examines its early history and proponents, but mentions only the "safe period" or rhythm method approved by the Catholic Church. This method is noted, but other means of contraception are neither enumerated nor described.

Such examples indicate that revision is not enough to insure superior coverage in the social sciences, since the outlook of the editors and their contributors may reflect the interests of special groups, rather than modern ideas.

Although changes have been somewhat erratic in the social sciences, more attention has been paid to the physical and biological sciences. Many fresh articles have been added on comparative anatomy, and a set of transparent acetate plates graphically portrays successive layers of human anatomy. Antiquated accounts of Mars, Heat and the Compton Effect have been replaced—and new essays appear on such subjects as Stars, Aeronautics, Space Exploration and Low-Temperature Physics. Because of such outstanding entries, the natural sciences are often treated with a thoroughness and lucidity that cannot be matched by other reference works.

These excellent articles must be attributed to the enterprise and enthusiasm of individual contributors, since the editors have accepted hopelessly pedantic material as well as outstanding contributions. An example is the essay on Germanic Languages which discusses Proto-Indo-European in the following way:

> PIE had a spirant s, a few obscure consonants called "laryngeal," and at least the following stops (perhaps more): p t k k^w, b d g g^w, bh dh gh g^wh. By a change known as the Gmc consonant shift (Grimm's law) the stops developed as follows:

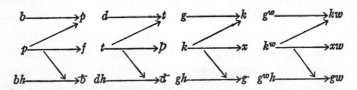

This tabular material is not explained or interpreted—and such learned mumbo-jumbo continues to enter the *Encyclopaedia*.

In chemistry, some entries have been simplified, such as Camphor and Naphthaline, but others rely on a highly technical style. The essay on Carbohydrates contains a host of complex figures and formulas—and the analysis of Molecular Rearrangements employs a dense array of chemical reactions. The article on Organometallic Compounds offers such revelations as:

> Treatment of the product of the interaction of cyclopentadienylsodium and chromium (III) chloride with nitric oxide gas produces cyclopentadienyldinitric oxide-chromium chloride, $C_5H_5Cr(NO)_2Cl$. Reaction of the latter with methylmagnesium iodide gives cyclopentadienylmethyldinitric oxide-chromium $C_5H_5Cr(NO)_2CH_3$, while treatment of $C_5H_5Cr(CO)_3H$ with diazomethane results in cyclopentadienylmethylchromium tricarbonyl, $C_5H_5Cr(CO)_3CH_3$.

The entry on Conformational Analysis discusses the preferred shapes and configurations of organic molecules, and it reports:

> As a corollary to this rule it has also been established that electrophilic addition to the double bond give the trans diaxial product; in most cases this is the thermodynamically less stable one. Thus cholest-2-ene (XIX) gives mainly the diaxial 2β: 3α dibromocholestane (XX).

Since these articles are recent additions, they indicate that the editors have not been aware of the needs of their readers, but have allowed authors to display their erudition ostentatiously. This failing is quite plain in mathematics, where very few entries have been simplified. Rather the reverse has occurred. Topology is now examined in two separate articles—one on Algebraic Topology and the other on General Topology. They analyze such advanced topics as point sets and topological spaces, but omit any simple explanation of their subject. Highly technical essays have been introduced on Algebraic Geometry and Continuous Groups, and the practice of addressing research mathematicians is illustrated by a long article on Complex Analysis. It considers a variety of concepts including "new notions from algebraic topology, namely fibre bundles and chohomology with coefficients in sheaves." But instead of describing these concepts so they can be understood by intelligent laymen, the article supplies thirty-six footnotes referring to original papers in French, German and English.

The treatment of Tensor Algebra illustrates the *EB*'s esoteric approach. It observes:

> If $\phi_{j_1} \otimes \ldots \otimes \phi_{j_s} \otimes e^{i_1} \otimes \ldots \otimes e^{i_r}$ is the tensor which gives the value 1 on $(e^{j_1}, \ldots, e^{j_s}, \phi_{i_1}, \ldots, \phi_{i_r})$ and 0 for any other choice of base vectors, then

$$T = \sum_{i,j=1}^{d} T_{i_1,\ldots,i_r}^{j_1,\ldots,j_s} \phi_{j_1} \otimes \ldots \otimes \phi_{j_s} \otimes e^{i_1} \otimes \ldots \otimes e^{i_r}$$

Such articles demonstrate that editors have not secured contributors who can present scientific information in a form that is meaningful to educated laymen. Instead they have abdicated their editorial function by permitting professors to instruct their colleagues and ignore the public. This misguided policy is evident in forbidding essays on Vector Spaces and Abstract Analysis. The latter discusses Hausdorf and Banach spaces, and one of its simpler passages notes:

> The Fourier expansion theorem and the theory of Fourier series in general have a considerable generalization in which functions of period 2π on the line are replaced by functions on a locally compact abelian group G and integration is carried out with respect to the Haar measure of the groups.

Despite such esoteric material, the Company boasts about the stimulating contents of the set. A recent broadside announces: "EVERY ONE of the 24 volumes of your *Britannica* is a treasure of fascinating reading!"—and it maintains:

> What do you want to know more about? . . . Just name it. Then turn to your *Britannica* and read the fascinating information on the subject. Or, if you want to read just to relax, there's nothing better for the purpose than the "fun reading" you'll find in every page of your *Britannica*. . . .
>
> Pick up any volume—turn to any page and *start reading*. Here, you will discover not a page of dull, dry facts—but the liveliest kind of reading—reading that will keep your eyes glued to the pages until you lose all track of time.

Such claims are not based on the *Encyclopaedia*'s contents, but are designed to increase the sales of the work, and this apparently is the only justification they require. The Company has spent millions of dollars in promoting and advertising the *EB* to establish its reputation for accuracy, utility and modernity. As a result, the public has been led to believe that the claims of the *Britannica* and its actual performance are synonymous. But despite this massive effort to identify the *Encyclopaedia* as a final authority, the 1963 edition contains so many serious faults that it is impossible to equate it with the best in American learning.

[19]

The 1963 Edition

EVERY year a new edition of the *Britannica* is published—accompanied by a flood of press releases and promotional material extolling the set. And each year the Company attempts to capture the interest of consumers by identifying the latest edition as an outstanding contribution to knowledge and a major advance in the *EB*'s development.

Unlike a daily newspaper which is read one day and discarded the next, an encyclopedia may be used for a decade or more. Most families purchase an encyclopedia only once in a lifetime, while libraries may keep a set for five or ten years before replacing it with a later edition. Such a work is consulted for many years, so that the latest edition represents only a small fraction of the sets in the possession of the public. This limits the influence of a given edition when annual revision is employed. As a result, even when drastic changes are made in an encyclopedia, their impact can only be felt gradually, as older copies are replaced and new ones acquired. Therefore the *Britannica*'s image cannot be identified merely with the latest edition, but is derived from editions published over the last decade or more.

An examination of the latest edition offers an opportunity to gauge the *EB*'s reputation for scholarship and the effectiveness of current editorial procedures. The treatment of contemporary artistic movements is a good diagnostic test, because the ebb and flow of artistic taste soon expose editorial neglect. Such a test reveals the inadequacy of the 1963 edition. Its survey of the Music of the 20th Century contains only a few sentences on American composers, and these are primarily lists of names. The account of Post World War II Painting in America measures exactly three inches; and the section on English and American Poetry of the 20th Century treats developments since 1940 in two inches of type containing the names of twenty-seven poets.

The *Britannica* ignores the existence of abstract sculpture. A plate of works in the modern idiom originally appeared in the article on Sculpture Technique, but it has been removed from the 1963 edition, and the text has been reprinted without change. Consequently the entry says nothing about direct methods of metal working favored by many contemporary sculptors—and the vintage of this discussion is obvious from the following:

> It seems strange that in these days of keen athletic youth, great action and intense living, many sculptors are still content with the portrayal of well-rounded and rather phlegmatic female figures usually reminiscent of days long past, in form, position and in name.

The *Encyclopaedia*'s essay on Sculpture is equally retrograde. It fails to acknowledge abstract sculpture as exemplified by the work of Henry Moore, Jacques Lipchitz or Alexander Calder. With the exception of a small Brancusi head, not a single illustration of abstract sculpture accompanies this essay. The most recent information offered is: "Present day (1940) tendencies in sculpture are diverse and seem chaotic."

Although many new entries have been added on modern creative personalities such as Rouault, Léger and Brancusi, striking omissions still persist in the 1963 edition. There are no articles on Sean O'Casey, André Malraux and Jacques Maritain. The entry on Henry Miller refers not to the author of the *Tropic of Cancer,* but to a turn-of-the-century American actor and playwright. The essay on Music identifies Heitor Villa-Lobos as an "outstanding exponent" of music based on national folk themes, but he does not receive a notice. Similarly, Roger Sessions is described as having written "important and skillful works" in the "styles of the Renaissance and middle ages"; but he is not given a biographical entry. Finally, there is no article on the pioneer Charles Ives, but individual notices are devoted to such obscure American composers as Horatio Parker and Amy Beach.

Although the editors provide a good deal of material on notables from earlier generations, they still neglect well-known contemporary figures. In the latest edition, there are entries on the American actresses Julia Marlowe and Mary Anderson, but not on Katherine Hepburn or Judith Anderson. Articles are assigned to the British actors John Hare and Frank Benson, but not to Laurence Olivier or John Gielgud. As a result, the *Britannica*'s biographical coverage often resembles an old *Who's Who* rather than a modern reference work. The danger of obsolete material increases with the number of entries, so that the *Encyclopedia Americana* with 59,000 entries contains even more superfluous biographies and insignificant geographical notices than the *Britannica.*

The latest edition of the *EB* treats a number of major literary figures in a very superficial manner. Although Thomas Mann and André Gide have had international reputations for more than a generation, they are allotted brusque entries that do little more than list the publication dates of their principal works. In a similar fashion, the biography of D. H. Lawrence sums up *Lady Chatterley's Lover* in a single misleading sentence: "He was increasingly obsessed by the problems of sex, as in his famous novel *Lady Chatterley's Lover* (1928)"—and the brief bibliography at the end of this article is more than thirty years old.

The inadequate coverage of contemporary figures is vividly illustrated by the following complete entry:

HESSE, HERMANN (1877–   ), German-born Swiss writer and poet, was born at Calw on July 2, 1877. He wrote a long series of novels, Indian travel sketches and other works. His collected poems appeared in 1942. Four years later he received the Nobel prize in literature.

Bibliographies are an important aspect of an encyclopedia's coverage because they assist readers seeking additional information, and allow them to verify facts presented in particular entries. To be useful, they should emphasize recent studies reflecting modern knowledge. The *Britannica* frequently fails in this respect because many of its bibliographies were prepared more than fifty years ago. This is illustrated by the article on Tacitus which observes:

> Tacitus has been many times translated, in spite of the very great difficulty of the task; the number of versions of the whole or part is stated as 393.

But the most recent translation listed is dated 1904. This is only one of a series of bibliographies taken from the eleventh edition. The latest reference on Sparta is dated 1878, and the latest one on Thebes, in Greece, is for 1890. Such antiquated citations are not unusual. The most recent biography of the English martyr Hugh Latimer is dated 1899, and the article on Samuel Richardson, author of *Pamela*, notes "recent lives" which appeared in 1900 and 1902.

Such obsolete lists are easy to detect because references are usually accompanied by their date of publication—and it is quite obvious that such archaic references are not a reliable guide to contemporary scholarship. Such bibliographies reflect the aged character of the articles to which they are attached, and in some cases they have been retained even though they are useless to the average person. An illustration is the essay on the Hanseatic League. It contains almost a score of references from the turn of the century, all of which are in German.

In other cases, comprehensive articles appear without any bibliography. Examples include the entries on the Schleswig-Holstein Question and the Hundred Years' War—and an extreme instance is the sixteen-page essay on Heraldry which concludes:

> The student may be advised to turn his attention to all works dealing with the effigies, brasses and other monuments of the middle ages, to the ancient heraldic seals and to the heraldry of mediaeval architecture and ornament.

With the exception of a few references in the final paragraph, this advice is not supplemented by a bibliography; yet the article has been reprinted for more than fifty years.

The large number of obsolete bibliographies in the 1963 edition must be due to a deliberate policy of editorial neglect, since the aged character of these references is quite obvious. An example is the following:

> *See* Lunzi, Περὶ τῆς πολιτικῆς καταστάσεως τῆς Ἑπτανήσου ἐπὶ Ἑνετῶν (Athens, 1856); Ansted, *The I.I.* (1863); Viscount Kirkwall, *Four Years in the I.I.* (1864) vol. i.; F. Lenormant, *La Grèce et les iles ioniennes* (1865); P. Chiotis, Ἱστορία τοῦ Ἰονίου κράτους (Zante, 1815–64); Mardo, *Saggio di una descrizione geografico-storica delle Isole* (Corfu, 1865) (mainly geog.); De Bosset, *Description des monnaies d'Ithaque et de Céphalonie* (London, 1815); Postolakas, Κατάλογος τῶν ἀρχαίων νομισμάτων τῶν νήσων Κέρκυρας, Λευκάδος κ. τ. λ. (Athens, 1868); Wiebel, *Die Insel Kephalonia und die Meermühlen von Argostoli* (Hamburg, 1873) . . . .

This comprises one-third of the bibliography accompanying the article on the Ionian Islands, and many similar lists are reprinted from the 1911 edition. Yet the function of a bibliography is to assist readers in locating additional information; this requires as far as possible that references be given to books published in English during the last generation. But this principle has not been adopted by the *Britannica*.

Despite the lavish claims advanced for the 1963 *EB*, it continues to rely on remnants from the famous eleventh edition. As a result, many articles in the field of religion represent the knowledge of 1910, rather than contemporary learning. Examples include entries on historical topics such as the Huguenots, Hussites,

Waldenses, Sūfiism and Monasticism; erudite treatments of the books of Genesis, Leviticus, Samuel and Kings; plus material on Infallibility, Incense, Priest, Pilgrimage, Procession and Sacrifice.

These articles reflect the ponderous approach of an earlier generation—and they are supplemented by ancient bibliographies referring to the scholarly and theological literature of an earlier era. Outmoded essays can be found in other areas of the humanities as well, so it is idle to pretend that the 1963 *Britannica* can be identified with modern scholarship.

Despite the hundreds of *EB* employees engaged in continuous revision and the tens of millions of words that have been changed in the last few years, obsolete relics still survive in the latest edition. A long article on the Niger River traces its course in West Africa, but its most recent information is that the British began dredging the river in 1910. The Victorian essay on the Tamils deals with the language and people who inhabit southern India and Ceylon. It reports:

> The art of printing . . . has also been the means of perpetuating and circulating a deal of literary rubbish and lasciviousness which would much better have remained in the obscurity of manuscript.

And it smugly remarks: "English influence has . . . as in Bengal and elsewhere in India, greatly tended to create a healthier tone in literature both as to style and sentiment."

It is difficult to understand why this two-page article has not been disturbed, particularly when it contains many references to books published in the 1860's and 1870's. Continuous revision demands that *every* entry be inspected at periodic intervals, yet this principle has not been followed.

The publishers claim that the "*Encyclopaedia Britannica* keeps pace with the changing world of knowledge"—and they maintain that the *EB*, "perhaps better than any other work of its kind, reflects today's swift changes in the body of man's knowledge." But readers who examine the 1963 edition may come to different conclusions. The article on Shop Front Design records: "As a matter of solution of design, the stores in America have not shown great brilliancy in spite of the tremendous opportunities that have been presented"—and its latest information is:

> In more recent days through 1935, the tendency has veered more and more toward simplicity—note the stores in the new Rockefeller group in New York.

The entry on Linen was written before the invention of modern synthetic fibers. It asserts:

> Bleached linen, starched and dressed, possesses that unequalled purity, gloss and smoothness which make it alone the material suitable for shirt-fronts, collars and wrist-bands. . . .

The essay on Feathers states that one of their principal applications is in quill pens, and it declares:

> Swan quills are better than those from the goose, and for fine lines crow quills have been much employed. Only the five outer wing feathers of the goose are useful for writing, and of these the second and third are best.

It is obvious from such examples that neither the editors, their consultants, nor advisors know the true age of entries in the set. If all articles were plainly dated, the likelihood of such blunders would be sharply reduced. However, the editors are unlikely to introduce such a daring innovation as long as they are able to deceive the public about the age of the *Encyclopaedia*'s contents.

Despite the rapid pace of industrial progress, a number of entries on technological subjects have been reprinted from the 1929 edition. They include the essays on Lace, Weaving and Glove Manufacture; Hose-Pipe, Gas Holders, Water Turbine, and the Mercury Vapor Boiler. There are even articles, such as Woolen Manufacture, from the 1911 edition. This antiquated approach is exemplified by the essay on the Pianoforte, which discusses the manufacture of pianos with the aid of information and figures gathered fifty years ago.

Despite such obsolete material, the Company has been concerned with the impact of technology on modern life. It sponsored a conference on technological order because, in the words of one official, "the *Britannica* wants to make clear to its readers what technology is, what it means, and what should be done about it." Although the proceedings of the conference fill 280 pages in *Technology and Culture* (Fall, 1962), the practical problems of dealing with this subject in the *Encyclopaedia* were not discussed. Consequently one participant ruefully complained that the only reference to technology in the 1962 edition consisted of two sentences.

For an encyclopedia to bridge successfully the academic and lay worlds, it must keep up with advances in science and scholarship, and offer articles on significant new discoveries. An illustration is the establishment in 1955 of a new phylum in the animal kingdom, Pogonophora, by the Russian zoologist A. V. Ivanov. The importance of this development may be appreciated when it is remembered that all vertebrates are members of a single phylum—Chordata. The Pogonophora were not recognized until recently as a separate phylum because they live inside hollow tubes at the bottom of the ocean. The identification of this phylum was one of the striking events in biology during the last decade, but it is not recorded in the 1963 edition.

Such lapses are inevitable unless the scientific literature is systematically examined for significant material. A good example is the entry on the card game Baccarat which reports: "The banker's advantage cannot be exactly calculated, but has been estimated to be 7% of all the money bet against it." However, a complete theoretical solution of baccarat was presented in 1957 in the *American Mathematical Monthly*. It specifically noted that the *Britannica* was in error, since the banker's advantage is only 1.3 percent, or less than one-fifth the value quoted by the *Encyclopaedia*.

Such lapses are not limited to isolated entries. Sometimes major fields are neglected. The treatment of the Gene has not been disturbed since 1947; therefore the article fails to describe the revolutionary advances in genetics during the last decade. It states that biochemical "studies have not led to a satisfactory explanation of the gene's fundamental property, self-copying"; and this idea is repeated in the article on Genetics. Yet it is contradicted by an essay on Nucleic Acids which discusses the fundamental role of DNA in transmitting hereditary data.

Relying on the *Britannica* as an authority can sometimes lead to embarrassing results. This was illustrated by an editorial in the London *Times* on August 2, 1962. It compared English and German views of academic honors by declaring: "The normal British view is summed up by the *Encyclopaedia Britannica*: 'Degrees in law, medicine and theology still carry with them a license to practice the corresponding professions. . . .'" A few days later, the *Times* printed a correction from one of its readers who pointed out:

> It must surely be well known that to practice law in England it is necessary either to be called to the Bar or admitted a solicitor, for either of which the appropriate professional examination must be passed, degree or not.

Although the *Britannica*'s name emphasizes its British origin, its treatment of English history and ceremonies employs information gathered fifty and seventy-five years ago. Examples include the entries on Knighthood, Peerage, Lord Steward and Lord Chamberlain; as well as the biographies of Henry I–VI, Richard I–III, and George I–II; More, Gardiner, Wycliffe and Pitt; Fox, Sheridan, Hastings, Livingstone and Cardinal Manning. Outmoded facts also appear in other areas of British life. Articles on English law have been taken from the 1929 edition, and one can even find entries from the 1911 edition. Thus the legal analysis of partnerships refers to the Partnership Act of 1890, while the discussion of drunkenness is based on the Inebriates Act of 1879–1900.

Such relics cannot be defended because the editors have repeatedly stressed the importance of providing fresh information. John Armitage, head of the London editorial office which is responsible for history and the humanities, discussed the Company's editorial policies in a speech before the Royal Institution in London. According to the *Times Educational Supplement* (February 16, 1962), he explained that a major task of the eighty people on his staff was to check the accuracy of every new article submitted, and he stated that a fresh article should be written every twenty years, because each generation is dissatisfied with the evaluation of previous writers.

Despite this ideal, essays in almost every branch of history and the humanities have been reprinted from the eleventh edition. In American history, they include the entries on Garfield, McKinley, Patrick Henry and William Lloyd Garrison; as well as those on the Battle of Gettysburg, and the Petersburg, Wilderness and Shenandoah Valley campaigns. Such entries do not reflect current scholarship, and in some cases they have been retained despite serious defects. An example is a description of the Spanish-American War that deals only with the military aspects of the war—and neglects its political causes and subsequent influence on American foreign policy. The age of this account is obvious since it is accompanied by a fifty-year-old bibliography.

Although such old entries may have escaped notice, the editors like to boast about new material entering the set. A great deal of publicity has been given to a fresh article on Oliver Ellsworth, third chief justice of the Supreme Court, because it was written by John F. Kennedy. But there is no entry on Joseph R. McCarthy or McCarthyism. Despite the late Senator's profound influence on American intellectual life during the 1950's, the *Encyclopaedia* contains only a few scattered references to his extraordinary career. An earlier essay on Civil Liberties noted the pernicious effects of McCarthyism, but the current article ignores this sensitive topic.

William Benton during his three years in the Senate was an outspoken and courageous opponent of McCarthy and his reckless methods. In addition, Robert Hutchins as head of the Fund for the Republic was an active leader in the struggle against the excesses of McCarthyism. Yet the *Britannica* has failed to examine this threat to American freedom.

Although many prominent liberals are associated with the *Britannica*, its biography of Franklin Roosevelt only discusses his first term, so that readers must still turn to other entries for an account of his second and third terms. A fresh article on Herbert Hoover has been added which is written from a conservative Republican point of view. It maintains that "the U.S. had been making a slow but certain recovery from the recession when in 1931 . . . the European financial collapse occurred"; and it rather plaintively observes that despite Hoover's "extensive and constructive program for dealing with the depression . . . the electorate failed to return him to Office." If the 1963 edition examines Hoover's entire career, why should FDR's biography only treat four of his twelve years as President?

The difficult task of illuminating current history is often avoided by presenting a brief factual résumé of recent events. A new article on Concentration Camps occupies three columns. One column is devoted to Soviet labor camps, and another to Nazi concentration camps. Within such a brief space, it is impossible to explore the nature and operation of these camps in any real depth. At best, it can only skim over the subject. Even so, some of the facts supplied are misleading. The article notes:

> The most notorious of the extermination centers was the concentration camp at Auschwitz (Oświęcim), Pol. Rudolf Hoess, the commandant of Auschwitz, confessed to the extermination of 2,500,000 people in that camp alone.

This figure was first given by Hoess at the Nuremberg trials, but at his subsequent trial in Warsaw, he stated that about one million died at Auschwitz—and this estimate has been confirmed by later studies. Yet the article on Oświęcim reports that about four million people died there. Excessive statistics also appear in the essay on Anti-Semitism which employs 1945 estimates. It records that from 18 to 26 million people were killed by the Germans in concentration camps; but this figure was given as 12 million at the Nuremberg trials.

The *Britannica* is continually cited as an authority, yet its facts sometimes shift in a dramatic fashion. In 1958, it recorded that 300,000 people died in the bombing raids on Dresden in 1945. However, in the 1963 edition, this number has been reduced to 35,000 without any explanation. The Dresden fire storm is still described as "the greatest fire of World War II," yet on the next page the *Encyclopaedia* reports that nearly 84,000 people were killed by fire during the bombing raids on Tokyo in 1945. Such discrepancies may be disturbing, but a more serious defect is the systematic neglect of the human consequences of war. A new article on War Crimes examines the legal basis for trying war criminals, but it fails to describe any wartime atrocities. The essay on National Socialism has been revised by Hans Kohn, who wrote the earlier entries on Nazism. He declares:

> It was a stroke of genius on the part of Hitler to find this common denominator in the Jews and Judaism. This enabled him to discover the "Jew" behind all his changing adversaries . . . behind everybody and everything that at a given moment opposed his wishes or aroused his wrath.

Professor Kohn does not trace the results of this "stroke of genius," or examine the crimes committed by the Nazis. Instead he concentrates on the early history of the party, and devotes only two vague sentences to its wartime atrocities:

> In addition, however, to the now debased methods of the normal judicial process, special detention camps were erected. In these camps—of which some, such as Dachau and Auschwitz, achieved notoriety—the S.S. exercised supreme authority and introduced a system of sadistic brutality unknown in modern times and by far surpassing anything known in that respect in Fascist Italy or Communist Russia.

What insight can be possessed by an editor who accepts an essay on National Socialism that passes so hurriedly over Nazi deeds and describes Auschwitz and Dachau as "special detention camps"?

Despite the *Encyclopaedia*'s shallow treatment of contemporary issues, the Company maintains that it is a valuable aid in understanding current events. An advertisement in *Newsweek* (November 12, 1962) asks readers if they "know *how* things happen"—and asserts:

To be thoroughly informed on current events—to understand their implications for today and tomorrow—you need comprehensive background information. There is no better source than *Encyclopaedia Britannica*. *Britannica*'s clear, complete and authoritative coverage of every subject gives you new insight into events happening all over the world.

Despite such claims, the *Britannica* is not an adequate synthesis of current knowledge. It is an enormous jumble of facts; a collection of old and new articles; a mixture of legends and science, outmoded views and modern ideas. It is hard to believe that Mr. Benton's "Information Catalogue" is inspired by any large purpose or enlightened philosophy. It merely seems a product of American mass production—representing the labor of dozens of editors, hundreds of advisors, and thousands of contributors. The result is an enormous hodgepodge of 38 million words which is offered each year as a monument of contemporary learning—but which proves each year, despite incessant efforts to patch up its obsolescent contents, to be merely a makeshift substitute for learning.

Publicists may have successfully inflated this "Information Catalogue" into a national institution, but it cannot be accepted as the reference standard of the English-speaking world by anyone who is seriously concerned with intellectual values.

[20]

The Commercial Influence

I N addition to being a repository of knowledge, the *Britannica* is a business enterprise. Its owners, like other businessmen, hope their activities will yield a healthy monetary return—and many of their decisions are influenced by financial considerations. This attitude is reinforced by a traditional emphasis in the reference book field on sales, rather than scholarship. Consequently, commercial motives may explain many current policies.

The Company markets a number of products including a yearbook, an atlas, a two-volume dictionary, and a bookcase to house the *Encyclopaedia*. A subsidiary film company, owned by William Benton, is one of the largest producers and distributors of educational motion pictures in the United States. The idea behind the *Book of the Year* is quite simple: due to the inevitable progress of knowledge, the *Encyclopaedia* gradually becomes obsolete and new material must be added to cover general developments. Inevitably, the yearbook contains a great deal of ephemeral information. The rapidity of publication places a premium on topical themes, since there is little opportunity to explore significant advances in science and scholarship. The text often reads like a digest from the news columns of the *New York Times*, supplemented by photographs culled from *Life* magazine and other pictorial sources. This journalistic emphasis is reflected in the absence of references and bibliographies. However, motion pictures produced by the EB Film Company are carefully listed at the end of relevant articles, even though these films are not available to the average reader. Basically the yearbook is an annual review of a standard set of topics. But political changes, historical trends and scientific progress do not take place in twelve-month cycles. The use of such a short time-span does not allow transient events to be separated from significant long-range developments, which is necessary for an intelligent survey of contemporary knowledge.

The idea of a yearbook is not very practical, because to cover a single decade requires ten volumes occupying nearly half as much space as the *Britannica* itself. A much more sensible plan might be to issue a supplement every two or three years so that important advances could be covered in a reasonable number of volumes. This would provide editors with sufficient time to prepare surveys of different subjects with a depth and thoroughness impossible when an annual deadline must be met. Despite its limitations, the Company markets 800,000 copies of the yearbook annually. One reason for these large sales is that customers who order the *Encyclopaedia* usually agree to buy the yearbook at $4.95 a volume until they cancel their subscriptions. Its commercial character is emphasized by separate British and American editions which cater to special interests in each country, even though the same *Encyclopaedia* is published in the two countries.

The *Book of the Year* is only moderately successful as a means of preventing obsolescence. Two examples may be cited. The Dead Sea Scrolls were discovered in 1947, but a comprehensive article did not appear on the subject until 1958. Although radioactive fallout has been a matter of grave international concern since 1954, it was ignored until the 1960 edition, and then simply dismissed on the ground that its intensity is much smaller than natural radiation.

In the past, the yearbook carried biographical notices on leading personalities associated with the Company who were not in the *Britannica* itself. Such individuals included Robert Hutchins, William Benton, and the Chancellor of the University of Chicago. Sir Geoffrey Crowther joined this select circle after he was appointed chairman of the Encyclopaedia Britannica Ltd. in 1956. His biography appeared in the 1957 and 1958 *Book of the Year,* and reported that he is "bringing to this essentially Anglo-American enterprise a firm belief in the indispensability of the transatlantic alliance." However, in November, 1959, Sir Geoffrey was replaced as chairman of EB Ltd. by William Benton, who is also chairman of the American company. Needless to say, the biographical entry on Sir Geoffrey no longer appears in the American *Book of the Year.*

The *Britannica* has suffered from the practice of marketing subsidiary publications. The quality of its atlas in the last volume has deteriorated because the Company markets a separate *World Atlas* retailing for $27.50. As late as 1947, the *Encyclopaedia*'s atlas contained 224 pages of maps and a map index of 188 pages. A few years later, however, the size of the atlas was cut in half, so its maps now occupy a mere 108 pages with an index of 126 pages.

The 1959 edition of the *World Atlas* asserts that its program of periodic revision insures that its position "on the frontiers of Atlas production is held." Despite this claim, its political maps have been reprinted with permission from Rand-McNally, with only minor alterations from the latter's *Cosmopolitan Atlas* issued in 1949. The preface of the *World Atlas* distinguishes several types of atlases. One merely gives bare facts, another is an instrument of nationalism by orienting itself to the interests of a single nation, but:

> . . . the third kind is a true world atlas. Its subject matter is oriented to a world perspective, recognizing the common interests of all nations. Such is the *Encyclopaedia Britannica World Atlas*—an instrument of international education and understanding.

These sentiments are quite commendable in an age when international co-operation has become a necessity, but unfortunately the contents of the *World Atlas* fall short of this lofty ideal. There are 120 plates of political maps occupying 240 pages. But fifty-two of these plates are devoted to the United States, and ten more deal with Canada and its provinces, so that more than half the political maps are devoted to North America. This is hardly an international outlook, particularly when individual American states each receive a separate map, but only four pages are used to cover the entire continent of Africa.

The foreword reminds readers that "this *World Atlas* carries the dominant notes of world perspective, distinguished scholarship and technical excellence." One of its major innovations is a set of sixty plates offering a broad survey of cultural and demographic factors, linguistic areas and climatic conditions around the world. One section describes the territorial possessions of various colonial powers. The 1959 edition reports:

> Little Belgium and the large Congo comprise the most complete integration of the metropole and colony anywhere. Both units contribute to joint prosperity and stability through the reciprocal nature of their resources, brought to fruition by an intelligent policy. The test is, "Does it pay?," but an acceptable policy must go beyond francs to include long term satisfactions for both Belgians and Congolese. . . . The friction between Europeans and Africans that has engendered outbursts in many parts of the Negro continent has not yet appeared in the Congo.

One wonders about the "distinguished scholarship" that could describe Belgian colonial policy as "intelligent" in 1959 and ignore the "wind of change" sweeping the African continent.

One usually thinks of an atlas as a collection of maps, but more than half the *World Atlas* consists of statistical tables on a wide variety of financial and economic matters. Since most of the figures in the 1959 edition refer to 1955 and 1956, they were somewhat antiquated even when the *Atlas* was new. A more serious defect is the absence of graphs or charts that would make these statistics meaningful to the average person. At present, they are simply listed in a series of tables without interpretation or discussion—and it is hard to believe that three hundred pages of economic statistics on 150 different countries can be very useful to the general public, particularly when they are at least three or four years old.

In 1952 the *Britannica* completed one of its most ambitious projects with the publication of the *Great Books of the Western World*, edited by Robert Hutchins and Mortimer Adler. This fifty-four-volume set contains 32,000 pages and 25 million words. It includes 443 works by seventy-three authors ranging from Homer to Freud; and one of its novel features is the *Syntopicon*, a two-volume index, which is based on 102 "Great Ideas" divided into three thousand subtopics. This unusual index containing 163,000 references is quite helpful to scholars, because it allows them to collate different passages in the *Great Books* dealing with particular subjects or ideas. More than a million dollars was spent in preparing the *Syntopicon*, and this feature has been heavily stressed in marketing the set.

Although the *Great Books* set attempts to cover the major literary and scientific works of Western culture, it omits the dramas of Racine and Molière, the orations of Cicero and Demosthenes, and the poetry of Horace and Pindar. These omissions may be due to a shortage of space, yet the entire first volume is devoted to a long essay by Dr. Hutchins explaining the importance of the *Great Books*.

Although two volumes are assigned to St. Thomas Aquinas and one volume to St. Augustine, not a single Protestant religious thinker appears in the set. No attempt has been made to separate works possessing a contemporary interest from those which are significant for historical reasons. Consequently, two thousand pages are allotted to St. Thomas Aquinas who is concerned with such questions as:

> Whether Angels Know the Future?
> Whether there Is Sorrow in Demons?
> Whether an Angel Can Be in Several Places at Once?
> Whether the Woman was Fittingly Made from the Rib of Man?

Although more than two million dollars was spent in preparing the set for publication, it presents many of the classics in dull, archaic nineteenth-century versions. As a result, Homer, Sophocles and Euripides are given in the pedestrian prose of Butler, Jebb and E. P. Coleridge, respectively. This frugal policy has presumably been followed because these old translations are in the public domain and can be used without paying royalties. Nevertheless, the Company piously maintains in the reading guide on poetry issued with the *Great Books*: "Homer's *The Iliad* and *The Odyssey*, Vol. 4, and Dante's *The Divine Comedy*, Vol. 21, though given in prose translation, retain many of the poetic qualities of the originals."

Dwight Macdonald in a celebrated critique in the *New Yorker* (November 29, 1952) cited a number of other defects in the set. He observed that minor works by major authors are included, while major works by minor authors are excluded. Shakespeare's *Two Gentlemen of Verona* is reprinted—rather than Marlowe's *Dr. Faustus*, Webster's *Duchess of Malfi* or Jonson's *Volpone*. English poetry is restricted to Shakespeare, Milton and Chaucer—and there are no selections from Balzac, Stendhal or Flaubert. Six hundred pages are allotted to Kant, but there is nothing by Nietzsche or Kierkegaard. Three hundred pages are occupied by Montesquieu, but none by Voltaire or Diderot.

After analyzing the futile attempt to decompose the classics into 102 Great Ideas, Macdonald concluded:

> In its massiveness, its technological elaboration, its fetish of The Great, and its attempt to treat systematically and with scientific precision materials for which the method is inappropriate, Dr. Adler's set of books is a typical expression of the religion of culture that appeals to the American academic mentality. . . .
>
> The problem is not placing these already available books in people's hands (at five dollars a volume) but getting people to read them, and the hundred pounds of densely printed, poorly edited reading matter assembled by Drs. Adler and Hutchins is scarcely likely to do that.

The *Great Books* attempts to embrace the sciences as well as the humanities. Eleven volumes are devoted to scientific "classics," but this approach is handicapped by the enormous expansion of scientific knowledge. Brief technical papers have replaced long treatises as a means of communicating important discoveries, so it is impossible to supply a representative view of modern science with the aid of a small group of original works. Thus, electricity is represented in the *Great Books* by Faraday's *Experimental Researches* published a century ago, chemistry by Lavoisier's *Elements* of 1782, and astronomy by Newton's *Principia* of 1682. Indeed, the set does not include a single twentieth-century selection in the natural sciences—so it contains no information on atomic structure, organic chemistry or nuclear physics.

The Company has attempted to overcome this deficiency by issuing an annual volume, *Great Ideas Today*, to keep readers informed of recent progress. The 1961 volume contains a survey of physics and technology that discusses the application of the Mössbauer effect in testing Einstein's general theory of relativity. At the end of this survey, readers are reminded that if they wish to investigate such topics in greater detail they will find "much useful and interesting material" in the *Syntopicon* and the *Great Books*. They are then referred to the works of Fourier, Faraday and Newton. But suggesting these classics as a background for twentieth-century physics is like offering *Beowulf* and Chaucer as an aid to understanding Faulkner and *Finnegans Wake*.*

Most of the selections in the set are published in their entirety. Apollonius' treatise on conics occupies 205 pages, and Ptolemy's *Almagest* is a 494-page account based on the mistaken idea that the sun and the planets revolve about the earth. No effort is made to justify the particular works chosen, or suggest how laymen should tackle these formidable works. They are offered as a kind of sacred text. Thus readers are presented with 396 pages of Euclid's *Elements* containing such propositions as:

* Jean-Paul Sartre's *Existentialism* is reprinted in the 1963 edition of the *Great Ideas Today*, but Sartre does not receive a biographical entry in the *Britannica*.

If a rational straight line be cut in extreme and mean ratio, each of the segments is the irrational straight line called apotome.

If an area be contained by a rational straight line and a fourth apotome, the "side" of the area is minor.

The square on the major straight line applied to a rational straight line produces breadth as the fourth binomial.

The antiquarian spirit permeating the *Great Books* is illustrated by its neglect of modern mathematics. Its treatment of the theory of numbers is not based on Gauss, Dedekind, or later mathematicians—but on Nicomachus of Gerasa (*ca.* 100 A.D.). No distinction is made between important discoveries and traditional folklore, so that 160 pages are allotted to Hippocrates who reports:

In women, blood collected in the breasts indicates madness. When summer is like spring, much sweating may be expected in fevers.

In a woman when there is a stoppage of the menses, a discharge of blood from the nose is good.

When scientific selections are included in an anthology like the *Great Books*, they should be chosen because of their importance and accessibility to educated laymen. There is no point in offering treatises requiring intensive study by specialists, if the aim is to provide a liberal education for the average reader. Selection and interpretation are necessary because many scientific classics were originally addressed, not to the general public, but to other scientists whose training and background enabled them to evaluate fresh research. This is why discoveries of the highest importance may first be presented in a manner that is incomprehensible to the ordinary person.

Using original works to gain an understanding of science and its methods is a challenging task; its success largely depends on the skill with which suitable excerpts are chosen and explained. In examining the ideas and experiments of earlier scientists, it is necessary to separate their essential contributions from material superseded by later research. Their achievements must be placed in a historical perspective, and their terminology related to current usage. The need for such editorial help is ignored in the *Great Books*, which presents scientific classics without footnotes or critical introductions. This economical policy is defended by Dr. Hutchins in the first volume:

> The Advisory Board recommended that no scholarly apparatus should be included in the set. No "introductions" giving the Editor's views of the authors should appear. The books should speak for themselves, and the reader should decide for himself. . . . Since we hold these works are intelligible to the ordinary man, we see no reason to interpose ourselves or anybody else between the author and the reader.

However, it is difficult to see how the "ordinary man" can be expected to comprehend Apollonius' geometrical propositions or Archimedes' theorems.

Despite the obvious difficulty of scientific selections in the set, Dr. Hutchins maintains in the first volume:

> We believe that it is a gratuitous assumption that anybody can read poetry, but very few can read mathematics. In view of the countless engineers and technicians in our society, we expect many of our readers to find the mathematical and scientific masterpieces more understandable than many other works.

However, the geometrical constructions and proofs used several centuries ago are quite different from current mathematical methods. Therefore most engineers will be unable to follow the arguments of Copernicus and Newton.

Although the editors believe that scientific classics can speak directly to many people without the assistance of intermediaries, this faith is not shared by the Company's advertising which repeatedly emphasizes the need for such aid. A typical assertion appeared in *Life* magazine (February 10, 1961):

> Very few people have either the time or money to return to school, and to embark on a program of self-education without a teacher is both unrewarding and unproductive. Guidance, interpretation, discussion are necessary to help you relate the total experience of the whole human race to the problems of today.

Advertisements portray the *Syntopicon* as a "teacher" that will provide such assistance; but the *Syntopicon* is merely an index of ideas which is of little help in unraveling Ptolemy's mathematical reasoning or Fourier's differential equations.

Although a number of critics have questioned the scientific coverage of the *Great Books*, the editors have not attempted to rectify these faults by selecting new works, or supplying scholarly introductions and footnotes that would assist readers. Instead of attempting to provide an adequate comprehension of basic scientific principles, they have actively promoted the set as a means of meeting "life's challenges and problems with courage, confidence, and intelligence." In line with this policy, advertisements for the *Great Books* frequently carry personal sales messages from Robert Hutchins and Mortimer Adler. The resulting shift in their activity—from scholars to merchandising men—was aptly illustrated when Dr. Adler delivered the keynote address at the annual convention of the American Bookseller's Association in June, 1962 on the subject, "How to Sell a Book."

Despite its defects, the *Great Books* has been successfully marketed as a status symbol and a method of acquiring the "Great Ideas" of Western culture. According to *Time* magazine (April 20, 1962), sales have increased tenfold, from 5,256 sets in 1956 to 51,083 in 1961—corresponding to a gross income of $22 million a year. Thus whatever criticism may be leveled against the work, there can be little doubt that it has become a remarkably profitable way of marketing old classics by modern techniques.

The Company offers several special services to owners of the *Encyclopaedia*. If they supply the names of people who might be interested in acquiring the work, they are eligible to receive "home reading guides" on a variety of subjects. These guides are helpful in planning a course of home study because they contain a classified list of books on particular subjects. In addition to these optional guides, each purchaser receives fifty coupons entitling him to submit fifty questions over a period of ten years to the Britannica Library Research Service. The service supplies a written reply to each question provided it does not involve medical or legal topics, or infringe on professional ethics. In many cases, the answers are miniature library reports that not only contain a reply to a specific inquiry, but a detailed list of references as well. To limit the number of requests, only one question is answered at a time, and no more than ten questions may be submitted in any calendar year. According to the director of the service, only one thousand questions were answered in 1936, but a total of 110,000 were handled in 1959. Since about 150,000 copies of the *Britannica* are now sold each year, this means that an average of about one question is answered for each set sold.

The *Britannica* is more than a reference work dedicated to the diffusion of knowledge; it is part of a business empire. A separate mail order division periodically sends out circulars with special offers to individuals paying for either the *Great Books* or the *Encyclopaedia* on the installment plan. This division has successfully distributed many products including books, records, typewriters and movie cameras. In February, 1961, the Britannica became the largest firm in the reference field when it acquired *Compton's Pictured Encyclopedia.* As a result of this purchase, the Company now offers a full line of works including *Britannica* for adults, *Compton's* for high school students and *Britannica Junior* for elementary school students.

Competitors have shown that large profits can be made by emphasizing salesmanship rather than scholarship. The resulting conflict between commercial success and editorial standards has created a dichotomy in the Company's activities. On one hand, editors endeavor to pursue the goals of academic learning with the limited means at their disposal; and on the other, executives seek to increase sales by impressing the public with the *EB*'s accuracy and utility. Consequently the Company's image has been split into two contradictory components. One stresses the *Encyclopaedia* as a symbol of learning and authority; the other associates its salesmen with dubious claims and high-pressure salesmanship.

The educational director of the *Britannica* supplied a good illustration of these dubious claims when he asserted in an advertisement in the *Library Journal* (November 1, 1954): "It is so universally accepted as an authority that courts of law admit ENCYCLOPAEDIA BRITANNICA as evidence."

This claim has been repeated many times in the Company's direct mail campaigns, although it does not agree with established legal principles. Whenever a judge takes note of certain well-known facts without the testimony of witnesses, this process is known as judicial notice. However, it is an elementary legal principle that judicial notice can only be taken of scientific facts or matters that are generally or universally known, and which therefore can be found in encyclopedias, dictionaries or other reference works. These facts must be matters of common knowledge—and not questions where a difference of opinion exists. Thus scientific treatises and encyclopedias may be consulted by judges, but they are *not evidence*. One reason for this rule is that they cannot be placed under oath and cross-examined. Another is that citations in one book may be contradicted by other books unknown to the court. Therefore troublesome factual matters—such as disputed medical questions—require the testimony of expert witnesses.

There is one exception to this rule, however. Tables of weights and measures, as well as interest and mortality tables, are accepted as evidence because they are not subject to dispute. Seventy years ago, mortality tables were not available in convenient published form, but the ninth edition carried a set of the Carlisle mortality tables, which were widely employed in the insurance field. As a result, the *Encyclopaedia* was cited in several negligence suits against American railroads involving the death of the plaintiff (41 N.W. 26; 64 P. 203) in order to establish the plaintiff's life expectancy at the time of death.

With the exception of this special application many years ago, the *Britannica* has not been used *as evidence* in the courtroom, except as a source of juridically noticeable facts, because it would violate fundamental rules of legal procedure. This caution in relying on printed authorities is well founded. An illustration is the *EB*'s article on Ordeal which asserts:

> . . . The Bedouin will settle a conflict of evidence by the opposing witnesses licking a glowing hot iron spoon. This latter feat may be done with safety provided the iron be

clean and thoroughly white-hot, while if only red-hot it would touch and burn the tongue.

This is obviously nonsense. A white-hot spoon possesses a higher temperature than a red-hot one, so that if a red-hot spoon can touch and burn the tongue, an even more severe burn would be administered by a white-hot one.

Such claims are a reminder that an encyclopedia is a commercial product, as well as a repository of learning. Therefore it is necessary to consider how such a work is marketed, as well as edited.

[21]

Bold Advertising and the Hard Sell

THE publication and distribution of encyclopedias is a large and flourishing business. During 1960, $260 million were spent by the American public on reference works—an amount which was almost three times the dollar volume of adult trade books marketed through stores. The sale of encyclopedias has benefited from the mounting stress on higher education and the competition for entrance into a few select Ivy League colleges. This has made it much easier for salesmen to persuade people that knowledge is an important asset, and reference books are a valuable possession. Parents are now eager to acquire any aid that will assist their children in obtaining the higher education that seems essential for their future social success and financial prosperity. The publishers of encyclopedias have recognized this shift toward a child-oriented society and are acting accordingly.

This change may be seen in the *Britannica*'s advertising program. Once upon a time, appeals were directed primarily to adults who were told that ownership of the set would make them socially stimulating and intellectually respected. This was a natural approach because the *Encyclopaedia* is a reference work intended for adult readers. But that appeal has now been superseded by a new, more persuasive line aimed at the parents of young children. The New Look can be documented by a series of advertisements that appeared in the Sunday Book Section of the *New York Times* during 1959. On February first parents were asked (Plate I *detail*):

WHICH IS MORE IMPORTANT TO YOUR CHILD . . .
THE SIZE OF HIS HOME OR THE SIZE OF HIS MIND?

And they were told: "The first step in enlarging the mind is knowledge, and that is why thinking parents put the acquisition of the *Encyclopaedia Britannica* before any other possession." Such a positive statement has a powerful appeal for parents who observe their children taking more interest in television and comic books than in reading and studying.

On August 23rd a deeper note was struck when parents were asked (Plate II *detail*):

ARE YOU GIVING YOUR CHILDREN MORE THAN YOU HAD?

This question capitalizes on a strong American tradition which is epitomized in the immigrant's dream of a better life, not for himself, but for his children. Any suggestion that parents may not be doing their best for their offspring is bound to create anxiety, and once this feeling is aroused, parents are informed that if they "want to give their children this priceless gift of knowledge—the *Encyclopaedia Britannica* is an essential possession."

To lend distinction to these messages, they appeared under the name of Dr. J. Chapman Bradley, who presumably is an educator or eminent child psychologist. But there is some difficulty in determining Dr. Bradley's credentials. He is not listed in *Who's Who in America*, or *Who's Who in American Education*, or in any of the other standard biographical reference works. Fortunately, however, his background is briefly described by Herman Kogan in *The Great EB*. Mr. Kogan relates that

"Doc" Bradley served as an ordained Presbyterian minister for a decade, and then was a top executive of the American Bible Society. He invented display plates for automobiles and headed a company that marketed them. Since 1946 "Doc" Bradley has been with the *Britannica*—first as a salesman and district manager in the Bronx, and then as a division manager in Chicago. Presumably "Doc" Bradley's important sales position has made him an authority on why the *Encyclopaedia* is an essential aid in educating youngsters.

The Company has gone even farther in its hypnotic appeal to anxious parents. A high point was reached in the *New York Times* on September 27th, near the beginning of the school year, when parents were asked (Plate III *detail*):

HOW CAN YOU EXPRESS THE INEXPRESSIBLE LOVE YOU FEEL
FOR YOUR CHILD?

Lest parents be at a loss for an answer, they were instructed in the *EB* catechism: "Probably the most concrete way in which we show a genuine concern for our children is in the concern we have for their education. . . . There can be no doubt that a respect for knowledge exists in a home where the *Encyclopaedia Britannica* is a valued possession."

To make sure this point would sink home, the message was accompanied by a touching picture of a mother and her small son—who could hardly be more than five years old. Having successfully aroused the deep-seated instincts of parental love and responsibility, sales executives can confidently await the flood of little coupons which will bring parents an inevitable visit from a smooth-talking salesman. The fact that the *Britannica* is not intended for children—and cannot be used by children because of its scholarly and technical content—is immaterial as far as copywriters are concerned. Their mission is to increase sales, and the truth of their copy is secondary. Therefore they seek to create an irresistible message which will make the *EB seem* indispensable to parents concerned with the welfare of their children. It is only natural for advertising men to play on the sensitivity of middle-class parents who are frightened by the prospect that they may be unwittingly depriving their children of some precious asset required for their future success.

Executives are ready to use any emotion that will help sell their product. An advertisement in *Good Housekeeping* (March, 1961) shows a glowing picture of two starry-eyed youngsters and asks (Plate IV *detail*):

HOW WILL THEY MEASURE UP AGAINST THE KIDS NEXT DOOR?

Parents are reminded: "Uncomfortable as the idea is, this is the time to face it. Everyone wants more for his children. And your children will have to compete just as *you're* competing now in the adult world." Thus, it seems, not only must adults keep up with the Joneses, but their children must measure up against the kids next door. This sales message concludes: "The *Britannica* is more than words—and more than its brilliant illustrations. It is a seeking of the mind for truth and fact. It is priceless for your children. It can be equally invaluable to you."

The appearance of this advertisement in *Good Housekeeping* is of special significance because it offers a unique consumer guarantee: *"If any guaranteed product or service is not as advertised herein, it will, upon request and verification of complaint, be replaced or the money paid therefor refunded."* Products which are advertised in the magazine and approved by its Institute are entitled to use the familiar Good Housekeeping Seal, which is supposed to create a "climate of confidence" for consumers.

The May, 1961 issue of the magazine carried a special "Buyer's Guide" containing a list of approved goods and services. Its introduction stated: "All the fine products and services in this Guide and the advertising claims made for them in *Good Housekeeping* had to meet the requirements of the famous Good Housekeeping Institute before being accepted for advertising in

Good Housekeeping." Among the products listed were the *Encyclopaedia Britannica* and *Compton's Pictured Encyclopedia,* which is owned by the *Britannica.* One can understand how *Good Housekeeping* can test hair rinses, heating pads and vacuum cleaners, but how is it able to evaluate a reference work like the *Britannica?* What standards does it apply and how does it determine the accuracy and utility of a work of 38 million words?

Since the *Britannica* is in the "Buyer's Guide," it is entitled to use the Good Housekeeping Seal of Approval; and there is little doubt that such a privilege may be a valuable sales asset. This was stressed in an advertisement in the *New York Herald Tribune* (July 18, 1961) which declared:

> *Good Housekeeping* offers another open sesame, potent beyond all others: The magazine itself, the Institute, and the Good Housekeeping Consumers' Guaranty Seal open the mind and close the sale because . . . nothing persuades and sells like the truth.

Is *Good Housekeeping* ready to defend the "truth" of *Britannica* advertising that has appeared in its pages? Or is it ready to offer a refund to readers who have purchased the set and discovered that it is not suitable for youngsters? In short, is the Good Housekeeping Seal a shield for the public, or merely an added inducement for advertisers?*

Other reference works have advanced doubtful claims. An advertisement for the *Encyclopedia Americana* (*Saturday Review,* March 24, 1962) asserts: "Its accuracy, thoroughness, and ease of use make it equally indispensable to the junior high school student and the most advanced scholar." It is difficult to see

---

* Child-oriented advertising is still being employed. An advertisement in *Good Housekeeping* (September, 1963) states:
  Britannica covers every conceivable interest a child could have. It is made to make young minds grow. . . .
  Britannica keeps a child's mind actively growing and learning. No other reference work can do so much to develop hidden talents into successful careers.

how the *Americana*, or any encyclopedia, can be indispensable for *both* the junior high school student and the most advanced scholar, but such difficulties are ignored by the copywriters and executives responsible for such exaggerated statements.

The *Britannica*'s emotional appeals, which have been so successful in the United States, have been employed in the British Isles as well. On January 7, 1962, the Company launched a massive advertising campaign in leading Sunday newspapers in England. Large ads carried the bold caption: "The Britannica man opens the door to knowledge. . . . He represents a great cultural and educational organisation which is helping hundreds of thousands of families like yours to a better life." Readers were told:

> *How the Britannica man can advise you.* You can talk to him like a family friend. Tell him about your home, your children. Discuss school work, family hobbies, your interests, your hopes and your ambitions. Introduce him to your whole family, and let him judge for himself how he can best use his experience to help you, and your wife and children.

Thus the *Britannica* man becomes an educational counselor and a family friend, rather than a salesman trying to sell a set of books.

The marketing of encyclopedias is one of the last strongholds of direct selling. To attract likely prospects, many interesting techniques have been devised. One of the oldest is a phone call from a salesman who announces that you have been selected to receive a set free of charge because you are a distinguished figure or an "opinion leader" in your community. The mere presence of the work in your home, he tells you, will reduce the necessity for local advertising by publicizing the set among your neighbors. Later when he arrives to discuss the matter, he informs you, oh yes, there is a small charge (of several hundred dollars), but assures you that this is much less than the cost to an ordinary consumer. The figure mentioned, of course, is what everyone else pays.

This technique was described in the *Saturday Evening Post*

(July 28, 1945) by E. H. Powell, who served for many years as the *Britannica*'s chief executive officer. When Mr. Powell discovered that *EB* salesmen were using this devious approach, he was appalled and ordered a thorough reform of the sales staff to eliminate the unethical practice. But Mr. Powell left the *Britannica* in 1948. As many consumers have learned, this ancient method has been revived by salesmen and executives whose desire for additional income has overcome their moral scruples.

The Company's methods have attracted the attention of the United States Government. In 1952 the Federal Trade Commission in Washington issued a Cease and Desist Order to halt the School Advancement Program which was being used to sell the *Britannica Junior*, because the program claimed to be aiding schools when it was primarily a device for selling books. In this program (FTC Reports *48*, 1416), a school would receive a free set whenever a total of fifteen sets had been sold through the school. Under the plan, agents obtained the names and addresses of parents as prospective customers, but according to the FTC, the Company's agents often misleadingly represented that the school or its officials were sponsoring the sale of the set. Therefore the Commission ordered the Company to terminate this program.

In July, 1958 hearings were held by the FTC in Chicago to investigate charges that the *Britannica* was being offered at special prices. The initial decision of the hearing examiner (Docket No. 7137) was released to the public in September, 1960: it stated that *Encyclopaedia* prices for a combination of books and research material had been misrepresented. The examiner found the price of $511.50 shown in a typical brochure furnished to salesmen "is fictitiously padded in the amount of $120." This initial decision was disputed by the Company and the case was appealed to the full Commission because as a spokesman in Chicago explained, the *Britannica* has always adhered to the highest selling standards. On June 16, 1961, the Commission sustained the findings of the hearing examiner, but noted that the *Britannica*'s price was only padded to the extent of $49.50. It quoted from the Company's advertising material, as well as the claims made by its agents, which created the impression that consumers were being given a "MONEY SAVING OFFER," which would allow them "to acquire the WORLD'S MOST CHERISHED REFERENCE LIBRARY at a fraction of the cost of the material in any other manner." The Commission observed, however, that the price of the *Britannica* in the "Royal Red" binding of $294.50—or $298 including the Encyclopaedia Research Service—had not been changed since 1949. It therefore ruled that these claims of special savings were false and misleading because the prices employed were the same as the regular list prices.

Fictitious reduced prices have been quite common in the encyclopedia field because they are an effective means of increasing sales. On November 30, 1960, the Americana Corporation, publisher of the *Encyclopedia Americana,* was found in the U.S. District Court of Maryland to have violated an FTC Cease and Desist Order; its salesmen misrepresented that the *Americana* was available at a reduced price to a specially selected group of prospects. The Court entered judgment against the Corporation on eight separate counts fining it $16,000. This is only one of a series of legal actions against encyclopedia firms. An earlier case in 1948 involving the *New Standard Encyclopedia* (211 F.2nd 7) provides an account of some of the specious techniques employed. The court record discloses that salesmen would state that the encyclopedia or other books are free, that customers need only pay for the supplement or other services, that the offer is open only to a certain number of people in any given community, and that the regular price of the books and services is greater than the one now being offered.

Such deceptive practices have been cited a number of times. Perhaps the most famous case, FTC v. Standard Education Society (302 U.S. 112), was decided by the Supreme Court in 1937. Justice Black struck a vigorous blow against these methods by declaring:

> To fail to prohibit such evil practices would be to elevate deception in business and give to it the standing and dignity

of truth. There is no duty resting upon a citizen to suspect the honesty of those with whom he transacts business. The best element of business has long since decided that honesty should govern competitive enterprises, and that the rule *caveat emptor* [buyer beware] should not be relied on to reward deception and fraud.

To entice customers with special offers and premiums, salesmen must arrange an appointment with a likely prospect. Their chances of success are increased if a meeting can take place in a congenial atmosphere in which it will be difficult to resist a high-pressure sales "pitch." To achieve this goal, salesmen often phone prospects and tell them they are not members of the company's sales staff, but are connected with its advertising department which is engaged in a market research study or a brand identification program. This pose is maintained until an interview is arranged and a suitable rapport is established. Then the usual "once-in-a-lifetime" offer is revealed to an unwary prospect.

The FTC filed a complaint in January, 1960 against Crowell-Collier, the publisher of *Collier's Encyclopedia,* charging that its salesmen were using this deceptive method, as well as fictitious reduced prices. This case (Docket No. 7751), which is still pending before the Commission, and other actions taken by the FTC suggest that dubious sales practices may be the rule rather than the exception in the encyclopedia field. Agents for the *Great Books* sometimes take advantage of its association with the University of Chicago by pretending they are connected with the Publicity Department of the University. They tell consumers that they are conducting a program of public relations or adult education for the University, but once they secure an appointment, they abandon this pretense and launch a "hard sell" for the *Great Books.*

Sometimes salesmen make unauthorized claims on their own initiative. To prevent such occurrences, the Better Business Bureau has organized an industry-wide co-operative program with encyclopedia publishers. Under this program, which has been in operation for more than a decade, complaints received by the Bureau are forwarded to publishers for appropriate action. This program of self-regulation has not been very successful, however, since publishers have a vested interest in maximizing their profits. Sales divisions are organized so that executives will have a personal incentive for increasing the sales in their territory. They receive an "over-ride," or additional commission, on each sale made by their employees, and the rate of this bonus increases when sales exceed a prescribed figure. Therefore they are reluctant to curb successful salesmen who employ deceptive methods, unless they are forced to do so by adverse publicity or government action.

Although the *Britannica* stands alone by virtue of its coverage and authority, its sales practices have been similar to those of its competitors. Consequently the dichotomy between its imposing reputation and its high-pressure tactics is much sharper than for other firms in the field. The Company spends more on advertising and promotion than any of its competitors, and as a result of its aggressive sales tactics, its dollar volume has increased more than ten times in the last decade. In 1960, the Company grossed more than $90 million, and consumers have been repeatedly reminded of the benefits of this mounting sales volume. A typical claim appeared in a lavish two-page color spread in *Life* magazine (November 21, 1960):

> The latest edition of the *Britannica* . . . is the greatest in our almost 200-year publishing history. An *enormous printing* materially reduces our costs and under an unusual direct-from-the-publisher plan, we pass these savings on to you.

Despite this claim and the fact that about 150,000 sets are now sold each year, the price has not been reduced. Rather the reverse has occurred: the basic price of the set has increased from $298 to $398.

Several authoritative articles have described the Company's marketing methods. *Sales Management* carried an interview on July 20, 1956 with William Houghton, who is now an EB vice-

Plates
I-VI

Plate I

ARE YOU GIVING YOUR CHILDREN MORE THAN YOU HAD?

A THOUGHTFUL DISCUSSION

by Dr. J. Chapman Bradley

'When you look around your home with its comforts and conveniences, you will undoubtedly answer an unhesitating 'yes . . . my children have much more than I had.' But a moment's reflection may lead you to wonder— 'am I giving my children more of the really *important* things?'

"There is a distinction to be made between a *standard of living* and a *standard of life.* It is natural and good to want to give one's children more of the material things. But no material standard of living—no matter how high—is adequate preparation for the years to come. Your children must have a standard of life—to guide their conduct, to direct their thinking, to give them strength and wisdom.

"The first step in developing a high standard of life is knowledge. Knowledge 'the great sun in the firmament' that lights and warms our lives . . . gives us health and growth of mind. For parents who want to give their children this gift—the priceless gift of knowledge—the Encyclopaedia Britannica is an essential possession. With this world-famous treasure of knowledge in your home, your children will soon develop the habit of 'looking it up in Britannica'—a habit that will help them acquire a standard of life to sustain them throughout life."

Brand new edition

Plate II

HOW CAN YOU EXPRESS
THE INEXPRESSIBLE LOVE
YOU FEEL FOR YOUR CHILD?

A THOUGHTFUL DISCUSSION
by Dr. D. Alan Walter

"Most of the time I suppose we aren't really aware of the love we feel for our children. They worry us, amuse us, interest us, irritate and please us in turn. But running underneath those surface ripples is a strong, deep current of love, the intensity of which we realize only occasionally. A young, tousled head bent earnestly over a difficult task . . . a sleeping youthful face that suddenly looks defenseless and vulnerable . . . a group of youngsters with all their ideals showing as they sing around a campfire or in a school auditorium—at moments like these the love we bear our children rises in us with overwhelming force. We long to express it—and occasionally we try. We put an arm around a young son's shoulder—ruffle a beloved daughter's hair —and find it isn't nearly enough. What we feel seems inexpressible.

"Inexpressible in words, yes—but clearly expressed in other ways. Probably the most concrete way we show a genuine concern for our children is in the concern we have for their education. It is the essential tool every child will need to realize a full measure of success and happiness. And a child's attitude toward education depends more on his home than on his school. If yours is a home where a respect for knowledge is evident, your child will carry that respect to his schoolwork. There can be no doubt that a respect for knowledge exists in a home where the Encyclopaedia Britannica is a valued possession. Britannica is the symbol of knowledge—the accumulation of all man has learned since the world began. Children who are taught to 'look it up in Britannica' are taught to inquire, to seek, to learn, to think. Could you give the child you love a more priceless heritage?"

Brand new edition

Plate III

HOW WILL THEY MEASURE UP AGAINST THE KIDS NEXT DOOR?

Uncomfortable as the idea is, this is the time to face it. Everyone wants more for his children. And your children will have to compete just as *you're* competing now in the adult world.

That's one of the biggest single reasons why so many families have Encyclopaedia Britannica in their home. The Britannica is an easy source of reference the whole family can use. It is the world's most complete collection of facts and knowledge excitingly explained by leading authorities. In it, you can learn about sports, find a hobby, increase your appreciation of art, learn about gardening, missiles, philosophy, science . . . just about any subject you've ever heard of . . . and thousands you haven't.

The Britannica is more than words—and more than its brilliant illustrations. It is a seeking of the mind for truth and fact. It is priceless for your children. It can be equally invaluable to you.

New edition

ENCYCLOPAEDIA

Plate IV

Plate V

"How to achieve conviction and a point of view in troubled times"

A message from **The Honorable Adlai E. Stevenson**

United States Representative to the United Nations
Member, Board of Directors, Encyclopaedia Britannica

"When I visited Dr. Albert Schweitzer in his primitive jungle hospital in French Equatorial Africa, he told me he considered this the most dangerous period in history—not just modern history, but all human history. Why? Because, he said, heretofore nature has controlled man, but now man has learned to control elemental forces—before he has learned to control himself.

"Striving to understand how our mastery of elemental forces can be made to serve humanity in these troubled times, we instinctively turn to the sources of Western thought, to the searchings of great and immortal minds on the origins of government, the tenets of philosophy, and the nature of man. For man can control himself only if he understands both himself and the civilization he has created out of his longing for justice and peace.

"Here in the GREAT BOOKS OF THE WESTERN WORLD, is the mainspring of our civilization—the collective conscience which makes it run. In the pages of these beautiful volumes truth stands out—ready to guide anyone concerned with where our world is going."

Essential in the library of every thinking person

GREAT BOOKS
OF THE WESTERN WORLD

Published by the
Encyclopaedia Britannica
in collaboration with
the University of Chicago

Plate VI

president, which offered readers "lots of tips on how to sell in today's 'mass market.' " Mr. Houghton reported that the principal market for the *Encyclopaedia* is in the $5,000 to $7,000 yearly income bracket, and noted that the Company sends out 25 million pieces of direct mail annually to obtain leads for its two thousand full-time salesmen. This interview was accompanied by a sample of *EB* direct mail—a BRITANN-O-GRAM containing "an exceptional money saving offer" of the same type that was subsequently condemned by the Federal Trade Commission.

Mr. Houghton explained that leads received by the Company are forwarded to division and district offices, which in turn sell them to salesmen for two dollars each. He stated that by using such leads, salesmen usually manage to sell one out of every five or six prospects they see; and he concluded, "We pay high commission rates. It is possible for a good man to earn $25–30,000 a year."

Sales Management carried another article on June 3, 1960, entitled "How the Britannica Sells One out of Three," by G. Clay Cole, a senior vice-president of the Company. He described the *Britannica*'s intensive training program for its salesmen. Its objective is "the intelligent presentation of an item identified with knowledge and learning, and a politely aggressive presentation of a product for which a feeling of immediate need must be created." Mr. Cole stated that this training program has been quite successful; salesmen now make one sale out of every 3.7 presentations—a rate almost twice as high as that reported by Mr. Houghton four years earlier.

The Company has recently increased its payments to salesmen, because as Mr. Cole explained: "A keynote of our management philosophy is the opportunity for advancement and compensation—a necessary focus in order to attract and keep the high-caliber men we want to develop." In line with this philosophy, the Company has rearranged its sales organization and raised the commission of salesmen from 15 percent to 25 percent, so that an employee who sells the set and the supplementary books offered with the *Britannica* receives a commission of $75 to $100 for each completed sale.

The practice of marketing an encyclopedia together with other reference works is quite common in the subscription book field. Sometimes consumers do not have an option of purchasing these supplementary works, but are forced to take them as part of a combination offer if they wish to obtain a particular encyclopedia. The *Wall Street Journal* reported on February 16, 1961 that the cheapest edition of the *Americana* can only be obtained if one agrees to purchase *The Book of Knowledge* as well as a set of geography books. Until 1960, it was possible to order the *Great Books* without having to buy any other books, but subsequently a combination offer was introduced which required customers to choose two additional items, such as a Bible, a bookcase or a Seven Language Dictionary. This combination offer has increased the cost of acquiring the *Great Books* from $298 to $398, although the set has been reprinted year after year without change.

The *EB* is continually seeking additional salesmen because of the rapid turnover of its personnel; and it tends to exaggerate the ease of selling its products and the income a novice can earn. After joining the sales force, employees memorize a standard presentation and then search for promising prospects. The intensive exposure of the public to encyclopedia salesmen makes it difficult for a novice to find potential customers outside his own circle of friends and acquaintances. Sales managers carefully ration names obtained from advertisements because their income depends on the number of leads that can be turned into sales. Therefore they are given to experienced salesmen, or if a lead seems particularly promising, a manager may attempt to close a sale himself. Although many people have tried to sell encyclopedias at one time or another, few choose to remain in a field which requires such persistent, high-pressure tactics. A different evaluation of this activity was offered by Adlai Stevenson in a lavish sixteen-page advertising supplement in the *New York Times* (May 26, 1963). He declared:

> What interests me most about *Encyclopaedia Britannica* is not alone its contents, but the kind of mission that lies beyond sales and profits and perpetual editorial revision. I mean the *educational mission* of the people who go out and sell *Britannica,* who stimulate and satisfy the hunger for information, the appetite for enlightenment. Maybe this sounds a little lofty, but I think it must be satisfying to any salesman to be selling something that's educational and which has social usefulness.

Salesmen who succeed in overcoming the resistance of the public usually become sales managers, so they can direct and instruct others in this lucrative art. Managers generally earn a substantial income which increases as they ascend in the organization. The lavish rewards received by executives was suggested by William Benton in a speech at the Harvard Club in New York (*Advertising Age*, February 13, 1961). He reported that the nineteen division managers, who are at the top of the *EB* sales organization, earned an average salary of $125,000 during 1958; and he declared in the *Wall Street Journal* a few days later, "Any division manager of mine who doesn't earn $100,000 a year is not worth his salt."

The Company has gone to great lengths to obtain salesmen. In the summer of 1961 classified ads in the San Francisco area announced that college students could earn $480 a month without selling. Advertisements stated that they would be "trained to conduct field interviews for the sole purpose of obtaining public response and advertising for our Sales Department."

Students who qualified for the offer were engaged to present descriptions, advertising and promotional material on the *Great Books*. When they were hired, students were told they would be able to make a minimum of 120 presentations a month. However, after working a few weeks, students discovered that they were not going to be paid for these presentations—and that if they wished to receive any money they would have to sell the *Great Books* on a commission basis.

A somewhat similar scheme involving college students had been previously used in New York to obtain salesmen for the *Encyclopaedia Britannica* (*New York Post,* August 11, 1960). In San Francisco, however, a group of students filed a suit in Superior Court for damages against the *Great Books* (Daniel Rolfe, Jr., et al. v. Great Books of the Western World; No. 513619). After the suit was made public in the *San Francisco Chronicle*, the Company announced that it was discontinuing this employment practice. Subsequently, it arranged a compromise settlement with twenty-two of the plaintiffs who were minors. Under this settlement, the Company agreed to pay $24,-410 to the plaintiffs, in addition to the $3,420 they had already received; and similar settlements were made with other students who had been employed in this manner.

Thus in ethical terms, the Company's recruiting tactics, its high-pressure salesmanship and exaggerated advertising claims leave a great deal to be desired, even though they may be quite successful from a business point of view.

[22]

Men Behind the Britannica

INSTITUTIONS are guided by leaders who make their policies and direct their affairs—and they must be held responsible for their actions. The *Encyclopaedia*'s widespread acceptance has been aided by many prominent figures, who should be called to account if the set does not live up to its exalted image. A critic cannot escape the necessity for identifying these individuals.

The University of Chicago has been intimately involved in the *Britannica*'s recent history because it owns a one-third interest in the company. The article on the word "encyclopaedia" asserts: "The University's interest in Britannica enterprises is direct and active, although it assumes no management authority or responsibilities." This statement suggests the attitude of the University toward this repository of learning. It is a piece of property that is now yielding two million dollars a year in royalties, but the school assumes no obligation for its contents or business practices. Yet the University of Chicago's motto appears on the

332 / *The Myth of the Britannica*

Encyclopaedia's title page: "Let knowledge grow from more to more and thus be human life enriched." However, what is enriched is not so much human life in general, as the owners of the enterprise in particular. The University has received more than $18 million from the *Britannica*, but seems to avoid any responsibility for the deceptive salesmanship and inadequate scholarship that have helped to make these rewards possible. It furnishes the *Encyclopaedia* with an advisory committee composed of administrators and faculty members, and three of its trustees are members of the EB's Board of Directors, but the University apparently does not evaluate the Company's editorial or sales policies. Instead it seems to treat the *Encyclopaedia* and the *Great Books* as business assets yielding a handsome income. Such behavior is not surprising, if one assumes that the school resembles a modern business corporation rather than a guild of scholars. This would explain why it seems to be willing to abdicate its intellectual responsibilities and accept the myth of the *Britannica* in return for millions of dollars in royalties.

Many individuals connected with the University of Chicago have joined the *Encyclopaedia*'s roster. Robert Hutchins became chairman of its Board of Editors in 1948 while he was still chancellor of the University. Several of his academic associates were also given positions of authority including Ralph W. Tyler, dean of the Social Sciences, and Clarence H. Faust, dean of the Arts and Sciences. Dr. Hutchins' subsequent positions—first as an associate director of the Ford Foundation, and then as president of the Fund for the Republic—have led to an interlocking personnel associated with the *Britannica* and the educational activities of the Ford Foundation. This interlocking personnel is illustrated by the presence of Harry Ashmore, the *Encyclopaedia*'s editor-in-chief, on the Board of Directors of the Fund for the Republic, which is headed by Dr. Hutchins.

Paul G. Hoffman, the first director of the Ford Foundation, has served for fifteen years as a member of the EB's Board of Directors; and when the Foundation established several autonomous organizations, a number of Dr. Hutchins' former associates were appointed to important posts. Dr. Faust was selected as president of the Fund for the Advancement of Education, and Dr. Tyler was named as director of the Center for Advanced Study in the Behavioral Sciences.

Similarly, the head of the Fund for Adult Education (FAE) is C. Scott Fletcher, a former president of the Britannica Film Company. His group received some $47 million from the Ford Foundation from 1951 to 1961; and it has given over a million dollars to the nonprofit Great Books Foundation to promote a nationwide series of discussion groups devoted to the classics of Western civilization. Because of this interest in the humanities, it may be natural that Clifton Fadiman, who is also associated with the *Britannica*, should be actively engaged in FAE's educational program, since he is widely identified with the popular dissemination of literary culture.

A small group of men are simultaneously connected with the *Encyclopaedia* and the organizations founded by the Ford Foundation. They include Harry Ashmore, Clarence Faust, Ralph Tyler, Clifton Fadiman, Norman Cousins and George N. Shuster. Members of this exclusive club usually possess national reputations, as well as close ties with Dr. Hutchins; and they seem able to use these organizations as a means of extending their influence, or as a base of operations when there is a hiatus in their careers. Thus when Dr. Shuster retired as president of Hunter College, he went to the Center for the Study of Democratic Institutions, where he is a vice-chairman, to assist the Center in raising additional funds.

For some time, there has been a close association between the *Britannica* and the Center for the Study of Democratic Institutions. This relationship was solidified in 1960 when the *Encyclopaedia* entered into a financial arrangement with the Center to assist in planning future revisions of the set. Dr. Hutchins expressed the mutual interest of the Center and the *EB* by means of a rhetorical question:

> . . . What are the emerging problems that must be faced in the second half of the twentieth century if a free society is to survive, and how can those problems be presented so that any one who can read English can understand what they are?

This question states the common interest of *Britannica* and the Center.

This lofty formulation is characteristic of the Center. Its parent organization is the Fund for the Republic, founded in 1952 with a $15 million grant from the Ford Foundation. It was designed to defend the fundamental rights of free speech and political dissent that were being challenged by the hysteria of the Mc-Carthy era. Five years later, after $11 million had been allocated in grants, the Fund was reorganized—and the Center for the Study of Democratic Institutions was established in Santa Barbara, California to examine the fundamental problems confronting Western society. In the words of Dr. Hutchins:

> The Center deals with the basic issues affecting the maintenance of a free and just society today. The object is to clarify these issues, not to settle them. The method is discussion. The staff meets every day to criticize a paper or an oral presentation by one of its members or by a visitor. Papers are then re-written and re-discussed. . . . A fraction of these documents is eventually published.

This mode of operation is quite congenial to the distinguished figures who direct the Center since it allows them to invite prominent guests to discuss important topics. The results of these conversations can then be recorded, edited and distributed without the necessity for laborious individual research. Most of the reports issued by the Center on such thorny topics as "The Corporation and the Economy" and "Religion and the Free Society" consist of informal discussions between guests and members of the Center. Needless to say, these reports lack the concentration and originality of studies undertaken by individual scholars; therefore they have had little impact on the academic community, or society at large.

The Center's research contract with the *Britannica* may be a natural development, since its endowment is rapidly being depleted. One problem that might be fruitfully considered by the Center is how the demands of scholarship can be reconciled with the *Encyclopaedia*'s meager payments to contributors and its lavish rewards to salesmen. Another problem is how the Center can advise the *Britannica* without becoming involved in its policies, particularly when its leaders occupy positions of responsibility in both organizations.

The association of many prominent scholars with the *Britannica* may be one reason why its policies have been rarely criticized. An apparent exception was an editorial in *Science* (July 14, 1961) which discussed a Cease and Desist Order issued by the FTC against the Company's sales practices. The editorial noted that many authorities are listed on the *Encyclopaedia*'s title page whose "cordial cooperation" make the work possible—and it suggested: "Perhaps, the FTC should not be the only group reviewing the business practices of the Encyclopaedia Britannica Inc. A committee of these authorities might also have some thoughts on the methods by which their efforts are being sold."

In response to this editorial, I submitted a letter citing some of the *Encyclopaedia*'s scientific deficiencies, and was informed by return mail, "We shall be glad to publish your letter of July twenty-eighth with two minor deletions." However, my letter did not appear. Three months later, when I inquired about the matter, I was told:

> . . . We have decided to reverse our opinion and not publish it. This is of course an unpleasant decision for us to have to make, but upon further consideration we have decided that for us to publish a gratuitous attack on the *Britannica* is not appropriate.

Science is published by the American Association for the Advancement of Science; and the president of the Association during 1961 was Thomas Park, professor of zoology at the University of Chicago, who is also chairman of the University's Advisory Committee to the *Britannica*, and a member of its Board of Editors.

The *Encyclopaedia* has been honored on a number of occasions. It was awarded the Wisdom Seal of Approval in 1959, and an entire issue of *Wisdom* (Volume 30) was devoted to the set. The cover carried a large photograph of William Benton who was presented the Wisdom Magazine Award for "Significant Contributions to Knowledge and Distinguished Service to Mankind." This award was given in behalf of the Wisdom Society of Beverly Hills, California, "a non-profit educational publishing institution dedicated to the advancement of American education and to the highest aspiration of the human mind and spirit." Although single copies of the magazine cost five dollars, its publisher maintains:

> WISDOM is published not for profit but to advance the intelligence of the human mind. It provides for you a lifetime of education in a single compact magazine. It leads you to knowledge of our contemporary civilization. It is an indispensable aid in modern education. . . . It is a repository of all learning, a treasure of great ideas.

In presenting the Wisdom Award, the publisher described Mr. Benton in the following fashion:

> Recognized as one of the best minds of our age, William Benton is a profound thinker of great courage, creative imagination, intellectual and moral integrity. He has served America diligently with selfless dedication and devotion to public welfare, and to championing the cause of increased international understanding and world peace.

This generous praise was reiterated in a long biography in *Wisdom*, which opened with the observation:

> The most commanding figure in American education and publishing is William Benton—one of the most extraordinary men of our time. Enormously gifted, he possesses all the manifestations of greatness: he has intellect, energy, ideas, courage, one of the finest critical minds of the century, and he has devoted the overwhelming proportion of his time to public service. His place among the world's great individuals has never been more secure than at the present. He has outdistanced all competitors as a successful publisher, and stands first on the list of American educators, above and apart from all others. . . .
>
> The *Britannica* has made Benton's fame and prestige se-

cure. His work as an encyclopedia publisher is in sharp contrast with that of all his contemporaries. . . . He sets himself squarely against the educational apathy of our day, and throws the whole weight of his powerful intellect, his great learning and imagination, into the task of converting the *Encyclopaedia Britannica* to an essential part of everyone's life.

This extravagant panegyric was continued in the rest of the seven-page article devoted to Mr. Benton, and it was followed by six pages "from the Wisdom of William Benton"—a collection of excerpts from his speeches and writing. This material was supplemented by a collection of photographs portraying him in a variety of thoughtful poses surrounded by volumes of the *Encyclopaedia*.

"We are all imbued," says Cicero, "with the love of praise." This lavish issue of *Wisdom*, which expressed so much appreciation of the *EB* and its publisher, was apparently esteemed by the Company. A few months later, it co-operated in preparing another special issue of *Wisdom* (Volume 33) devoted entirely to the *Great Books*. The cover featured a set of portraits of the great men (Plate V). In the center were large pictures of Robert Hutchins, William Benton and Mortimer Adler. They were surrounded by smaller portraits of other great men—such as Plato, Aristotle, Shakespeare, Newton, Darwin and Freud. The magazine offered a selection of wisdom drawn from the *Great Books*, and reaffirmed the scale of values established on its cover by devoting four pages to the wisdom of Hutchins and three to the wisdom of Adler, but only one page to the wisdom of Aristotle and one to the wisdom of Shakespeare.

The adulation expressed in this issue is illustrated by a caption under a photograph which reported: "Publisher William Benton and Editors Robert M. Hutchins and Mortimer J. Adler have preserved the accumulated wisdom of the human race for generations to come in the *Great Books of the Western World*, the outstanding literary and intellectual achievement of our time." The unique value of this work was explained in a special section entitled, "Great Thoughts of the Great Men about the Great Books." Some representative quotations were:

"Great Books make us heirs of all eternity."—SHAKESPEARE

"A great book is the precious life-blood of a master spirit, embalmed and treasured up on purpose to a life beyond life."—MILTON

"Great Books are the legacies that a great genius leaves to mankind, which are delivered down from generation to generation, as presents to the posterity of those who are yet unborn."—ADDISON

"The true university these days is a collection of great books."—CARLYLE

"All that mankind has done, thought, gained or been: It is lying as in magic preservation in the pages of great books. They are the chosen possessions of men."—CARLYLE

Not every product can utilize endorsements prepared by great men, but unfortunately this copy has been edited. Shakespeare speaks of honor, not great books, and Milton of "a good book" rather than a great one, while Addison and Carlyle refer merely to books.

Such alterations seem rather shortsighted, since these quotations can be easily checked. With the exception of the fictitious Shakespearean passage, they may be found in Bartlett's *Familiar Quotations*. These selections are not the only ones that have been doctored. The excerpts from Thoreau, Browning, Bacon, Bennett, Channing and Eliot have been edited by changing "books" into "great books." Such alterations have been necessary because authors in the past were content to praise books. They felt no need to single out "great books" for special attention. This idea has been exploited only during the last generation by Robert Hutchins and Mortimer Adler, who have sought a convenient short cut to the fundamental ideas of Western culture. To gain the support of earlier thinkers, it has been necessary to alter their words. The *New Yorker* exposed three of these fictitious quotations on September 24, 1960, but the Company has continued to use this issue of *Wisdom* by prominently displaying it in sales booths set up at conventions and other public places. Apparently the bold picture of Hutchins, Benton and Adler on the cover—surrounded by that astonishing bevy of lesser men—attracts the attention of passers-by, and the array of garbled quotations inside helps to confirm the intellectual importance of the work.

The Company has made a special point of using prominent figures in selling the *Great Books*. Its promotional material often contains photographs of celebrities who own the set such as Adlai Stevenson, Paul Hoffman and Irene Dunne—and its advertisements feature testimonials from distinguished individuals. The Company occasionally receives additional publicity from movie and television stars who attempt to impress interviewers with their intellectual attainments by stating they read the *Great Books* or the *Britannica* in their spare time. A good example is a newspaper profile on the television personality, Dave Garroway, which appeared in the *New York Post* (March 14, 1960). It reported:

> He spends much of his time on what his employees call "that disconnected plane" where he can be equally absorbed in a page-by-page reading of the *Encyclopaedia Britannica* and a mail order catalogue.

Mr. Garroway is one of the few individuals who is said to have read through the entire *Encyclopaedia* in his spare time, and therefore it may be natural for him to endorse the Company's products. He asks in an ad in the *New York Times* (December 4, 1960), "Are you an interesting person?"—and then offers some advice:

> The startling thing is that the way each of us can become truly interesting is, in itself, most enjoyable: it is the act of reading the right books—after you find out what the right books are. And the best of these are now collected together for you in the GREAT BOOKS OF THE WESTERN WORLD.
>
> Consider this—the GREAT BOOKS contain every significant idea that man has pondered since the written word began. They are the best source I can think of to familiarize yourself with the great thinking on every topic fundamental to the development of our civilization.

Mr. Garroway confidently offers a key to social success and states with an assurance that many professors would envy: "The

Great Books contain every significant idea that man has pondered since the written word began." Since Freud is the only twentieth-century thinker in the set, Mr. Garroway apparently believes that no other significant ideas have been created or developed during the last sixty years.

Sometimes testimonials for the *Great Books* supply an unconscious commentary on the behavior of individuals connected with the enterprise. Clarence Randall, former president of Inland Steel, asks in the *New York Times* (December 25, 1960), "What has become of the self-made man?" and declares:

> Fifty years ago industry was dominated by self-made men. . . . They knew what they believed. Above all, they knew themselves. Trained for nothing, they were prepared to tackle everything.
>
> America needs to recapture that boldness, that magnificent confidence in our own abilities. Among the barriers is the very perfection of our educational process. Fear marks the modern specialist. He dares not attempt that for which he was not trained, dares not speak out on a subject that was not on his examination papers.

This gap is now being filled by individuals promoting the *Great Books*. Mr. Garroway tells us how to be interesting, and John Mason Brown informs us: "If your search is for vision, force, certainty—new curiosity and mental strength—you could not do better than to explore the world of the *Great Books* with the *Syntopicon* to guide you."

In itself, the pursuit of economic self-interest is such a common feature of American life that it hardly merits special comment. Many individuals associated with the *Britannica*, however, claim to be moral leaders who are beyond such mundane considerations. They maintain their role as public benefactors while promoting the *Great Books* and endorsing the Company's editorial policies. Their attitude has perhaps been inadvertently described by Mortimer Adler, who is now a member of the *Encyclopaedia*'s Board of Editors. He asks in an advertisement for the *Great Books* (*Time*, September 5, 1960), "Is a well-rounded man sometimes a hollow man?" and replies:

We work hard in business—but with no well-defined principles to give us a sturdy, inflexible integrity. We busy ourselves dutifully in civic activities but with no real understanding of a dedication to service. We are hollow men.

Encyclopedias have often engaged prominent figures to lend authority and distinction to their work. An illustration was the appointment of Dwight D. Eisenhower as chairman of the Editorial Advisory Board of the *Encyclopedia Americana* in December, 1961. When he was appointed, it was announced that Mr. Eisenhower would serve without remuneration and would meet periodically with the editors to discuss matters of broad editorial policy and the selection of contributors. However, it is rather difficult to see how Mr. Eisenhower can make a significant contribution to the *Americana*, since he has not shown any serious interest in scholarly or intellectual matters. Indeed, when he was in the White House, it was reported that his personal reading was confined to westerns and other light fiction.

Other well-known figures have been active in the encyclopedia field. In 1954 Adlai Stevenson was appointed to the Board of Directors of the Britannica Film Company, and the following year he joined the Board of Editors and Board of Directors of the *EB*. In 1959 he became chairman of the Board and head of the Executive Committee of the Film Company—and in 1960 he toured South America with William Benton. During this two-month tour, they announced in Rio that a Portuguese edition of the *Britannica* would soon be issued.

Mr. Stevenson, by virtue of his eminent position and eloquent prose, has become one of the elder statesmen in American life whose public pronouncements are widely disseminated. When *Life* magazine and the *New York Times* sponsored a series of essays on "The National Purpose" in May, 1960, he was commissioned to prepare a leading article in the series. In discussing the quality of life we want, he emphasized the importance of education and the arts by insisting:

> We mean, in short, new standards of respect and reward for the intellect and culture. And we mean more stable

financing for basic research, more concern for advancing knowledge for its own sake. . . . And we mean that the pursuit of truth in itself is the highest activity of man.

No one can argue with such lofty sentiments; yet while Mr. Stevenson calls for new rewards for the intellect, the *Britannica* continues to pay two cents a word to its contributors. One wonders whether Mr. Stevenson has ever protested against these low rates, particularly since he is intimately aware of the financial problems facing writers. When he visited Russia in 1958, he represented the Authors League in an effort to secure Soviet royalties for American authors.

Mr. Stevenson has prominently endorsed the *Great Books*. A full-page advertisement in the *Saturday Evening Post* (March 18, 1961) carried a message from "The Honorable Adlai E. Stevenson" under the provocative caption, "How to achieve conviction and a point of view in troubled times." He noted (Plate VI *detail*):

> When I visited Dr. Albert Schweitzer in his primitive jungle hospital in French Equatorial Africa, he told me he considered this the most dangerous period in history. . . .
> Striving to understand how our mastery of elemental forces can be made to serve humanity in these troubled times, we instinctively turn to the sources of Western thought, to the searchings of great and immortal minds on the origins of government, the tenets of philosophy, and the nature of man. . . .
> Here, in the GREAT BOOKS OF THE WESTERN WORLD, is the mainspring of our civilization—the collective conscience which makes it run. In the pages of these beautiful volumes truth stands out—ready to guide anyone concerned with where our world is going.

Dr. Schweitzer has nothing to do with the *Great Books,* but Mr. Stevenson invokes his name to lend distinction to his sales message. This advertisement is accompanied by a large photograph of Mr. Stevenson who is identified as:

> United States Representative to the United Nations
> Member, Board of Directors, Encyclopaedia Britannica

There is little doubt that this sales appeal has been quite effective, since it has been repeated in many publications including *Time, Life, Esquire, McCall's,* and the *New York Times.*

Of course, Mr. Stevenson may believe he is acting in the public interest by endorsing the *Great Books* and serving on the Company's Board of Directors. After all, the function of a myth is to induce a belief in its assumptions and to eliminate the necessity for rational thought. Without believers, there would be no myth —and sometimes the very people who initiate a myth unwittingly become its victims. This may perhaps explain why William Benton can present himself as an advocate of academic ideals, and Robert Hutchins can maintain that the *Britannica* represents modern scholarship—and the imposing image they have created may explain why so many prominent people have lent their names to the Company's products.

The development and elaboration of the Britannica Myth is a brilliant achievement. Under cover of the myth, Mr. Benton seems able to out-huckster the hucksters, and enlist the help of such respected institutions as the University of Chicago and the Center for the Study of Democratic Institutions.

The myth enables him to associate the *Britannica*'s commercial aims with the lofty goals of education. This was aptly illustrated during a recent visit to Russia, which he described in the *Saturday Review* (October 27, 1962). In Moscow he had a two-hour interview with Anastas Mikoyan, Deputy Premier of the Soviet Union. Mr. Mikoyan charged: ". . . Your encyclopedia articles distort the picture of the Soviet Union. Why don't you correct the untruths?" Mr. Benton told the Minister he was misinformed —and replied that his challenge was not to the *Britannica,* but to world scholarship, since "Soviet editors knew full well that the *Encyclopaedia* has reflected the best in world scholarship for almost 200 years." He concluded that Mr. Mikoyan's "ignorance of the *Britannica* shows the depth of his misunderstanding of American institutions."

Thus Mr. Benton does not treat the *Encyclopaedia* as a privately owned work whose editorial and business policies he controls; instead he implies that any attack on its accuracy and veracity is in effect an attack on American institutions. And by wrapping the Flag around the set, he reaffirms its mythological status and its elevated position as a symbol of learning.

Mr. Benton's zeal is understandable. He advanced $100,000 to enable the University of Chicago to accept the *EB* as a gift in 1943. A scale of royalties was worked out, with Mr. Benton receiving two-thirds of the Britannica's stock, and the University one-third. According to *Book Production Magazine* (March, 1963), the University of Chicago has received more than $18 million from the Britannica, so one can assume that this arrangement has also been beneficial for Mr. Benton. At the same time, he has successfully cast himself in the role of an enlightened public citizen concerned with intellectual values and cultural ideals. His ownership of the *EB* has helped make him a multimillionaire, enhanced his status, and provided him with a convenient platform for expressing his views on education and foreign affairs.

His public services were acknowledged in March, 1963 when he was appointed American representative to the Executive Board of UNESCO. When the President made this appointment, he elevated Mr. Benton to the personal rank of ambassador; thus conferring added distinction on the publisher of the *Britannica*.

[23]

Future Prospects

WHEN the Athenians decided to replace the buildings on the Acropolis which had been sacked by the invading Persians in 480 B.C., they made no effort to preserve the ruins that remained. Damaged statues, standing columns and the remnants of ancient temples were used to fill holes and level the site. The Greeks did not attempt to save these monuments, which had once been sacred objects, because they were confident they could surpass them. With the aid of Pericles' financial support and under Phidias' brilliant direction, the Parthenon and its heroic ornaments and decorations were completed in the brief space of fifteen years. This feat was justly praised by Plutarch in his life of Pericles:

> The speed with which these works were erected is most deserving of admiration. Stately was their appearance, inimitable their shape and beauty, for the artists vied with each other to make the decorations transcend the buildings in splendor. It might be imagined that every one of these works

could scarcely have been erected during many terms of office or generations, and yet they were all completed during one man's energetic term of office.

This exuberant burst of creative energy was inspired by the Greek pursuit of *arete*, or excellence. But today such enthusiasm is a liability whenever business considerations are paramount. This is illustrated by the frugal practices of the modern encyclopedia in which old and new material is fitfully combined to preserve relics from the past. Such editorial activity deals only with surface defects and not fundamental faults, because encyclopedias are regarded by publishers as commodities designed for public consumption, rather than as cultural monuments.

The *Britannica* has been successfully promoted by aggressive salesmen and lavish advertising. The resulting decline in its intellectual quality is not surprising, since the objectives of scholarship and the goals of salesmanship are not synonymous. At best, sound works are produced when there is active competition and a large well-defined market. This is the case with collegiate dictionaries and junior encyclopedias; but the commercial spirit is incapable of supplying an incentive for scaling the heights of scholarship. Massive projects, such as the *Oxford English Dictionary,* which took seventy years to complete, would never have been carried through if they had relied on their commercial prospects; yet the progress of learning depends on such scholarly undertakings.

Today there is a definite need for a new encyclopedia that will encompass the enormous range of contemporary knowledge and represent the values of the English-speaking world in the same way that the eleventh edition did for an earlier era. Such a synthesis might require fifty or sixty million words, and cost perhaps twenty or thirty million dollars to complete. But it would be difficult for a commercial publisher to justify the expenditure of such large sums by the number of potential consumers, particularly when others have shown how large profits can be obtained from mediocre reference works.

Ideally a new encyclopedia should be subsidized in much the

same way that educational institutions receive financial support. However, it is unlikely the government will enter a field dominated by private enterprise, or that foundations will disturb the economic interests of the University of Chicago. This was illustrated in 1960 when I received a long letter from a leading official of the Rockefeller Foundation who described a host of *EB* errors in his own special area, the Far East. Later, at his invitation, I had lunch with a group of officials in the Foundation's private dining room and discussed the *Encyclopaedia*'s defective state. A few months later, the editor of the British magazine *Encounter* saw his letter and found it so interesting that he asked for permission to reprint it. This request was refused because as the official explained:

> While I have a very real personal interest in this problem, I am afraid that it is not very practicable to get into a public debate with regard to the *Britannica*; such an act might conceivably involve the organization for which I work and cause misleading implications as to its practical concern with this problem.

This cautious attitude encourages the spread of popular illusion by silencing effective criticism. Once a myth assumes an institutional form and is converted into a financial asset, men in authority are reluctant to challenge it, so the myth can flourish undisturbed.

Once the *Britannica*'s policies have been widely publicized, some changes may be introduced, since scholars may be unwilling to donate their services—and the University of Chicago may be unable to avoid its intellectual responsibility for the work. This may lead to a spirit of reform, but it remains to be seen whether it will be sufficient to correct the *EB*'s shortcomings.

If the Company wishes to demonstrate its good faith, it can begin by dating the *Encyclopaedia*'s articles to show when they were written and when they were revised. This would indicate the true age of its material and stimulate efforts to supply fresh information on subjects that have been neglected. Another step would be to offer contributors a decent rate of payment so that editors could reward authors for their scholarly labor instead of exploiting it.

The Company may decide to ignore these recommendations, as well as the findings in this book, by launching a massive advertising campaign to bolster public confidence in the *Britannica*. When I criticized the 1959 *Encyclopaedia* in the *Columbia Forum*, William Benton replied in *Newsweek* (February 1, 1960) that of 90 articles mentioned, fourteen were being rewritten or revised for the 1960 edition, and another thirteen for 1961. Three years later, when I was interviewed by the *New York Times* (wetern edition; February 25, 1963), I cited a number of obsolete and antiquated entries in the 1963 *EB*. The executive editor of the *Britannica* replied to this criticism by noting alterations that would be made in the 1964 and 1965 editions. Therefore, when this book is published, the editors may issue press releases describing changes being made, but such statements will not redeem past failures, because hundreds of thousands of consumers have purchased editions already in print—and not ones that will be issued in the future.

To defend the *EB*'s scholarship, the editors should demonstrate that the examples presented as evidence are either insignificant or incorrect. Since hundreds of illustrations have been supplied on a wide variety of subjects, the Company cannot refute this unfavorable critique by pointing out that thousands of articles have not been cited, because a reference work must stand behind *all* its material.

Many entries have not been discussed because this book is less than one three-hundredth the length of the *Encyclopaedia*. But enough examples have been given to demonstrate the general quality of this grand myth among reference works. I think I have shown that in many important ways the *Britannica* does not fulfill its function as an authoritative reference work. If a researcher wishes to check a dubious point by referring to its pages, he may get accurate information, but in my opinion he may also be misled. And carping about the number of articles that have not been criticized will not change this unpleasant fact.

This book has attacked many idols and illusions, but perhaps its findings may lead to positive results. Textbooks suffering from defective scholarship may be revised; the public may adopt a more sophisticated attitude toward standard reference works; and authors may be encouraged to turn to primary sources of information. Thus this book may possibly stimulate some needed reforms and help raise intellectual standards which have been debased by the pursuit of commercial gain.

During the Renaissance, men of vision like Bacon, Montaigne and Erasmus were inspired by the belief that knowledge would liberate men from the superstitions of the past. Living in an age when science was an ideal, rather than a reality, their faith in the power of learning was a dream that looked toward the future. Today, more than three centuries later, their vision has been vindicated. Science and scholarship are major activities supported by the state and society, and their discoveries have shaped the intellectual outlook and physical environment of modern man. It is no longer necessary to defend the quest for knowledge; the great problem is to make its fruits available to educated citizens. Information is multiplying so rapidly that it must be synthesized and presented in a form that can be assimilated by people who are not scholars or specialists. Since an encyclopedia seeks to unify and record man's knowledge, it can play a significant role in furthering the ideals of education and the acquisition of learning which are essential elements of a free society. Therefore the creation of a major new encyclopedia would be a valuable means of elucidating the advances of science and scholarship. The utility of such an endeavor was emphasized by the director of the University of Chicago Press in the Winter, 1963 issue of *Daedalus*. He urged that "in view of the scandalous deterioration in the quality of existing English-language encyclopedias," university presses should "venture collectively upon the preparation and production of more specialized encyclopedias that would be worthy of contemporary scholarship in the English-speaking world." Such activity would exert a beneficial influence on commercial encyclopedias and would allow the academic community to re-examine the problem of providing a synthesis of current knowledge. In addition, it might offer a bulwark against those who seek to identify mediocre reference works with the rigorous standards of scholarship. Finally, it would permit the encyclopedia to act as an instrument of adult education and a significant expression of modern learning.

Notes

NOTE I, PAGE 104

Perhaps the most famous victim of the Victorian code was the Irish leader, Charles Parnell, who fell within a few months from the heights of political authority to the depths of personal despair as a result of a marital scandal.

As the year 1889 drew to a close, Parnell reached the summits of popularity and political power. He had just been triumphantly vindicated in a dramatic state trial of charges brought by the London *Times*, which sought to link him with the Phoenix Park murders in which a mob of Irish terrorists had slain two leading British colonial officials. After Parnell's acquittal, Home Rule seemed only a few months away, as Gladstone and the Liberal Party joined forces with the nationalists in pressing for this peaceful solution of the Irish question. Then without warning, a crushing blow fell. Captain William O'Shea sued his wife for divorce and named Parnell as the guilty third party. Parnell's allies and associates were stunned by this unexpected turn of events. The shocked sentiment of the English middle class was expressed by Queen Victoria when she wrote in her diary, "Parnell is shown up not only as a very bad character, but as a liar, and devoid of all sense of honour or of my sort of principle." And she added, "Now Gladstone is put in great difficulties by it." The article on the Irish leader records:

> Parnell's intimacy with Mrs. O'Shea had begun in 1881, though at what date it became a guilty one is not in evidence. . . . It is not known why O'Shea suddenly took action in 1889.

The facts in the case have been known since 1931; they make the affair seem like a farfetched romance, rather than an incident in the life of a prominent politician. When Kitty O'Shea met Parnell in 1881, she had separated from her husband and was living in a cottage on the estate of her rich aunt, Mrs. Wood, whom she visited every day. Parnell and Mrs. O'Shea soon became lovers, and regarded themselves as husband and wife, but kept their connection a secret from Mrs. Wood.

Mrs. O'Shea made no attempt to divorce her husband, but was content to live secretly with Parnell. Since Parnell was a Protestant, there would have been no religious obstacle to a divorce and remarriage. One fact, however, prevented the lovers from legalizing their union—the wealth of Kitty's aunt. Since Mrs. Wood was eighty-eight years old when the lovers met, she could hardly live much longer. After her death, Kitty would inherit a large fortune as the sole heir, but if Mrs. Wood were to learn of her divorce, she might decide to disinherit her. To avoid this danger, the lovers decided to wait until she died before taking any legal action. Their plan seemed reasonable enough, but Mrs. Wood confounded their expectations by refusing to die. Instead, the old woman continued to live on year after year. When she finally died in May, 1889, she was ninety-six years old. She left her niece a legacy of £144,000. Seven months later, Captain O'Shea sued his wife for divorce in an attempt to obtain part of this inheritance. Parnell refused to answer O'Shea's charges by contesting the divorce because he wished to marry Mrs.

O'Shea. His tacit admission of adultery was a political disaster that wrecked his career and the prospects of Home Rule.

Oddly enough, the article on Katherine and William O'Shea in the 1959 edition refers to the publications of Henry Harrison whose book *Parnell Vindicated* gives the full story behind the affair, but the article itself presents a garbled account of the matter. It does not explain the central role played by Mrs. Wood and attempts to exonerate Captain O'Shea:

> It is not clear when he became aware of the existence of intimate relations between his wife and Parnell, though he subsequently alleged that only his wife's intercession prevented a duel in 1881.

Captain O'Shea, however, knew about his wife's infidelity almost from the very beginning. He invented the story of a duel to put himself in a good light with the Court, although it had no foundation in fact. Almost a decade earlier, he had gone to the Home Office after the Phoenix Park murders to ask for police protection for Parnell and himself because he thought their lives were in danger. At the time he gave Parnell's address as the cottage at Eltham where his wife was living—and this was in May, 1882!

The article on Gladstone claims:

> . . . In 1890 when he was over 80, momentary excitement led him into a dangerous quarrel with Parnell about the political consequences of the O'Shea divorce. (Gladstone had never believed the rumours about Parnell's liaison, holding that Parnell would never "imperil the future of Ireland for an adulterous intrigue.")

This is not true. Gladstone knew about Parnell's intrigue long before the divorce trial. He learned the true nature of the affair within a week of the Phoenix Park murders when Harcourt, the Home Secretary, told the Cabinet that the Kilmainham Treaty, which the government has just concluded with the Irish nationalists, would never be popular when the public discovered it had been negotiated through Captain O'Shea, the husband of Parnell's mistress.

The English Government had taken the trouble to investigate Parnell's private life early in his career because he was head of a potentially dangerous movement for Irish independence. The Home Secretary had him shadowed and soon learned the truth about his domestic arrangements. Gladstone's knowledge that Parnell was engaged in "an adulterous intrigue" had little effect on his subsequent collaboration with the Irish leader because he was bound by the realities of political life rather than the moral sentiments expressed by Victorian novelists. Gladstone himself was no prude; two members of his Cabinet were living more or less openly with women who were not their wives. Such arrangements were not unheard of. In itself a clandestine "affair" was no great matter as long as it was concealed from the prying eyes of the public and the notoriety of the divorce courts. Morality consisted in certain conventions and the leading rule was: You must not be found out.

There could really be little secrecy in Parnell's affair with Mrs. O'Shea. When he was arrested in October, 1881, along with other leaders of the Irish Land League, Kitty was pregnant with his child, who was born four months later. While Parnell was in prison, he sent her letters which opened with the tender salutation, "My Own Darling Wifie," and closed with the signature, "Your Own Darling Husband." Although Captain O'Shea occasionally visited his wife for the sake of appearances, he could hardly be ignorant of what was going on. While the affair was in progress, Parnell was forced to placate O'Shea, and on one occasion in 1886 attempted to foist him off as a candidate for Parliament on the indignant voters of Galway. After the divorce trial, O'Shea gained custody of the two children that resulted from the affair, and he used them until his death as a means of extorting money from his former wife.

Parnell's downfall had a powerful impact on subsequent Irish history. The *Encyclopaedia* discusses the case in the entries on Gladstone, Parnell and O'Shea, yet in all three instances it supplies erroneous information. It is a curious fact that perhaps the most significant development in this celebrated scandal took place after O'Shea divorced his wife. The dramatic turn occurred when Parnell refused to submit to the Victorian code by resigning as leader of the nationalist cause. Blind to the hostile wave of public opinion sweeping over England and Ireland, he struggled to remain in a position of authority. Headstrong and obstinate, he refused to heed the advice of Cecil Rhodes who telegraphed: RESIGN, MARRY, RETURN. Instead he vainly demanded the respect and obedience he had formerly enjoyed. The results were tragic. Parnell was deposed and Ireland, which had been united in the cause of national liberation, was split into feuding Catholic and Protestant factions, into Parnellites and anti-Parnellites— and the conflict between the two groups raged for almost a generation.

Parnell died a broken man, less than two years after the O'Shea divorce trial. But after his death he became a symbol of Ireland's oppressed condition. This was possible because the true circumstances surrounding his fall were unknown, so patriots could mistakenly believe his downfall was caused by treacherous agents of the Church and the State. Had they realized that this scandal was due to their leader's desire to obtain his mistress' inheritance, they might not have cast him in the role of a proud hero falsely betrayed. If these facts had been made public in 1890, Joyce would hardly have written, "The priests and the priests' pawns broke Parnell's heart," and Yeats would scarcely claim, "The Bishops and the Party/That tragic story made."

After the disaster of the Parnell case, many young Irish writers turned away from the political struggle, which seemed hopeless, to devote themselves to the cause of literature. Under the leadership of Yeats and Lady Gregory, their efforts led to a remarkable literary revival that made Dublin a center of creative activity from which Yeats, Joyce, Synge and O'Casey emerged as world figures. Although Parnell's downfall exerted a profound influence on the course of modern Anglo-Irish literature, the *Britannica* does not acknowledge or discuss this obvious fact. One can, perhaps, understand the reluctance to explore the unsavory aspects of Parnell's personal life, but there is no reason why the literary effects of his disgrace should be ignored, particularly when his checkered career left a mark on the work of Joyce and Yeats.

The Parnell affair is an illuminating illustration of the wide disparity that sometimes occurred during the Victorian era between the realities of private life and the demands of public morality. The widespread shock and outrage produced by the revelation of Parnell's and Kitty O'Shea's "adulterous intrigue" furnishes a striking confirmation of the reality and intensity of Victorian moral sentiments. Yet it should be pointed out that while it is convenient to identify a fixed set of ideas such as sexual prudery, social respectability and moral rectitude with the Victorian period, such an identification should not be pushed too far. At any given moment, the ideals accepted by different members of society form an amorphous complex of judgments and attitudes that are constantly changing in response to new conditions. Thus, the ideals of propriety and respectability elevated by the pillars of Victorian society did not spring up suddenly: they acquired their sacred position gradually over a period of several generations. They began to gain ground early in the nineteenth century, before Queen Victoria ascended the throne, when scattered attacks were leveled against the sexual levity exhibited by earlier English writers.

NOTE II, PAGE 154

An illuminating case is the entry on Jonathan Swift, abridged from the eleventh edition. A passage describing his impudent exposé of a London almanac-maker supplies the same facts as the original, but differs significantly in style. The original version exploited the humorous possibilities of the affair:

> In his Almanac for 1707 a Protestant alarmist and plot vaticinator styled John Partridge warned customers against rivals and impostors. This notice attracted Swift's attention, and in January 1708 he issued predictions for the ensuing year by Isaac Bickerstaff, written to prevent the people of England being imposed upon by vulgar almanac makers. In

this brochure he predicts solemnly that on the 29th of March at 11 o'clock at night Partridge the almanac maker should infallibly die of a raging fever. On the 30th of March he issued a letter confirming Partridge's sad fate. Grub Street elegies on the almanac maker were hawked about London. Partridge was widely deplored in obituary notices and his name was struck off the rolls at Stationer's Hall. The poor man was obliged to issue a special almanac to assure his clients and the public that he was not dead: he was fatuous enough to add that he was not only alive at the time of writing, but that he was also demonstrably alive on the day when the knave Bickerstaff (a name borrowed by Swift from a sign in Long Acre) asserted that he died of fever. This elicited Swift's most amusing *Vindication of Isaac Bickerstaff, Esq.* in April 1709. The laughter thus provoked extinguished the *Predictions* for three years, and in 1715 Partridge died in fact. . . .

This delightful account has been severely condensed in the current article:

> The next few months witnessed one of the most amusing hoaxes ever perpetrated against the quackery of astrologers, the victim being a Protestant alarmist and plot vaticinator styled John Partridge. In Jan. 1708, Swift, under the name of Isaac Bickerstaff, issued a solemn prediction that the notorious almanac maker, Partridge, would die at 11 o'clock P. M. on March 29, and on March 30 he published a letter confirming this prophecy. Partridge's fatuous denial and reply to Bickerstaff elicited Swift's amusing *Vindication of Isaac Bickerstaff, Esq.,* in April 1709.

Both passages contain the same information—but the modern version is a pale reflection of the original. Space may be saved, but interest is lost.

NOTE III, PAGE 163

After *Aida* and the *Requiem* were completed, Verdi felt his career was over, for he said, "Music needs youthfulness of the senses, impetuousness of the blood, fulness of life." When a friend protested against this idea, the sixty-one-year-old composer replied that he was finished with the clamor of the public and the applause of audiences and concluded, *"le partite sono saldate"*—"the account is closed."

Despite this pessimism, Verdi finally relented and returned to the lyric theater because of the efforts of a fellow composer, Boito, who furnished him with a masterly libretto based on Shakespeare's *Othello*. Aroused from his slumber, Verdi transformed the libretto into the most perfect realization of a great play ever achieved on the operatic stage. From the triumphant entry of Otello in the first scene to the fateful strangling of Desdemona in the last act, he traced the fearful consequences of a jealous passion that poisons conjugal love and destroys the proud and the innocent alike.

Verdi was seventy-three when *Otello* was completed, yet his career was not over. Within a few years Boito succeeded in rekindling the creative spark in the composer who had said after the première of *Otello*, "I have fired off my last cartridge. . . . Tonight the public has torn away the veil that concealed my last mysteries. I have nothing left." Boito again played the role of a faithful collaborator by preparing a brilliant new libretto based on the blustering, swaggering figure of Falstaff—one of Shakespeare's most endearing creations. He obtained the plot from *The Merry Wives of Windsor,* and added the larger humanity present in *Henry IV* and *Henry V* to create a rich, full-bodied portrait of the admirable rogue whom Prince Hal called, "This sanguine coward, this bed-presser . . . this huge hill of flesh."

When Verdi began to set the libretto to music, more than fifty years had passed since the composition of his first opera, and yet when he finished, he had succeeded in transforming a rowdy charade taken from one of Shakespeare's minor plays into a great comic tableau, whose central character fills the imagination—and whose misfortunes, like those of Don Quixote, illuminate the gulf separating man's dreams from painful reality.

While working on the score, Verdi wrote his publisher: "In writing *Falstaff* I have thought neither of theaters nor singers.

I have written it to please myself." The result is an opera that moves with a swirling swiftness and a bubbling gaiety belying the heavy years and dark pessimism of its creator. The *Britannica* says very little about the fruitful collaboration of Boito and Verdi who wove the varied strands of Shakespearean drama into two resplendent musical tapestries that are among the chief glories of Italian opera. Readers who are dissatisfied with this brusque treatment may turn to the survey article on Opera in hope of finding further information, but they will be disappointed. All they will learn is that *Falstaff*, "written when the composer was 80, is his most perfect work, flawless in every particular and . . . incomparably refined."

NOTE IV, PAGE 172

The article on Betsy Ross identifies her as the heroine of one of the most picturesque legends about the origin of the American flag. It relates that Washington ordered the first flag and that she altered the design from six-pointed stars to five-pointed ones by showing they "could be made with a single clip of the scissors." The essay on the Flag, however, questions this patriotic tradition. It observes that the story was first made public in 1870, almost a century after it was supposed to have occurred, when a grandson of Betsy Ross read a paper before the Pennsylvania Historical Society. He presented an account which he said had been preserved orally through several generations of the Ross family: how George Washington, Robert Morris and George Ross entered Betsy Ross' shop on Arch Street in Philadelphia in June, 1776, before the Declaration of Independence had been ratified, with a commission from the Continental Congress to obtain a new flag for the "United States."

No record exists, however, of any continental flag before June, 1777; and George Washington, who is supposed to have ordered the Stars and Stripes, failed to raise it when he had the Declaration of Independence read before his assembled troops in New York on July 10, 1776. In addition, he never mentioned the flag of the United States or the Stars and Stripes in his voluminous diaries or correspondence, although he is a central character in the Betsy Ross saga. Consequently, historians have rejected this claim which was advanced long after her death.

The article on the Flag notes that the same honor has been assigned to Francis Hopkinson, an artist and signer of the Declaration of Independence,* but the entry on Betsy Ross maintains:

> No contemporary documentary evidence has ever been found to support the story, nor has any, on the other hand, been found which gives the honour to anyone else. All that has been verified is that there was a Mrs. Ross living in Philadelphia at the time of the flag's adoption, and that she was an upholsterer and flagmaker by trade.

This tradition was popularized by the American Flag Society which launched a national campaign in 1898 to raise funds to buy the "Betsy Ross House" in Philadelphia. The Society sold portraits and post cards of Betsy Ross, and schoolchildren contributed nickels and dimes to the cause. Through these efforts, the Society raised over $120,000. Of this sum, $25,000 was paid for the house—and almost all of the remainder was pocketed by the individuals who had promoted the scheme. Ironically, Betsy Ross never lived in the house purchased at 239 Arch Street, which had once been a beer tavern, and the portraits sold were all spurious since no authentic picture of her exists. However, such minor details can hardly check the creation of an edifying patriotic tradition.

The *Britannica* acknowledges the work of the Flag Society by including an engraving of the Betsy Ross House in the article on the United States. Underneath the picture is the caption:

> The little house on Arch Street, Philadelphia, where Mrs. Ross lived at the time she is said to have made the first American Flag (1777). . . .

---

* In May, 1780, Hopkinson sent a bill to the Board of the Admiralty for a series of designs he had executed which included "the flag of the United States of America." This assertion, which was repeated several times, was made only three years after the Continental Congress had authorized the first flag, and it was directed to men who either knew or could ascertain the facts about the flag.

This date cannot be correct because George Washington was not in Philadelphia during 1777—so he could not have visited Betsy Ross' shop. It was precisely this difficulty that led her grandson to invent June, 1776 as the date of their meeting—a solution that disposed of one difficulty only to create fresh problems.

The Betsy Ross House is not the only landmark with a fictitious pedigree. One of the show places of Kentucky is the house where Stephen Foster is said to have written the song "My Old Kentucky Home." The site is the old Rowan Manor House near Bardstown, Kentucky—known as "Federal Hill"—which was the spacious residence of Judge Rowan, who was a cousin of Stephen Foster. Like the Betsy Ross House, the Rowan Manor was purchased by public subscription; $65,000 was raised and the house was presented to the State of Kentucky in 1922. It is now open as a museum and ranks with Mammoth Cave as one of the major tourist attractions in the state. The entry on Kentucky contains a picture of "Federal Hill" which is described as "The House in which Stephen Foster wrote 'My Old Kentucky Home.'" This identification was first made in 1893 by the *Louisville Journal* which reported that the song had been written during a visit to the Rowan Manor in 1852, forty years earlier. No documentary evidence, however, was offered to support this claim, which was said to rest on a local tradition. No proof has ever been found in contemporary letters or local newspapers that Foster visited the Rowan estate during 1852, let alone that he wrote his famous song there. This story was contradicted in 1886, seven years before it was made public, when Morrison Foster stated in a letter that his brother's lyrics and songs including "My Old Kentucky Home" were composed at Stephen's home in Allegheny County, Pennsylvania.

The attempt to link "My Old Kentucky Home" with Rowan Manor is rather curious because the lyrics of the song describe the harsh lot of "darkies" inhabiting a slave cabin, not the luxury associated with the ante-bellum South. When the song says, "Weep no more, my lady," the lady referred to is a Negro living in a humble cabin, and not the white mistress of a plantation manor. This observation is confirmed by Foster's workbook which shows the song was initially called "Poor Uncle Tom, Good Night." This suggests it was inspired by Harriet Beecher Stowe's novel, *Uncle Tom's Cabin,* published in 1851. In the original draft, the first line of the song was,

De sun shines bright in de old Kentucky home

and the last line of each verse and the chorus was,

Den poor Uncle Tom, good night.

Foster later changed the title and refrain to "My Old Kentucky Home" so the song would have a wider appeal, but it is rather ironical that a song written in Pennsylvania about a slave cabin should become identified with a large manor house in Kentucky representing the gracious life of a white aristocracy. Mere facts, however, are seldom sufficient to destroy a flourishing patriotic industry. Tourists visiting Philadelphia will continue to view the Betsy Ross House as an authentic colonial shrine, and travelers passing through Kentucky will be shown the manor where Stephen Foster wrote "My Old Kentucky Home," even though both sites are modern inventions.

Appendix

The following is a list of articles in the 1963 *Encyclopaedia Britannica* which have been taken from the ninth edition of 1875–89, the tenth edition of 1902–03, or the eleventh edition of 1910–11. The 666 articles in this list include only entries occupying at least a half-page in the *Britannica*. Although occasional articles may be "classics" possessing an historical interest, it is difficult to understand why so many others have been retained. Therefore, this list may suggest the extent of obsolete material in the latest printing of the *Encyclopaedia*.

Assize
Beheading
Boyle, Robert
Brehon Laws
Buckingham, Earls, Marquesses
    and Dukes of
Burnet, Gilbert
Burton, Sir Richard Francis
Casaubon, Isaac

Ceará
Dalberg
Derby, Earls of
Eylau
Fabius
Fable
Fabliau
Fairfax of Cameron, Thomas
    Fairfax

Fairy
Farnese, Alexander
Fathers of the Church
Fatimites
Febronianism
Fehmic Courts
Fénelon, François de Salignac de la Mothe
Ferdinand I (Roman emperor)
Ferdinand II (Roman emperor)
Ferrara-Florence, Council of
Ferrers
Feudalism
Fictions
Fielding, Henry
Filigree
Fisher, John
Fitzgerald
Flood, Henry
Font
Fontenoy
Forster, William Edward
Fouché, Joseph
Fox, Charles James
Fox, Richard
Francis II (Roman emperor)
Francis I (king of France)
Francis, Sir Philip
Franco-German War
Frederick I (Holy Roman emperor)
Frederick II (Holy Roman emperor)

Frederick III (Holy Roman emperor)
Frederick II (king of Prussia)
Frederick III (king of Prussia)
Frederick III (king of Sicily)
Frederick Charles (Friedrich Karl Nikolaus)
Frederick William I
Frederick William II
Frederick William III
Frederick William IV
Free Church of Scotland
Freiburg im Breisgau
French Revolutionary Wars
Frisians
Frobisher, Sir Martin
Froissart, Jean
Fronde, The
Froude, James Anthony
Fürstenberg
Galatia
Gallatin, Albert
Gambetta, Léon
Games, Classical
Gardiner, Stephen
Garfield, James Abraham
Garibaldi, Giuseppe
Garrett, João Baptista da Silva Leitão
Garrison, William Lloyd
Gautier, Theophile
Gawain
Genealogy
Genesis
Gentleman
Gentz, Friedrich von

Heraldry
Herbert, George
Hero
Herod
Heroic Romances
Hertzberg, Ewald Friedrich
Hesiod
Hincmar
Hindu Kush
Hippolytus, The Canons of
Holberg, Ludvig Holberg
Horn
Hudson's Bay Company
Huguenots
Humboldt, Alexander
Huns
Hunt, James Henry Leigh
Huss, John
Hussites
Hutten, Ulrich von
Hyder Ali
Hymns
Ignatius
Imperial Chamber
Imperial Cities
Incense
Infallibility
Ikerman, Battle of
Inspiration
Investiture
Ionian Islands
Ionian School of Philosophy
Irenaeus
Irving, Edward
Ivan IV ("the Terrible")
Ivan III

Jacobins
James (Biblical)
James (prince of Wales)
Jansenism
Janissaries
Jenghiz Khan
John (king of Bohemia)
John (king of England)
John III (king of Poland)
John (duke of Burgundy)
Joinville, Jean
Jomini, Antoine Henri
Jonson, Ben
Jordanes
Joseph II (Roman emperor)
Joshua, Book of
Jubilees, Book of
Judges, The Book of
Jugurtha
Julian
Junius
Justinian I
Justin Martyr
Kālidāsa
Karnak
Karun
Kavirondo
Keble, John
Kelvin, William Thomson
King
Kings, First and Second Books
    of
Kingsley, Charles
Klopstock, Friedrich Gottlieb
Knighthood and Chivalry
Knight-Service

Perth (Scotland)
Peter I ("the Great")
Petersburg Campaign
Phigalia
Philip II (king of France)
Philip VI (king of France)
Philip the Good
Philistines
Phoenicia
Pianoforte
Pilgrimage
Pindar
Pippin
Pisa
Pitt, William
Poitiers
Pole (family)
Politian
Polo, Marco
Polycarp
Pompeii
Pope, Alexander
Porphyry (Greek scholar)
Porson, Richard
Porter, David Dixon
Possession (in Law)
Prayer
Preaching
Prescott, William Hickling
Prester John
Pretorius
Priest
Primitive Methodists
Procession
Prose
Ptolemies
Punic Wars

Pushkin, Alexander
Pyrenees
Rabelais, François
Racine, Jean
Raleigh, Sir Walter
Ranke, Leopold von
Ravenna
Renaissance
Renan, Ernest
Repoussé
Rezánov, Nicolai Petrovich de
Rhetoric
Richard I
Richard II
Richard III
Richardson, Samuel
Richelieu, Armand Jean Du Plessis de
Richmond, Earls and Dukes of
Richter, Johann Paul Friedrich
Rimbaud, Jean Arthur
Ritual
Robert I, "The Bruce"
Roberts, Frederick Sleigh Roberts
Robespierre, Maximilien François Marie Isidore de
Rodney, George Brydges Rodney
Roger II
Rogers, Samuel
Roland, Legend of
Roman Army
Romance
Roses, War of the
Rossetti, Christina Georgina
Rossetti, Dante Gabriel

Index

[Italicized page references indicate *Encyclopaedia Britannica* articles that are either cited or discussed in the text.]

Love, *104-06*, 286
Low-Temperature Physics, *288*
Ludendorff, Erich, *144-45*
Lucas, F. L., 270
Luck, *199*
Lucretius, *83*
Lucy, Sir Thomas, 8
Lynching, *218, 286*
Lyrical Poetry, *7*
Lys, Battle of, *199*

Macaulay, Thomas Babington, *7*, 36, 98
Macdonald, Dwight, 309
Macfarquhar, Colin, 29
Machiavelli, Niccolò, *7*
Macmillan, Harold, 206, *271*
Madariaga, Salvador de, 283
Mahler, Gustav, 61
Malays, *214*
Malinowski, Bronislaw, 220
Malraux, André, 293
Malthus, Robert, 35
Mann, Thomas, *293*
Manning, Henry Cardinal, *299*
Manton, S. M., 235
Manship, Paul, *90*
Maori Land League, 14-15
Maritain, Jacques, 293
Marlowe, Christopher, 81
Marlowe, Julia, *293*
Marne, Battles of, *199, 201*
Marriage, *220*
Mars, *237, 288*
Marshall, George C., 68
Marsupialia, *230*
Mary (Queen of Scots), *7*
Mary (Virgin), *66-67*
Marx, Karl, *213-14*, 216, 224
Marxism, *276*
Masai, *215*
Masks, *111*
Masonry, *238*

Mass Communications, 221
Mass Production, *52*
Masturbation, 111
Materials, Strength of, *238*
Matriarchy, *220*
Maxwell, James Clerk, 40, *253*
Mazurka, *273*
Mazzini, Giuseppe, *9*
McCall's, 343
McCarthy, Joseph R., 300
McDonald, General John, 143
McKinley, William, *300*
Mead, Margaret, 220
Media, *9*
Medici, *7*
Melchers, Gari, *62*
Melville, Herman, *81*
Mencken, Henry L., 52
Menstruation, *110*
Merriam-Webster Unabridged Dictionary, 233
Mercury Vapor Boiler, *297*
Metals, Fatigue of, *238*
Metternich, Clemons, *9*
Michelangelo, *88*, 162
Middle Ages, *193-97*, 211
Middle East, 287
Midhurst, England, *274*
Midway, Battle of, 201, *286*
Midwifery, *32*
Michelson, Albert, 239
Michelet, Jules, 197-98
Mikoyan, Anastas, 343
Mill, James, 35-36
Mill, John Stuart, 225
Miller, Henry, 80, *293*
Milton, John, *83, 92, 276*, 338
Milyukova, Antonia I., 109
Minoan Linear B Script, 11-12, 277
Mirabeau, Honoré, *7*
Molecular Rearrangements, *288*
Molière, 168, 308